MW01069453

So, Like Dude…

What it Was Like Growing up in the San Fernando Valley in the 50's 60's and 70's

By Richard Sain

Copyright 2018
By: Richard Sain

"The Only Thing That Is Constant Is Change "

— Heraclitus

1

Introduction

The San Fernando Valley has changed dramatically since I was a kid – as most places have. There are no more horse ranches or orange groves to be seen and many of the places I used to walk past on my way to Robert Fulton Junior High School and Monroe High School, such as the General Motors Plant on Van Nuys Boulevard and the Broadway Department Store, no longer exist. The building that housed Food Giant Market and then Ralph's Market was also erased by time.

In my mind, I remember what the streets and structures and landscapes all looked like as I was growing up through the 50's, 60's and 70's. I felt compelled to capture that period of time on paper so others could reminisce along with me. Leaving behind a permanent record of that era, was also important to me. As I revisited the San Fernando Valley through the miracle of the internet and Google's streetscapes, I felt like Doc Brown in the movie "Back to the Future". So much of the world that I grew up in has been lost. It is hard to reconcile the images that I retain in my mind with the reality that exists today. This troubling dichotomy reminds me that time waits for no one.

We all have memories that we carry with us and cherish no matter what age we are. We all cling to whatever good times and interesting places we have experienced. But, as time progresses, the distance grows between what has past and what exists today. This can be particularly baffling to older folks. So, we should be patient when we hear an older parent or grandparent talk about the way things used to be. Those memories of what "used to be", even though they may have occurred decades ago, are still fresh in the minds of many older people.

So, no matter what age you are, step into Doc Brown's time machine with me and cruise back down Van Nuys

Boulevard during the mid-1950's when nearly all the cars on the road were built by GM, Ford or Chrysler, when TV used to only have three major channels – ABC, CBS and NBC, when kids played outdoors from morning till night in the summer months, when all electronic devices actually had to be plugged in, when there was no fast food and moms stayed at home while dads went to work, when moms prepared fresh food for dinner and everyone ate at the same time around the dinner table, when there were no personal computers or internet, when teenagers listened to music imprinted on vinyl records, when stereo music didn't exist, when washing machines had "wringers" you had to run your clothes through after they were washed, when people hung up clothes to dry outside, when we had incinerators where we burned our trash, when families went to see movies together in "drive-ins", when nobody had credit cards...
Sheesh! Can you imagine?

Chapter 1

I was in a dark and cozy room tucked into my bed when I heard voices outside my window. I couldn't make out what they were saying. The roof of my room was suddenly being peeled back like a sardine can and an intense white light began flooding in. I heard murmuring and saw a couple people staring down at me. They were wearing blue surgical masks and gloves. One of the guys reached into my room and grabbed me. He held me firmly in his hands and slowly pulled me into the light. I was blinded by the brilliant white light! Suddenly, I realized that there was something wrong. I looked down at my stomach and saw that there was a cord coming out of it! Holy shit! I was just being born!

NEWS FLASH: On January 31, 1957, a Douglas DC-7B operated by Douglas Aircraft Company was involved in a mid-air collision with a United States Air Force Northrop F-89 Scorpion and crashed into the schoolyard of Pacoima Junior High School located in Pacoima, a suburb in the San Fernando Valley of Los Angeles, California. - Wikipedia

I was five years old and just getting out of Haddon Avenue Elementary School. As I was walking home, I was seeing all this pink shit hanging in trees and blowing in the wind down Terra Bella Street. So, what was up with that? When I got home, my mom was all freaked out and telling me that a plane fell on Pacoima Junior High School and my brother, John, was in the hospital. She started telling me that she and my dad were going to visit him and that I should stay at home with my grandma who was busy praying on her rosary beads. So, this was a total drag and life would never be the same for our entire family.

John was lying in a hospital bed with body parts that were char broiled. Doctors were saying that he might lose an arm. Meanwhile, I was thinking: "How the fuck do you lose an arm?" I had lost toys and shit like that but I never lost any body

4

parts. WTF? My folks told me that they wanted me to go to the same hospital and have my tonsils pulled out. I was thinking: "Hell no! I don't even know what a fucking tonsil is but I don't want to go to a place where people are losing limbs and shit. No way dude! I wanted to remain whole and keep all my body parts. What was up with that?"

Well, I lost that argument and the next thing I knew this doctor dude was asking me to lay down while he jammed a needle in my arm and asked me to count backwards from 100. Who does that? So, I started counting backwards and before I got to 96 the lights went out bro. When I snapped out of the darkness I was lying on a hard ass operating table with the same damn blue surgical masks and gloves staring down at me. Then some nurse started telling me some stupid ass story about three little bears and I was thinking: "Had the whole freaking world gone mad?"

The next thing I knew, I was lying in a hospital bed with some nice old guy lying in a bed next to mine asking me if I was all right. Like dude, I was in a damn hospital feeling like someone just ripped my fucking throat out and I was hurting so badly that I couldn't answer his question if I wanted to. So, I just laid there pondering my fate and wondering what the hell was going to happen to me next. Sheesh! What a fucking nightmare!

So, I finally went home. Home was the Model Motel located at 10601 San Fernando Road between Pierce Street and Terra Bella Street directly across from a set of railroad tracks and Whiteman Airport in Pacoima. We lived in a two bedroom one bath California bungalow and I got to sleep in the living room on a scratchy pink couch that folded down into a bed. I hated that bed. There was a big gap down the middle of the damn thing and sometimes my arm would get wedged in that gap. It also had big ass buttons on it that would get jammed between my toes while I was sleeping. The stupid sheets never stayed on it and I ended up dancing cheek to cheek with that crappy excuse for a bed. I hated sleeping on that couch so much that I pissed on it every night. My folks took me to a freaking doctor to see if there was anything that could be done to stop me from pissing in bed. All I could think was, dudes, just get me a real bed and maybe I'll stop pissing on it.

My oldest brother, Tony, was the first one to check out of the Model Motel after graduating from San Fernando High school. He ended up getting his girlfriend pregnant and moving in with her family. They had lots of land and horses and their property was right next to Hansen Dam Park so they were able to ride on trails that wound through there. Tony would take me over there sometimes and let me ride with him on the back of his horse, Babe. It was totally cool!

John was evicted from the Model Motel next because he dropped out of high school and just got drunk all the time. My folks shipped him to his Uncle who lived in Germany. Dude, I could have told them that it was a bad idea sending a budding young alcoholic to Germany where they drink beer out of big ass steins any time of the day or night! Who would do that?

Enroll today!

¡Inscríbete hoy!

Visit

GoDirect.gov

or call us at

1-800-333-1795

**Phone operators are available
Monday – Friday | 9 a.m. – 7 p.m. ET**
Saturday, April 2nd | 11 a.m. – 3 p.m. ET

Para español, visite

DirectoasuCuenta.gov

You will need your:

- Social Security number
- Information from your most recent federal benefit check or claim number
- Date of birth *FOR DIRECT EXPRESS*
- Financial institution's routing transit number *FOR DIRECT DEPOSIT*
- Account number and account type (checking or savings) *FOR DIRECT DEPOSIT*

For quick access, scan this QR code using your smartphone camera to enroll.

Do not discard your benefit check. Cash your check as you normally would after you enroll.

DIRECT**EXPRESS** ❯

DIRECT❯DEPOSIT
Simple. Safe. Secure.

Exercise your right to vote. To learn more, visit vote.gov.

0422

Save time, save paper, save energy.

Make your life simple and more secure by converting your paper check to direct deposit or a Direct Express® card.

Chapter 2

So, like dude, I was floating along with several enormous black slabs that were rotating in slow motion and extending outwards into space . It was dark. We were all moving in unison. There it was, all laid out in front of me: Eternity; Infinity; Divinity. And I was asking myself what did it all mean? It was totally awesome but frightening as well! All I wanted was my mother.

I woke up in total darkness. I was laying in my crib crying for my mom. I stood up grabbing the crib's railing. My nerdy brother, Joe, opened my bedroom door and poked his head inside. His goofy face was bathed in bluish light from a black and white TV in our living room. I could see reflections of the TV show he was watching bouncing off the lenses of his horn rimmed glasses. He was the last person in the world that I wanted to see! I collapsed onto my crib crying uncontrollably. Eventually, I was enveloped in darkness once again.

My crib was parked in my parent's bedroom and they frequently woke me up arguing about something. I would stand up staring silently at them thinking WTF? It's like 2:00 am in the morning. Give me a frickin break! I'm a young kid who needs his sleep! Do you guys have any freaking idea what kind of psychological damage you are doing to me right now? My mom, pointing in my direction, would say, "Look, you woke the baby!" Yeah, you're frickin right you woke me up! So, shut up, turn off the light and go to sleep.

I was three years old when my parents told me that my grandmother was coming from the "Old Country" to live with us. Her name was Kate. Her husband had died back in Croatia and my mom and dad made all the arrangements for her to travel to the Valley. They took me along to pick her up at the airport and I was wearing my coolest yellow sleeper with built in slippers. Greatest PJ's ever! So, this really old woman, who was my mom's mother, came walking down a set of stairs that were rolled out to an airplane parked on the tarmac. As soon as she saw me, she grabbed me and hugged me. She held me in her arms in the backseat of our car the whole way home! Dude, I was smitten. I loved my grandma even though she couldn't speak a word of English. I learned to speak her language so I could talk to her and understand her.

My parents' marriage was not the greatest. My dad was always complaining about being forced out of Croatia after the country was taken over by communists during World War II. The way he said "communists", whatever that was, he made it sound worse than an invasion of cockroaches. He would say, "We were rich back in Croatia and my brother was the Minister of Finance under the King." Like dude, who has kings anymore? Another chronic complaint was, "Things were always better in the "Old Country." It was his mantra. He also complained about having to do manual labor at the Budweiser brewery on Roscoe Boulevard. He was totally unappreciative of his job even though he was earning union wages while drinking beer on his breaks. I mean, how tough was that dude?

He was an alcoholic and marathon smoker who picked up his tobacco habit when he was nine years old back in the "Old Country". Every night at dinner he had a jug of Gallo wine sitting on the kitchen table that he would chug down while criticizing his children and ridiculing his coworkers. The dude had an attitude. I felt like telling him that this was the "New World" where you had to show some initiative, work hard and save your money. Instead, he groaned about work, spent his money on cigarettes and booze, and gambled away whatever was left over in Las Vegas.

I hated those trips to Las Vegas! The kids, all four of us, would all sit in the backseat of the car with all the windows wide open including the little triangular wind wings that old cars had. It was like a blast furnace back there! The desert heat would be blowing through our hair and onto our parched faces while we teetered on the brink of heat stroke. Occasionally, we would stop at a rundown gas station where the bathroom was filled with graffiti. People wrote stuff like: "Here I sit, broken hearted, came to shit but only farted." I mean, who writes shit like that? And why?

Back in the 1950's the Las Vegas Strip consisted of a handful of casinos: "The Flamingo"; "The Sands"; "The Sahara"; "The Dunes"; "The Riviera"; and "The Tropicana". But we didn't stay in any of those. No way, we stayed in a rundown "Travelodge". It had a sign outside with a caricature of a bear sleepwalking while wearing white pajamas and a white night cap. Their motto was: "Sleep Like a Log at Travelodge." How lame was that dude?

After we checked in, my dad took off and we wouldn't see him again until he lost all his money. So, we were all stuck hanging out at the Travelodge pool burning up in the desert sun. At night, we would all be in pain suffering from sunburned skin. My mom would rub calamine lotion on us but it was pointless because it did nothing to ease the pain. The coolest part happened several days later when we all sat around our dining room table to see who could peel the largest patch of dead skin off of our bodies!

Occasionally, my parents drove us to San Pedro to visit their friends from Croatia - at least it was closer than Las Vegas. We would visit with Lena, who was my God mother, and her husband, Frank. He was a bigger sad sack than my old man and he always wore his suit pants pulled up way above his stomach. Dude, he looked like he had a six inch torso! I mean, what kind of odd ball style of dress was that? When I first met him, I thought he was just goofing off. But he wasn't. Lena spoke English better than my parents did and Frank just refused to speak English at all. She was a tough talking lady who always had a cigarette in her hand and was constantly berating her husband. I would look at Frank after she zinged him and the dude just sat there like it was business as usual. I had never met such a spineless creature in my entire life, short as it was, but I guess it explained why he was always hunched over.

The first movie my parents took me to was "The Ten Commandments" and it played at the Panorama Theater in 1956. I was four years old and watching this color movie on a full sized theater screen was transformational for me. I had no idea that anyone could create an alternate reality that was so stunning and magical and meaningful. Moses, as a baby was found floating in the Nile River by the daughter of Pharaoh who adopted him and he grew up to lead the Jews to the Promised Land. The scene of God parting the Red Sea to allow his people to escape was totally awesome dude!

My parents never took me to another movie at the Panorama Theater but they did take me to the Van Nuys Drive-in a few times. After seeing a full length feature film in a theater, the drive-in was a letdown. Listening to the soundtrack coming out of a small tinny speaker that hung on the inside of the car window was less than ideal and watching the movie from the backseat was annoying as well because the rear view mirror blocked a good part of the movie screen. Another amazing kid moment that occurred in 1956 was being taken to Disneyland shortly after it had opened. I was astonished that grownups created this incredibly beautiful "Magic Kingdom" for children to enjoy. It was a wonderful adventure and Tom Sawyer's Island was the best bro!

Chapter 3

Something was chasing me and I was terrified. I tried running, but I felt the air suddenly turning into molasses. I started flapping my arms in desperation like a person drowning in the sea. And then, I started lifting off the ground! I started flapping my arms harder and harder and I went soaring into the sky. The predator chasing me was no longer a threat. I was so relieved. A wave of euphoria swept over me. I looked down and suddenly realized I was as high in the sky as an airplane. Dude, I freaked out! Fear gripped me like a vice and I lost control of my flying ability. The next thing I knew, I was sinking down to the ground. Faster and faster I fell. I was terrified and I forced myself to wake up. I jolted upright in my bed and sat there soaking in sweat.

My mom and grandma spent their days cleaning up rooms and running the motel while I kept myself occupied as best as I could. There were always interesting people coming and going each day and a couple of families who were long term residents. My mom had this freaking ancient washing machine that had wooden rollers on it. You could use them to wring out your clothes. One of the motel guests got her hand too close to the rollers and ended up running her arm all the way through the wringer. My mom heard her screaming and ran over to the machine and unplugged it. She helped the woman get her arm out. My mom was cool. She never complained about working hard or talked about the "Old Country". She just moved on with her life. "In Croatia," she once told me, "we have an expression: "Napred". It means forward." I immediately understood the profoundness of what she was telling me. So dude, from that moment on, I never looked back.

My mom told me that when I was younger, she would put me in a playpen outdoors while she cleaned rooms. One day, she came out and discovered that I had broken out. Apparently, I had busted a couple of the slats and then ran for it. After frantically searching everywhere for me, she finally found me standing on the curb of San Fernando Road. I was staring at the cars whizzing by me. The speed, size, and noise that the vehicles made must have convinced me that venturing further would be a bad idea. So, I was just standing there frozen in awe.

The manager's unit of our motel was in a duplex. Our next door neighbors had lived there ever since I could remember. They had a daughter who was a couple years younger than I was and her name was Yolanda. Her mother, Dolores, was kind and sometimes invited me into their home. Dude, they had something called a "Murphy bed" that folded up into the wall! It was so cool. So, at night they used the room as a bedroom and during the day it was their living room. When I visited, Dolores would always heat up some homemade flour tortillas on the open burners of her stove. She would spread butter on them, roll them up and give them to us as a snack. They were delicious!

Our motel was on an acre of land that fronted on San Fernando Road and ran all the way through to Ilex Avenue. I liked hanging out on Ilex for two reasons, it was quieter and there was a huge pepper tree next to the street that I loved to climb. I decorated the tree with postcards and some of my drawings. I loved that tree and it felt so good just to be standing or sitting in it. I could tell that it was old and solid and alive and being with that tree made me feel secure.

Our front yard was confining and so close to San Fernando Road that it was always loud. There were trains and planes and cars going by all day long and the only time of year that I enjoyed playing out there was when the bushes fronting the road were in bloom. They had these cool flowers that were multi-colored with bright yellow, red and orange blooms. When the bushes were blossoming, moths would perch on the small flowers with their wings slowly opening and closing. I would wait until their wings were closed before plucking them off the flowers with my thumb and index finger and carefully slipping them into a glass jar with a threaded metal lid. As I stood barefoot on tall, cool grass under the warm sun I had a great time watching them flutter about.

My brother, Joe, and I would stare out our front window when we were bored. I loved watching small planes landing at Whiteman's Airport which was across the road from us. It was a beautiful sight dude. The planes were so graceful as they slowly floated down to the runway and then gently touched down. Occasionally, a pilot would dip a wing too far to the right or left while landing and that would always scare me but I never saw anyone crash.

Whenever we heard a train coming we would rush to the window and start counting the number of cars that it was hauling. The number of locomotives in front would typically indicate how long or short the train was going to be. One locomotive would be pulling 50 or less cars. Two locomotives would be pulling less than 100 cars and three would be pulling more than 100. There were boxcars, flatbeds, cattle cars, hopper cars and tankers. The shortest train I ever saw had a locomotive pulling a caboose. Dude, that cracked me up so much, I kept laughing until tears came to my eyes.

Joe and I would also spend hours watching out the window and calling out the make, model and year of the cars that passed by. In the 1950's most cars were either, Fords, Chevys or Chryslers with the occasional Rambler, Studebaker, Cadillac, Pontiac, Buick, Oldsmobile or Mercury. Dude, all of them were gas guzzlers spewing out poisonous gasses. The air in the Valley was sometimes so thick with smog that it turned the air a purplish grey color cutting visibility down to a couple hundred yards. When the sun was low in the sky, it formed a small dull circle of red light that was surrounded by an orangy brown color and you could stare right at it without even squinting. Playing outside in that kind of smog was always a bad idea, and afterwards, I would complain to my mom that it felt like someone was sticking knives down my lungs every time I took a breath. It was bad dude.

If you went out in that kind of smog, even if you weren't running around in it, it made your eyes sting. They would start watering and quivering and you couldn't even keep them open. It was a drag. And whenever it rained you couldn't look up because the rainwater was so full of petrochemicals that it would burn your eyes! When autopsies were done on young people who were killed in automobile accidents the doctors found severe lung damage had occurred as a result of breathing in all that poisonous air. Dude, I started thinking that there had to be a better place to live.

Chapter 4

I was in school and I asked to be excused to go to the bathroom. My teacher said that it was okay to do so. I got out of my seat in a hurry and rushed into the boy's room to relieve myself. It took a long time but it felt good to reduce the pressure that had built up in my bladder. When I was done, I walked over to the sink to wash my hands. As I stared into the mirror, I realized that all my clothes had disappeared. I freaked out dude! How did this happen? Immediately, I headed out the door to find something to cover myself with. When I stepped outside some older students were standing there and they started pointing at me and laughing. All I could do was run away feeling horribly embarrassed.

I began pondering my earlier schooldays and remembered the most humiliating day of my short little life. My mother had dropped me off on the first day of my kindergarten class and wished me well. After sitting in class for a long time, doing what the teacher asked us to do, I realized that I needed to go to the bathroom. I looked around the schoolroom and realized that there was no bathroom within the confines of our four walls. Man this was totally messed up! I was too shy to tell the teacher I needed to go to the bathroom and I didn't want my bladder to burst so I just let it all out. I felt relieved and revolted at the same time and was so happy at the end of the day when my mom came to pick me up. I had lingered in my class sitting cross legged on the floor allowing all the other students to leave before I stood up. I figured that this would minimize my embarrassment. After all the students left, I stood up revealing a large circle of wetness on the front side of my pants. Dude, I had to walk all the way home like that. Sometimes, life just sucked!

Our kindergarten was completely fenced off from the rest of the school creating our own mini- schoolyard with our own play equipment. We were allowed to play outside every day after we had our milk and graham crackers. Occasionally, some of the older students would line up along the fence and stare at us chanting: "Kindergarten baby, born in the gravy." What did that even mean? I stared at them in shock while trying to make sense of what just happened. Slowly, each one of them dropped their gaze to the ground, turned around and never said another word. Dude, people are frickin strange.

During our play sessions, my teacher would separate the girls from the boys. The girls got to play house with cool little stoves and cupboards and cookware while the guys sawed boards. After I sawed one board, I decided that I was done with that activity. I wandered over to where the girls were playing and joined them until the play session was over. I did this repeatedly and sometimes my teacher would redirected me back to where the other boys were.

In first grade all I remember was reading about a couple lame little kids named Dick and Jane. By the way, who would name their kid Dick anyway? Do parents even think about the psychological damage that a guy walking around with that name would suffer? Or the trauma that a whole country would suffer being led by a President with that name? Sheesh! We also did lots of crafts which was fine with me because I liked working with my hands.

My second grade teacher always assigned trash pick-up duty to yours truly because I didn't pay any attention to him whatsoever. This was the consequence for choosing to talk to a kid sitting next to me instead of paying attention to my teacher. So bro, I was basically being punished for being sociable and talkative. Like what's wrong with that? If I could, I would have signed the dude up for a personality enhancement class and a speech class where he could learn to lose that boring monotone he spoke in which resulted in most of the class falling asleep.

One day, when I was out picking up papers, I heard this little Hispanic dude talking about last night's episode of the

"Toilet Zone". WTF? The "Toilet Zone"? Did I hear that
correctly? So, I perked up my ears and started listening to him.
As it turned out, he was retelling the plot to the previous night's
"Twilight Zone" television program. When I corrected him, he
got all pissed off and insisted that the show was called the
"Toilet Zone". Okay, so the little dude couldn't figure out that
someone in his family was joking about the name of the
program. I didn't want to insult him, so I just shrugged and kept
cleaning up.

During second grade, I was called into the nurse's office
for a checkup. When she asked me to read the eye chart I could
only read the big E on the first line and the F P on the second
line. That was it. She gave me a note that I was supposed to
give to my parents. It was a good thing that I asked her what
the note was about. She said that I needed glasses and if I
didn't pass the eye test with my glasses on, I would be sent to
the school for the blind. You've got to be shitting me lady! No
way am I going to a school for the frickin blind. So, I asked her
real nice and politely how many lines down would I have to read
in order to stay in my current school and she told me that I
needed to be able to read at least four lines down. I had very
cleverly worked my way closer to the eye chart before asking
her. And I immediately memorized the letters on all four lines:

E

F P

T O Z

L P E D

My folks set up an appointment for me at an
optometrist who worked out of a Montgomery Ward store in
Panorama City. The dude hooks me up behind something that
looks like a periscope and starts asking me which one is better
"A" or "B". And I'm thinking WTF? Is he talking about school
grades? Is he some kind of dumb ass that doesn't know that an

"A" is always better than a "B'? So, I politely responded by saying that I didn't understand what he was asking. We finally got it right and he goes on flipping lenses and asking which one was better "A" or "B". Like dude, this goes on forever. Finally we finish up and he tells my folks that the glasses will be ready to be picked up in a couple of weeks. Then the man turns around to me and says that even with my poor eyesight I could still be successful and maybe someday even become a foreman. WTF? Dude, my aspirations were way higher than that! Growing red with embarrassment, I looked down at the ground as I began turning away from the guy and headed for the exit thinking that this guy would totally fail as a fortune teller.

So, the first day walking to school wearing my new glasses was a bit challenging. I could definitely see a little better but it was weird looking out of two pieces of glass surrounded by black horn rimmed frames. It took some time before I felt somewhat comfortable walking with them on. About halfway to school one day, some older kid looks at me and calls me "Four Eyes". I felt so sorry for the dude. I mean, I knew that I didn't have the greatest eyesight, but at least I wasn't seeing double like he was! I reported to the nurse's office with my new glasses and read the letters I had memorized the last time I was in her office:

E

F P

T O Z

L P E D

In third grade, I had this teacher named Mr. Schneider who didn't like me at all. He was a violent little dude with a short fuse. He yelled at me several times and told me not to talk in class but I couldn't help it bro. We sat at a two person table and I thought that not engaging in friendly conversation with the person sitting next to me seemed totally inhospitable and rude. He tried moving the guy to a different spot in the classroom thinking that this action would make me shut up. Leaving me alone in the back of the room with no table partner to chat with was boring. Pretty soon, I was leaning over to talk with one of the kids sitting at the table next to me.

Schneider absolutely freaked out one day. He came running over to my table, grabbed me by the ear and pulled me out of my seat. As he started leading me out of the classroom, he was mumbling something about teaching me a lesson. I was thinking, holy shit this dude was going to kill me! After stepping into the hallway, he looked both ways making sure no one was watching him and he grabbed each of my shoulders with his hands and started shaking me violently. I thought my frickin neck was going to break! After he was done, he told me that he didn't want me talking in his class ever again and he went on saying that if I did so, he would do the same thing to me again. When he let go of my shoulders, I could barely walk. The hallway was still swaying, my legs felt like rubber, my head felt like it was going to explode and I thought I was going to barf.

So at eight years old, after being assaulted by my teacher, I resolved to never speak in class ever again. And dude, this violent act had a profound effect on me. I didn't like being victimized but realized I was too young and small to do anything about it other than comply with my attacker's demands. This event planted a seed deep in my little brain that budded into: Resentment of authority; A deep seated anger toward society in general; A hatred of anyone who would use physical force to make someone comply with their own will; A hatred of bully's; And a deep fear for my own personal safety. It also made me wonder how many other kids had suffered a similar fate or would suffer a similar fate at the hands of this sick little man. Sometimes bro, life is a bummer!

Chapter 5

I started laughing my head off when I first saw this freaky little dude dressed in a trench coat and wearing black horn rimmed glasses. I was fully grown and staring down at a boy who was about eight years old. As odd as it may seem, he was already going bald and he had this horrible comb over where a pitiful few black hairs laid across his bare scalp. As I looked more closely at him, I totally freaked out. I suddenly realized that it was a miniature version of my dad who was complaining to me about some grave injustice that he had suffered. So, I'm looking down at my miniaturized old man wondering how was it possible? How could I be the father of my father? Dude, my little brain couldn't handle this conundrum and everything froze as we stared into each other's eyes with great astonishment.

So, my dad was worse than Mr. Schneider. He had struck everyone in my family and we all carried around the trauma of the physical and psychological damage that occurred as a result. My mom suffered the most but my brother, Tony, was a close second. One night my dad came home crying while holding his ribs sobbing to my mom telling her that Tony had hit him and broken his ribs. Tony had already been married for a while and was living in an apartment with his wife. The concept of a son striking his own father was shocking to me.

The next time I saw Tony, I asked him what happened and he explained to me that my dad came over to his place and started yelling at him and pushing him around in his own home. Tony, who also had a hot temper, responded by punching my dad in the ribs. Tony was a scary dude. I remember driving with him to Roger Jessup Dairy for some milk and stuff and on the way back home some guy cut him off. Tony went ballistic and pulled his aqua colored Chevy pickup to the side of the road, jumped out, and barked at me to climb out of his truck. He pulled the back of the bench seat forward and started digging through stuff that was stored back there and finally grabbed a steel lug wrench. I started thinking WTF? He didn't have a flat tire or anything so what was going on? While I'm mulling over the possibilities, he shoves the seat back, yells at me to jump back into the truck, and pulls out into the road at an alarming speed. After building up my courage, I asked him what he was going to do with the lug wrench and he quickly responded that he was going to through it through the windshield of the guy who cut him off. Like dude, who does that? Fortunately for everyone, we never caught up with the bad driver.

My dad didn't limit himself to hitting family members. One day, he grabbed a young kid who was riding his bicycle through our motel parking lot and smacked him around while yelling at him to never ride his bike through our property again. That night there was a knock on our back door. When my dad opened it, the father and uncles of the boy he had slapped around earlier in the day were standing outside brandishing knives and yelling at my dad. My mom freaked out. While gathering her two youngest children together, she screamed at us to stand behind her. She got into a protective stance gripping a broom and readying herself to do battle with the angry men.

Our visitors were Hispanic and I heard my father speaking to them in Spanish – both he and my mom went to night school to learn the language so they could communicate with our non-English speaking neighbors. Fortunately, the men calmed down after a while and then left peacefully. Apparently, my father's dad was also involved in a similar altercation in Croatia that ended with a group of townspeople beating him to death with boards that had nails hammered through them.

Shortly after this bad encounter of the worst kind, my parents sold our motel and moved to Thousand Oaks. They had purchased an aqua colored home at 763 Avenida de los Arboles which was built on a quarter acre lot. There were no homes directly behind our property and that provided us with an unobstructed view of the countryside. It was fun not having fences up. The neighborhood kids all played together running through each other's yards.

We moved into our new home in January of 1961. My dad joked about President Kennedy moving into the White House while we were moving into the aqua house. Like dude, why did I remember that dumb comment? Probably because it was my dad's first attempt at humor. My dad had Nixon bumper stickers on his car at the time but thankfully, it wasn't Tricky Dick's turn to be President. During the 1960 Presidential campaign, I had heard both candidates speak and I was totally impressed with John F. Kennedy. Nixon, on the other hand, just sounded like a dour and insincere person.

Before buying our home, my mother had cautioned my dad about the length of the commute he would have from Thousand Oaks to the Budweiser brewery in Van Nuys. He reassured her that he wouldn't mind the drive but his 1959 Pontiac with its big V-8 engine was costing him more to drive than he had anticipated. Coupling that with the lost revenue from the sale of our motel, he felt squeezed financially. Dude, this income reduction and cost increase totally worked in my favor resulting in no more miserable trips to Las Vegas! They even cut back on their trips to San Pedro!

My mom signed me up to attend Ladera Elementary School where I was placed in a third grade class. It was a brand new school with plenty of open space around it. The teachers there were much nicer and the atmosphere was more relaxed. But dude, there was something missing. Pacoima was a multi-ethnic and multi-racial environment and Thousand Oaks wasn't. It was pure vanilla. The kids had no depth of character and they were not nearly as nice as my old friends from Haddon Avenue Elementary. There were no mom and pop grocery stores like

Del Guadio's Market which was run by Sal and Esther Del Guadio who had incredibly big and colorful personalities. There was no Ritchie Valens or Cheech and Chong. It was really dull bro. I felt like I was abducted by aliens and dropped onto another planet entirely stripped of joy and brightness.

One day, I went for a walk down a street forming a tee intersection directly across from our home. Looking out our kitchen window, you could see all the way down to the end of this road. Model homes were built on this side street and colorful flags were fluttering at the top of twelve foot wooden poles anchored in bare dirt. I tried climbing up one of the flags but it started bending as soon as I was a few feet off the ground. I kept on walking until the road ended. There was a huge, white wooden barrier anchored in gravel with red, plastic reflectors plastered all over it. Beyond the barricade was a junk yard surrounded by a tall chain link fence with busted up cars stacked all over the place. When I approached the fence, I was startled by a large Doberman that started barking and jumping up onto the fence.

It was my first encounter with a vicious guard dog. As I was backing away from the fence, I bent down and picked up a handful of gravel just to make myself feel more secure. Once I was on the other side of the barricade, the dog stopped barking and I stood there staring at a bunch of red reflectors while clutching a fistful of rocks. Soon, I was throwing the pebbles at the plastic targets and then checking to see if I had managed to crack any of them. I was starting to get bored and hungry so I did a 180 and headed back home.

I was nearly in front of my home when I heard a car roaring up behind me. I turned around and saw a white 1959 Chevy Impala swerving toward me. The car came skidding to a stop with the driver's side parked next to the curb. The driver swung open his door, jumped out of his car and started yelling at me about breaking the windshields on his junk cars! And I was thinkin' no frickin way dude. The balding driver wearing a white tee shirt grabbed me while muttering something about teaching me a lesson. I immediately flashed back to Mr. Schneider muttering the same thing and I was thinking no way dude!. I didn't want another lesson so I started struggling and screaming my head off yelling kidnapper, kidnapper!

So, the child abductor shoved me into his car from the driver's side telling me he's going to take me to the Sheriff's office. Eyeing the door handle on the passenger side of the car, I started thinking about opening the car door when the driver would have to stop at the tee intersection directly in front of our home. As the guy brought his car to a stop, I had my hand on the door handle ready to swing it open as he looked to his left for oncoming traffic. At that moment, I heard my mom yelling as she bolted across the street stopping right in front of the dude's car with both hands on his hood screaming, "Let my son out!"

The dude was pissed off. I instantly sprang out of the car. He put it in park but left the engine running as he stepped outside to talk his way out of his predicament. My mom told me to go into our backyard where my dad was doing some landscaping. I rushed across the street, opened our gate and ran to my dad. He was standing there with a cigarette hanging out of his mouth with no shirt on while shoveling dirt into a wheelbarrow. I felt so relieved escaping another lesson from a child abductor!

Chapter 6

I was in my backyard walking along the top of our cinderblock fence when our neighbor's German shepherd ran over and started lunging at me. He was barking ferociously and baring his teeth as he repeatedly tried to bite my feet. As I worked at keeping my feet away from his mouth I tripped and fell into our neighbors yard landing on my back. The dog ran over to me growling loudly and I shook myself trying to wake up. When I woke up I still heard the growling in my bedroom and I was totally freaked out. How did the dog get into my room? Where was it? I was frozen with fear. I just laid there motionless and listening and trying to piece together what was happening. I finally realized that our furnace was on and my bedroom door was shut and making a loud rumbling sound as the air was being forced out of my room and sucked toward the cold air return located down the hallway. Dude, I was sweating bullets but was so thankful that our neighbor's freakin' dog wasn't in my room!

My brother John came back from Germany in 1962 and was living with us again. He had brought back a German phrasebook, some German coins and a huge collection of beer coasters from the bars he had hung out in. He also brought back a chess set and he taught me how to play. We spent many evenings sitting across from one another playing chess. Dude, it may have looked like a laid back game but we were battling mightily in our minds looking for ways to corner one another's kings. My dad and my brother Joe also spent time sitting across from me. I beat my dad easily but Joe and John were formidable opponents who won about half the games we played.

One day, after school, I saw an RV parked across the street from Ladera Elementary School that had the name of a local newspaper stenciled on the side of it. They were trying to recruit kids to deliver newspapers. About 15 kids at a time were ushered in for a short spiel about how we could earn money as paper boys. At the end of their presentation they handed out bags of M&M's to everyone who participated. I ended up going through the line about a dozen times stuffing candy into my lunch pail. The guys handing out the candy didn't seem to mind.

Afterwards, I started heading home. A classmate of mine caught up with me and I showed him all the M&M's I had. Dude, his eyes got as big as saucers and he was so jealous. We passed by a couple of other kids who had a BB gun with them and my classmate walked up to his gun toting friend and whispered in his ear. A big grin spread across the face of the kid with the BB gun as he lifted it up and pointed it at me. Holy shit! Was this a frickin hold up? Was I stuck in a time warp and back in the wild West where I was facing down a gun slinger?

The little dude told me to hand over all my candy. I was so pissed off! I had never been shot by a BB gun and didn't want to know how much it would hurt so I reluctantly opened up my lunch box and handed over the goods. I was a victim of armed robbery by my peers! This little situation made me realize that I would have to spend the remainder of my public school years surrounded by future felons of America. I'm telling you bro, public school was a dangerous place.

John ended up finding work as a construction worker and it seemed to suit his needs. He was enthusiastic and interested in learning more about building. When he turned 18 in November of 1961, he was given the money the court had awarded him for his injuries resulting from the plane crash at Pacoima Junior High School. The first thing he did with it was purchase a brand new 1962 Pontiac Grand Prix coup. It was a sleek looking car with clean lines and painted a beautiful deep shade of maroon. It was loaded with all the latest gadgets like automatic windows and air conditioning. Definitely a cool ride. It was the first year that Pontiac came out with a hardtop convertible. But bro, talk about following in your dad's alcoholic, smoking, new car buying, Pontiac driving blue collar worker footsteps. Sheesh!

My dad was diagnosed with lung cancer near the end of 1962. His forty year smoking habit caught up with him and as soon as he heard the word "cancer" it was all over for him. After coming back from the hospital one day, he lifted up his shirt to show me a massive rectangular, dark brown swath of skin that had been burned into his chest as a result of an "experimental" radiation treatment. After the procedure, whatever bit of fight that was left in him was extinguished as quickly as one of his own cigarettes. He went into his room, laid in his bed for a few weeks, and then was admitted to the hospital where he quickly passed away in January of 1963. I was ten years old. Two months later, my grandmother died from intestinal cancer.

Dude, it was a huge shock for all of us. I began pondering what life would be like without my dad and grandmother around anymore. My mom became anxious and concerned about how we were going to survive. She wanted to sell our home and move back to the San Fernando Valley where shopping was within walking distance. My dad had never allowed her to get a driver's license so she needed to be close to bus lines as well. She was entitled to Social Security survivor's benefits and had a small income from a note and deed of trust she was carrying back from the sale of our motel in Pacoima. She put the house up for sale and we ended up moving back to the Valley in the summer of 1963.

Chapter 7

I was in a strange room trying to fall asleep when I heard what sounded like a baby crying outside my window. It would cry a little and then stop... Cry a little more and then stop... This went on for the longest time and it bothered me to think that a baby was outside crying. I looked out the window where two huge elm trees were standing across an asphalt driveway. The crying was coming from high up in the tree. WTF? How could a crying baby climb all the way up a huge elm tree? I listened some more and worried some more. Maybe someone else would hear it and call the fire department. Was it really my responsibility to do something? Dude, I was only a kid and I didn't know what to do, and then everything went dark and quiet.

John used some of his money to buy a house in Panorama City located at 8343 Tyrone Avenue. It was a three bedroom one bath home with a built in pool in the backyard. He said that we could all live there with him. My mom didn't have much of a choice. John did a great job finding a home in an established, suburban, middle class neighborhood that was close to Food Giant and The Broadway department store located on Van Nuys Boulevard. We were also close to Roscoe Boulevard which had several bus lines running down it. The neighborhood had plenty of kids my age living on our block and I was excited about that.

A few days after we moved in, there was a knock at our front door. I walked over, opened it, and stared into the eyes of a strange little dude with a shaved head holding a flat basketball. He had a big smile on his face and asked me if I wanted to come over to his house and play basketball. WTF? Was this kid like mentally challenged? Was this a joke? Play basketball with a flat ball? I was taken aback by the entire situation and the only thing I could think about was getting rid of this strange little kid standing on our front porch. I told him that I would have to ask my mom to see if I could go out to play. I quickly closed the door and stood behind it for an appropriate length of time and then opened it up again and told him that my mother wouldn't allow me to play right now. The little dude looked dejected as he hung his head and tried to bounce his ball which just made a plop sound and sat motionless at his feet. I told him I was sorry and slowly closed the door. Dude, I felt bad but it was all too weird for me.

Later that day, a small crowd of kids congregated on the sidewalk in front of our home and just hung out together chatting and joking and having fun. I snuck peeks out the window and realized that they were all waiting for the appearance of the new kid on the block. It was an embarrassing moment for me, but I mustered up the courage to face the inevitable and walked out the door. Everyone was friendly and excited to meet the new kid and they all told me their names and I filled them in on where we moved from and why. It was the beginning of the best summer that I ever had dude.

Alan was a Jewish kid who lived up the street and we hit it off immediately. After the crowd dispersed, he asked me if I wanted to ride bikes with him. I told him that I would love to but I didn't own a bike. He said that I could borrow his brother's bike. I stepped inside my home to let my mom know what I was up to. Alan and I walked over to his house where we got onto bikes and started cruising around our neighborhood. We rode over to the Food Giant parking lot dodging around parked cars and riding up and down the aisles. We had a great time and I got a better idea how the neighborhood was laid out. After riding back to Alan's house, his mom came out and told him that it was time to get ready for dinner. I thanked him for letting me borrow one of their bikes and walked back down the block to my new home.

After dinner, kids started to gather in front of our home again. I went outside to join them and we all decided to play a game of hide and seek. Every night, for the rest of the summer, we either played hide and seek, pom pom pull away, tag, or tug of war until the street lights came on. That was the signal that the day was done and everyone's parents wanted their kids to come home for the night. We all had a blast playing together bro and I was having the time of my life.

The name of the kid with the flat basketball was Tony. He was a Hispanic kid who was creative and fun to talk to and hang out with. One time after dinner he told me he wanted to buy me an ice cream cone at the Thrifty Drug store located across an alley from the Food Giant Market. Dude, no kid ever volunteered to buy me anything in my entire life! I asked him if he was sure and he said yes. After walking over to Thrifty's, I ordered one scoop of vanilla and Tony got the same for a grand total of a dime. We hung around a magazine rack thumbing through several issues of slick magazines filled with lots of full color glossy photos while licking up our ice creams. When we were done, we headed for the front door. Tony stopped next to a candy display, lifted up his foot while resting one hand on a shelf full of candy and adjusted his shoe with his free hand. As his shoe came back down to the floor, he managed to nonchalantly grab a candy bar and stuff it into one of his pockets before walking out of the store.

After we had walked away from Thrifty's, Tony pulled out the candy and asked me if I wanted half of it. Dude, I was mistified. I didn't see him pay for any candy so I asked him if he bought it? He said no, he stole it. I couldn't believe how matter of fact his response was. He must have read the perplexed look on my face and told me that he did it all the time. Wow, the little dude was a big time thief! I felt uncomfortable being his accomplice and he picked up on the bad vibe. He said it was no big deal but I wasn't so sure. Finally, I put my hand out and accepted the contraband. As we walked on, he said that taking a candy bar from a store wasn't hurting anyone. I pondered that comment as we headed back home.

That night, as I laid in bed, I began dissecting Tony's statement. Did it hurt anyone? It was just some big name chain store that made millions of dollars every year. How much could it hurt them? It was just a loss of a few pennies. But what if we got caught? My mom would freak out dude! The moral debate raged on and on, and it was keeping me up a long time. Finally, everything went dark and quiet.

As the summer progressed, Tony and I took several after dinner walks for ice cream. Tony would always steal something on his way out and then share it with me along with some comment about how easy it was to steal stuff or how he never got caught stealing stuff. One night, while stopped at the candy display, Tony quietly leaned over and said why don't you take one, no one is watching? My heart raced. I had witnessed Tony doing this multiple times. I reached out for my favorite chocolate bar with a trembling hand and quickly stuck it in my pocket. Dude, my heart was pounding so hard I thought it would explode! We casually walked out the front door and headed back to our street. Once we were away from the Thrifty's, I pulled out my loot with shaking hands and ate it. I suppressed the fact that I was now a criminal. After all, it didn't hurt anyone.

Time passed quickly and our thievery grew exponentially. Soon Tony and I were walking into Food Giant, grabbing large shopping bags from a checkout stand and then filling them up with toys and candy and snacks. After the bags were full, we simply walked out the front door. It was a piece of cake. Afterwards, we would walk back to my front lawn and empty our booty into a large pile spending the rest of the day examining and playing with and munching on our treasure. Neighborhood kids would come over and we would share all the stuff we got telling them that Tony's mom bought it for us.

Skateboards were real popular that summer and a couple of the kids on the block had them and shared them with the rest of us. We took turns riding them up and down the block and sometimes one kid would ride his bike down the sidewalk while pulling someone else riding a skateboard. They were absolutely bitchin' dude!

Two brothers, Rick and Bill, lived across the street from us and they had a basketball hoop in their front yard that was attached above their two car garage. Rick was close to my age and Bill was older and way taller than I was. Occasionally, I would see them shooting baskets with their dad and I would head on over to their place to play a little 2 v 2 with Bill and me against Rick and his dad. They taught me all the rules and I picked up the game fast.

Lorie lived next door to Rick and Bill and she would sometimes let me into her house to watch TV. She was older than I was and usually pretty nice to me except for the time she wanted to show me a cool trick. I agreed to let her, so she took my hand and started rubbing the hairs on top of my forearm in a circular motion. For an eleven year old kid, I had extremely hairy arms. I was so embarrassed by them when I was in third grade that I used my oldest brother's electric shaver to cut off all the hair on both my arms. Anyway, when Lorie was done I had an arm full of knotted up hairs! She said that they would just wash out in the shower but they never did and It took me a couple of painful hours to untangle all the little knotted hairballs. Some of the nasty knots had to be cut off with a pair of nail scissors.

Mark, who was also Jewish, lived next door to me and was one of the kids that I hung out with. His dad had an east coast accent of some sort and frequently called out for his son with a booming voice – Maaaak! You could hear that voice from a block away. Mark always looked nervous when his dad called him and he would immediately start running home. Mark's cousin worked at the lunch counter inside of Thrifty's and one day he invited Mark and me to have lunch with him one afternoon. His cousin was from Israel. Mark and I took him up on his offer and he was quite nice to us. It made both of us feel like "big kids".

Chapter 8

I was lost in a strange neighborhood and it was dark. I thought if I climbed a tree I would be able to check out my surroundings and get some idea of where I was. One of the houses, on a corner lot, had a big tree in front of it

. So, I climbed to the top of it and looked around the neighborhood. I could see lights on in people's homes but I couldn't recognize where I was. I wondered if I could jump from one tree to the next until spotting something familiar. There were plenty of trees around and they were all close together. I took a big jump and landed safely and softly onto a neighboring tree. Dude, it was so much fun! I was so ecstatic that I just kept jumping from one tree to another not worrying about where I was.

Summer was coming to a close and I was facing the prospect of entering a new school and enduring the trauma associated with that. I collected school supplies with my mom from Panorama Stationery on Van Nuys Boulevard while wondering how the school year would unfold. I was registered to start a sixth grade class at Chase Street Elementary School which was located on Chase Street – duh – and Hazeltine Avenue. Before school officially started, I walked there and back home again a couple of times just to get an idea of how long it would take me and to familiarize myself with the neighborhood.

I resented being dragged to another new school and it made me angry. One of the items that I stole over the summer was a slingshot. On a bright sunny day, just before the school year was to begin, I pocketed my slingshot and went outside to search for pebbles. I found a pile of gravel in a neighbor's driveway and shoved a handful of rocks into my pocket. As I got on my bike, I started riding over to the Food Giant parking lot and began scoping out potential targets. There was a small, yellow kiosk sitting in the middle of the parking lot, and it had windows on all sides. It was a small business that made duplicate keys for people in the neighborhood.

Dude, I did a ride by first to make sure no one was inside. After passing right next to it, I determined that it was an ideal target. Slowly, I made a wide arc until I was facing the innocent and blameless structure. I peddled fast to gain some speed. As I approached my targeted window, I started coasting and steered the bike with my left hand. After placing the pebble into the leather strap of the slingshot, I began pulling the elastic bands back as far as I could then I released it. The thin window pane was no match for my swift little stone as it poked its way through the glass. It made a slight cracking sound and dozens of jagged cracks spiraled outwards creating a spider web pattern in the window. It was so cool dude! I peddled away with my legs pumping, my adrenaline flowing and my heart pounding.

After arriving back home breathless and sweating, I realized that my anger had been misdirected. Then I felt bad. After all, I was angry because I was being forced to change schools again. And then I realized my mistake. I should have targeted my new school! Well, as they say, better late than never. So, I hopped back on my bike and peddled over to my new school and proceeded to pop a few holes in a couple of windows. Dude, I have to confess, it didn't make me feel any better. I chucked my slingshot into a school trash can and rode back home feeling even more burdened than before.

Late that afternoon, there were a bunch of kids in my front yard looking up at a streetlight anchored to the sidewalk. The light was attached to a curved steel arm hanging over our street resting on top of a concrete pole. The kids in the neighborhood were challenging one another to see who could climb it. Everyone agreed that this activity required wearing jeans and sneakers because the concrete was so coarse that it would scratch our legs and feet if we tried climbing it while

35

wearing shorts and flip flops. A few of the boys, including myself, decided that we could climb all the way up and touch a large steel ball that adorned the top of the pole.

The climbers went home then reappeared wearing the appropriate gear. I decided to trade my tee shirt in for a long sleeved sweatshirt before rejoining my friends. One by one we attempted the climb with varying degrees of success. Some kids barely got off the ground, others made it halfway up but no one made it to the top until it was my turn. Slowly and deliberately I pulled myself up locking my legs securely around the poll to prevent any backsliding. I was in no rush.

As I reached the top, I made the mistake of looking down. Dude, I started freaking out and froze. Touching the top of the round ball required letting go of the pole with one arm. Dude, I was so scared I couldn't even think. I started taking deep breaths until my heart stopped pounding. There was no way I was climbing back down the pole without touching that stupid metal ball! It felt like an eternity passing before I slowly lifted my left arm off the pole and began reaching for that dumb ball. I totally lost control of the situation and fell all the way down to the street. I landed on my head busting my skull open and splattering my brains all over my friends!

Just kidding dude! But that was the fear I was dealing with. In reality, I gripped that pole as hard as I could with my legs and ever so slightly loosened my left arm making sure I wouldn't slide backwards. Slowly, I grew more confident. I carefully took care of the last detail by fully extending my arm and touching that freaking stupid round metal ball! Afterwards, I wrapped my left arm around that pole and ever so slowly and carefully slid all the way back down. My friends were patting me on the back with loud cries of congratulations. I was just happy I got back down safely. As I stared down at the ground, I was so happy to see my shoes firmly planted on terra firma. I was astonished to see the condition of my shoelaces though. They were completely ripped to shreads bro.

On the last day of summer vacation, we all realized that the days were becoming shorter and the streetlights were coming on sooner and a sense of impending doom was hovering over our heads. All the kids in the neighborhood were sad and walking around with their backs slightly bent and their heads hanging down. Santa Ana winds were blowing as we gathered together one last evening and started talking about how much fun we all had that summer. With school starting the next day we were all painfully aware of all the reading and homework that we would be forced to do during the coming school year. After moaning and groaning about it, we all decided to end our summer on a happy note by playing one last game of hide and seek. Our sorrow was soon drowned out by running, hiding and sprinting back to home base yelling FREE!

Just before the streetlights went on, I ran and hid in a tall cypress tree growing in a neighbor's front yard while the person who was "it" was counting out loud to 100. The Santa Ana wind was blowing hard as I quietly climbed to the top of the tree. As I was swaying back and forth in the wind, I had a 360 degree view of the Valley allowing me to watch a brownish orange band of twilight slowly sinking below the horizon.

Our streetlight came on and I heard a collective moan from all my friends as they abandoned their hiding places and began walking home. Lights were shimmering across the Valley and the foothills were turning into silhouettes. Standing on my perch hugging my huge friend, I lingered and watched the darkening sky. Soon the city lights were shining like brightly lit diamonds against black velvet . I was in a peaceful place, nearly sacred, just being with this living tree that was providing me with comfort and companionship. I felt safe and secure as its branches fanned out around me protecting me from a world that was cold and cruel. It quietly beckoned me and welcomed me to stay in its open arms where I found strength and encouragement. Dude, I miss that tree and the time I spent within its branches. As I climbed down and started heading home, I realized why the Mexican settlers named this place "City of the Angels". The warm days, the sweet summer nights, the cloudless skies, the colorful sunsets, the open landscape, the cooling sea breeze blowing in the sweet smell of sage from the mountains all combined in such a heavenly manner. No wonder people were moving here in droves!

Chapter 9

My first day at school was not as traumatic as the one I experienced in Thousand Oaks. I knew where the school was located and I knew how to get back and forth to it from my new home. It was an uneventful day but we were assigned text books and homework. We didn't have backpacks, back then, to carry our stuff in. Instead, we had to carry our notebooks and text books under our arms. And dude, there was always a practical jokester around who would walk up behind you, stick out his arm, place his hand on the top of your notebook and push down hard and fast. The notebook and whatever else you had balanced in your hand would flip backwards, crash to the ground and spread all over the place. A real bummer bro.

I thought of a brilliant idea that would resolve this problem. I asked my mom if I could use an old briefcase that she had sitting around our home to carry my school stuff in. She had no problem with that so I picked it up, took it to the bedroom that I shared with my brother Joe, and shoved all my stuff in it. It was a sturdy briefcase made of leather. It had a nice handle on top and a wide strap that you folded over when you wanted to close it. The end of the strap had a catch on it that you slipped into a brass latch that had a spring loaded button on it. You had to push the button downward if you wanted to release the strap once it was secured.

So, on the second day of school, I was carrying all my school stuff in my brown, leather briefcase. The handle fit into my hand nicely and it was way easier to haul my school stuff around like this. Man, I was such a nerdy little dude! When I walked into my classroom I could tell that my schoolmates found my briefcase intriguing. Many of them walked over to me to check it out. I showed them that the bottom of the case was like an accordion that would expand and contract depending on how much stuff you crammed into it. I also showed them the built in dividers that you could use to help you organize what you put inside. Before the day was over, my classmates started calling me "The Brain".

After the first few days of excitement were over, the days grew more mundane and began forming into a painful brain fog making it difficult to differentiate one day from the next. To protect your sanity your mind lumped all those days together and shrouded them in fog so you wouldn't freak out from remembering each and every boring day. Instead, you just remember it all as walking through a painful mist. School was so boring for me that it still causes me great pain just thinking about it.

When you were young and sitting in a classroom, time passed by in super slow motion and an hour seemed like a day. Time gradually speeds up as you age and by the time you are old, a day seems as long as an hour seemed to you when you were a kid in school. And dude, every single class I ever had to sit through had a big ass clock in it forcing you to watch every single second of the day tick by. Sheesh!

David was the first friend that I made in school. He had an identical twin brother named Daryl. I had never seen identical twins before and I was like totally fascinated. So I did some research on it and learned that identical twins were formed from a zygote, which is the cell that forms when sperm and ova are united in a woman's womb. A fetus grows through the process of mitosis, or cell division. Twins are created during that first division of the cell resulting in two cells that separate entirely forming two babies. Anyway, David was a cool dude and invited me over to his home to play ping pong and hang out together. Both twins were athletic and played little league baseball! I was so envious because I was still enamored with baseball. It sucked having poor eyesight!

I, on the other hand, lacking any other socially acceptable alternative to devote my considerable energy to, continued down the wrong path in life. In other words dude – I became a juvenile delinquent. During the school year, my friend Tony and I continued our friendship even though he was a year behind me in school. One day when we were walking around the Panorama Mall he came up with a game that he called "Titty Boom". It was simple enough. Whenever he spotted a young lady with large breasts, we would catch up with her from behind, split up so that one of us passed her on the right and the other on the left and then each of us would squeeze a breast and yell "Titty Boom"! Afterwards, we would run like hell laughing uncontrollably.

After repeating our little game a few times, we worked up a thirst and parked ourselves at Woolworth's lunch counter. We each ordered a Cherry Coke and sat there sipping our drinks and quenching our thirst. Suddenly, out of the blue, some lady comes up behind us and starts yelling at us right there in front of everyone. She started scolding us and telling us that we should be ashamed of ourselves and that we better stop doing what we were doing. As we slowly turned around to face our adversary, we saw one of the big breasted young ladies we had victimized earlier standing next to her angry mother. Her mom went on to tell us how disgusting we were and then turned and walked away in a huff.

We were totally embarrassed and red faced and shocked at the woman's outburst. It suddenly dawned on me, that we were doing something incredibly wrong and it wasn't a game at all. I never did it again bro. Meanwhile, our waitress came over and asked us what that was all about and we simultaneously shrugged our shoulders. She was a nice lady and she told us that the woman was probably just having a bad day. We nodded our heads, paid our bill, left a generous tip and scurried away with our heads hanging down.

One day, Tony came up to me during our lunch hour at school wondering how much saliva we could accumulate if we stopped swallowing our spit. We agreed to start saving our saliva half an hour before school ended. Dude, you have no idea how much saliva you can accumulate during that period of time! After school let out, I met Tony with his cheeks puffed out as big as mine and we started heading home. When we passed a bus stop on our walk home, Tony got all excited and began pointing at a bus as it was leaving. He ran up to it and unleashed the largest stream of spit you can imagine and then I did the same. Many of the windows were open and numerous passengers were moaning in unison as they were sprayed with all that nastiness.

The next day at school we decided to do the same thing. As we walked back home, Tony couldn't find an appropriate target for another spraying so we continued saving spit along the way. Dude, our cheeks were barely able to contain all that saliva. Finally, Tony starts tapping me and pointing down Chase Street. There were two guys riding on a small motor scooter and coming our way traveling close to the curb at a slow speed. Tony and I stood shoulder to shoulder with our toes on the curb facing the street. As the two boys approached, we spewed out our load of saliva showering both of them with our bodily fluids.

We took off running. As we were turning the corner onto Tyrone Avenue, I saw the guys pulling over and jumping off their scooter as they prepared to chase after us. So, I started wondering if that's why they called it Chase Street? Maybe this was like some weird corridor where dudes chased after one another. Anyway, after seeing how fast these guys were running I decided to hide in the backyard of the house on the corner. I barely made it up a driveway and behind the house when I heard them running by yelling "Let's get those assholes." I waited back there for a long time. Finally, I heard them walking back to their scooter as one of the guys said "I wonder where the hell they went?" I waited a while longer making sure they were gone, and then walked the rest of the way home.

My Brother Joe was also starting a new school this year. He had graduated from Camarillo High School as an honor student and had been accepted into UCLA. The bus rides to and from Westwood ate up quite a bit of his day and he started talking about staying in the dorms the next semester. He had gotten a work study job on campus so he was spending most of his time there. When he was at home, all he did was study.

Christmas was coming up fast and I was hearing quite a few carols on my little Sony transistor radio that I stole from The Broadway department store last summer. There was this one song that I heard multiple times and I was wondering what the hell it meant. The title of the song was: "I'm dreaming of a white Christmas". So, I'm outside playing in my tee shirt under beautiful blue skies the week before Christmas and the song comes on again on my Sony. WTF? I didn't get it dude. What the hell is a white Christmas? Were they talking about white flocked Christmas trees? They were very popular and quite a few of my friends had them in their homes. Dude, I couldn't figure it out and I was too shy to ask someone a lame question like what the hell is a white Christmas anyway? Maybe it was something racist.

Anyway, I wasn't too excited about Christmas because I never got anything that I liked. I usually got a bunch of clothes and occasionally a book or something. It was always hard for me to go back to school after Christmas vacation and listen to all the kids talking excitedly about all the fantastic gifts they got. I was getting used to it but it was still annoying. So, when I woke up Christmas morning and saw a bright green stingray bicycle with high rise handle bars and a banana seat I couldn't believe my eyes. Dude, it was so cool!

I untied the gigantic bright red ribbon resting on the long white seat and wheeled the bike toward the front door when I remembered that I was still in my pajamas. I also thought I should ask my mom's permission to take it outside.

After getting dressed, I rushed over to my mom's room, knocked on her door and asked if it was okay to take my new bike outside and ride it. She told me that it would be fine and she reminded me to thank my brother, John, for giving it to me. Dude, this was my best Christmas ever! After pushing my new bike out the door, I spent the rest of the day riding it around the neighborhood and trying to pull wheelies on it. I loved that bike!

Chapter 10

I was so excited to ride my bike to school for the first time. I hooked the handle of my briefcase onto the right side of my handlebars and slid it all the way down so that it was resting on the horizontal part of the bar where it was connected to the front fork. I hopped on my bike, cruised over to my school and locked my bike to the school's bike rack with my combination lock and chain. I was so proud to be riding my bike to school. It made me feel mature. People trusted me to be careful and to obey all the rules of the road. It was a busy day and after school let out, David, asked me if I wanted to walk home with him and I agreed. We had a great time chatting and enjoying one another's company as we walked. After doing my homework and eating dinner I went off to bed. As I woke up the next morning, I suddenly realized that I had left my bike at school! I was frantic and afraid that someone could have stolen my bike. My heart started pounding and I started shouting no, no, no... only to be woken up by my own screaming.

Dude, I hate violence and I hate bullies. At home, I was always able to keep Joe from beating the shit out of me by threatening him. Of course I was much smaller than he was and seven years younger as well; so, threatening him with physical harm would have been ludicrous. But, I quickly realized that I could control him with a different kind of threat. I set things straight with him at an early age by letting him know that if he ever hit me again, I would run to our dad and fink on him. My father was a violent man and he would get pissed off whenever he saw Joe hitting me. My dad would chase after him and give him a real licking whenever he could catch him. So, the next time he hit me, I ran and told my dad who immediately started chasing Joe and giving him a few good whacks after catching him. This immediately led to a truce that held for the rest of our time living at home.

Walking home from school could be a bit boring, so I decided to switch things up by occasionally taking a different route. On one of those days, I approached a house where this kid my age was standing at the edge of his driveway right next to the sidewalk. I figured he was just being friendly and was waiting there to say hi. Dude, I was totally wrong! When I got a little closer to him he started turning red and getting all agitated. Pretty soon the kid grabs my shirt and starts yelling right in my face telling me that he didn't want to see me walking in front of his house ever again. Then he gave me a good shove and told me to get the hell out of his neighborhood.

The next day at school, I talked to David about my encounter with the crazed bully and he was real cool about it. He just told me that he would walk home with me after school. We met up after the final bell rang at 3:00 pm and started heading home. We retraced my steps from the previous day and this weird little bully was standing guard at his driveway again. David and I were just minding our own business and not looking at the kid or saying anything to him. As I walked in front of him he grabbed me and started yelling at me again about not walking in front of his house. David, grabbed the kid by the collar telling him to pick on someone his own size and punctuated his statement by punching the bully in the nose. I was thinking, holy shit, this was getting ugly real fast. Instead, the bully just turned around, started crying and ran into his house. David and I didn't stick around. We just walked away like nothing ever happened. But dude, I never walked past that kid's house ever again.

One day a week David and his brother went to an after school class at Panorama City Presbyterian church at the corner of Roscoe Boulevard and Wakefield Avenue. They invited me to come with them one day after school and I did. The women at the church were real nice. After a little Bible study we worked on arts and crafts. We had a great time so I went with them a few more times. There was a kid named Dean who attended the class and he didn't like me from the very start.

One day after class, David and his brother and I were walking home when Dean came tearing after us and flat out tackled me to the ground. I was totally shocked bro! Realizing that there was no way out of this situation, I immediately counter attacked. Dean was older and bigger than I was but I was quicker and stronger. I dug my feet into the grass and used my legs to push him off me and ultimately turned him over and got on top of him. David was yelling and telling me that I could take him. I quickly got the kid in a headlock and raised my body off the ground with only my feet touching the grass. My upper body was resting on his neck and burying his face into the grass. Soon, the dude started yelling uncle. WTF? I'm not this kid's fricking relative! What the hell is he talking about? Then he started yelling I give, I give. That I could understand, so I let him go and he immediately ran away.

One day at school, this kid named Wesley and his buzz cut buddy named Bill were running around with a long hat pin that had a white oval head on it. Wesley brought it from home and the two of them went roving around the playground sneaking up on kids and poking them in the butt with the pin. They would run away laughing hysterically. Later on that day, they were threatening me with it so I told a teacher and she took the pin away from them. What a couple of dipshits!

The playground at school was a menagerie of prepubescent children of all shapes and sizes. You had the budding young criminals like Wesley and Bill along with another kid named Troy who was already smoking cigarettes. You had a small group of one, who went by the name of Pete and nobody wanted to be around him because he was always scratching his butt. Most of the prissy girls would be out playing two square or the more daring ones would be found playing four square. The more athletic girls would be jumping rope or playing hopscotch while the more athletic boys would be playing socco or kickball.

We all ate lunch out on the playground where they had picnic tables and benches to sit on. I always brought my lunch from home in a brown paper bag and so did most of the other kids. It was always interesting to see what other kids ate for lunch. The most popular sandwich was peanut butter and jelly between two slices of "Wonder Bread". My mom usually made me a ham and cheese sandwich or a tuna sandwich between two slices of "Oroweat Honey Wheat Berry" bread. I felt like the oddball because I was the only one with different bread but after watching a kid compress an entire slice of "Wonder Bread" into a ball the size of a marble, I knew that my bread was more substantial and filling. My mom almost always gave me some orange wedges to go along with my sandwich. One day, after eating my orange slices, I stuck a peal between my teeth and my lips so that when I smiled all you could see was the orange peel. My lunch buddies thought it was so hilarious that they paraded me around other tables telling my classmates that they had to watch "The Brain" smile. When I flashed my orange smile, It was so unexpected that everyone totally cracked up.

Chapter 11

I was hanging out at Tony's house one day after school and he was showing me how to give rocket rides. He laid down on his back with his knees tucked into his chest and his feet pointing up at the ceiling. He told me to sit on his feet and then he started counting backwards three... two... one... blast off. And as he said blast off he pushed me up with his legs as hard as he could. This sent me up and forward. Dude, it was totally cool! He did this repeatedly to me and then he asked if he could have a ride. I got on the floor, Tony sat on my feet and I proceeded to do the countdown. I shouted blast off and pushed him up as hard as I could.

That was a mistake. I had no idea my legs were that strong! I sent Tony sailing up to the ceiling and saw him bouncing off of it and landing hard with his hands behind his back breaking his fall. He not only broke his fall he also broke his wrist! I had never seen anything like it in my entire life! Dude, his hand was all limp and there was a bone shoving up the skin on the bottom of his forearm. Tony was crying his eyes out and I was feeling horrible. I told him he needed to call his mom right away and have her take him to the hospital. He gathered his strength, walked over to his phone and dialed his mom's work number. His mom came rushing home and took him to the hospital.

The next day, Tony showed up at school with a cast on his arm. He had painted it florescent green and kids in his class were signing their names on it. I went over to Tony's house after school to let him know how sorry I was about breaking his wrist. His doctor told him he needed to spend a few days resting and not playing any active games. Tony showed me a painting he made and it was beautiful. I told him that he was a super talented artist. Dude, I was totally blown away by his creative ability.

We decided to pass the time by making crank calls on his telephone. We just dialed random numbers with the same prefix as ours and when people answered I altered my voice to make it sound deeper and would say, "Hello, I'm with the Department of Water and Power and we have reports of a

power outage in your neighborhood. Could you please check your refrigerator to see if it's running?"

Then I would wait until the person came back to the phone and they would say, "Yes, my refrigerator is running." And then I would reply: "Well, if it runs down my street I'll catch it for you!" And then I would hang up. We took turns making the calls and both of us would laugh uproariously every time we hung up. I visited him at his home over the next few days and we chatted about all kinds of life issues that typical twelve year old boys talk about. We spent most of our time trying to unravel the mystery of the female mind and body. Tony didn't know much more about young women than I did but I did run across a reference book at the Panorama City Library titled the "Kinsey Report". It was totally cool and it had way more answers than I had questions! I read through the entire two volumes over the next few weeks. Dude, it's amazing what you can learn from reading books!

After Tony was allowed to go outdoors and return to a more active lifestyle, we resumed our usual shenanigans. We decided to walk over to the Panorama Shopping Center and along the way we would ring people's doorbells and quickly run away. Our first stop was the trash bin behind the US Post Office on Chase Street near Van Nuys Boulevard. The postal workers threw away undeliverable mail in a bin and Tony and I would frequently scrounge through it. One day, we were so excited because they threw away tons of direct mail ads that had a penny attached inside every envelope! Our busy little hands were ripping and tearing into those ads and peeling pennies off as quickly as we could.

During our marathon effort, we each collected a couple hundred pennies. Our pockets were bulging as we walked over to Thrifty's. We each bought several cellophane packages of Planters peanuts which were much lighter than lugging around a bunch of pennies. We leisurely popped peanuts into our mouths as we walked over to Robinson's Department Store. It was a new store and neither of us had ever been inside of it. They had interesting escalators that had a balcony surrounding them. After riding up, we circled around the escalators checking out the gently curving glass banisters topped with a curved wooden handrail. We leaned over the railing and could see people walking below us on the first floor. Most of the people were older women with grey hair.

I was awestruck by the openness of the design and the elegant curving handrail. We were still munching on our last packets of peanuts when Tony looked at me with a devilish grin. He asked me if I thought he could drop a peanut and land it on an elderly lady's head. I spurred him on by nodding my head. He took aim and released his first little peanut over the edge eagerly watching it sail down and missing its mark. Soon, both of us were launching peanuts over the edge occasionally hitting our targets and then quickly ducking back away from the railing so we wouldn't be seen.

Dude, we were having so much fun until we both ran out of peanuts. Tony suggested hitting our targets with wads of spit and I immediately agreed. One of the elderly victims must have reported us to the store manager who snuck up behind us, grabbed us by our shirts, marched us over to a backroom office and sat us down on a couple of folding steel chairs. She demanded our names and phone numbers and we gave her erroneous information. Afterwards, she got up and told us to wait in her office. After a few seconds, Tony said that we should make a run for it and we quickly sprinted back through the store and down the escalator.

A bunch of elderly women were waiting for us at the bottom of the escalator. Tony was in front of me and his florescent green cast was swinging hard and furious. None of the women wanted to get smacked with a hard cast so they stepped aside and let him go. The gap immediately closed up and several pairs of wrinkled arms were grasping at me and several angry wrinkled faces were yelling at me. It was a frickin nightmare bro! We were both apprehended and ushered back to the dreaded backroom. The manager was pissed off and she told us that she called the police and they were on their way. We started crying and bawling and wailing to no avail.

When the LAPD officer arrived he asked us for our names and phone numbers and this time we told him the truth. He tried calling Tony's mom but she was at work so he called my mom. When she answered the phone the officer explained the situation to her and told her that he would be driving us home. The officer led his teary eyed young perpetrators through the store with our heads hanging down and feet shuffling slowly and heavily along the highly polished floor. It felt like a death march bro. As the officer drove down my street, I saw my mom walking toward us a couple of blocks from our home. WTF? What was she doing?

I told the officer that the woman walking on the sidewalk was my mother. He stopped and rolled down the window and my mom started begging him to let us out of the car right there on the spot. The officer told her that he couldn't do that and asked her if she would like a ride back home. My mom repeatedly voiced her concern about what the neighbor's would think if a cop car pulled up to our home. Finally, my mom declined the invitation to ride in the cop car and she told him that she would prefer to walk back.

The officer drove onward and parked his car in front of my home where we waited until my mom got back. The officer walked us up to the front door, told my mom what we had done, released us into her custody and then turned and walked back to his squad car. After the officer left, my mom told Tony to walk back home. After walking into our house, she proceeded to scold me for what I had done and told me repeatedly that I should be ashamed of myself. She also let me know how embarrassing it was for a police officer to come to our home. Dude, it was a terrible, horrible, no good very bad day!

A few weeks later, Tony told me that his dad took him to this place called "The Classic Cat" on Van Nuys Boulevard. He said that there were waitresses there who weren't wearing any tops. WTF? I thought he was kidding me so he took me on over there. We went in through the backdoor. Dude, it was so dark in there that I could hardly see anything. There were some guys playing pool in the backroom as we walked past them and into the lounge area of the bar. My eyes adjusted quickly and got as big as saucers when I saw a waitress walk right by me with her breasts passing by at eye level. Dude, this was a first for me. I had never seen a woman's naked breast before! Some dude told us we didn't belong in there and Tony told him that our dad was playing pool in the backroom. We hung around until the guy returned and informed us that no one in the backroom had come in with any children and that we better get the hell out of there. We busted out of that place in a hurry!

Sometimes, Tony and I would go to a local coffee shop and order breakfast on a Saturday or Sunday. After we were done, we would pay close attention to the tables around us. When we saw that there were a few tips on the table tops we started eyeing the waitress. As soon as she would go into the kitchen, we would make a quick dash for the exit grabbing all the cash laying on the vacant tables. Once we were outside we ran hard and fast for home!

Chapter 12

John had met a young woman named Sandy shortly after moving into our home on Tyrone. Apparently, he got his fifteen year old girlfriend pregnant and her parents kicked her out of their home. Sandy came to live with us and she was a bunch of fun. She taught us all how to play Rummy 500 and we spent hours and hours playing that game together. Sandy was a short Italian gal who had incredibly large brown eyes that would totally envelop you. She was funny and sweet and my mother hated her. Sandy soon gave birth to my second niece, Gina. John had three more children with Sandy: Angela, Richard and Joseph.

Unbeknownst to me, my mom was shopping for her own home which she purchased in January of 1964. It was a tiny two bedroom one bath home built in 1949 on a small lot located at 8018 Wakefield Avenue. The home was only a few blocks away from our current home but I was pretty pissed off about moving again. My mom wanted to show me our new home so John drove us over. Dude, it was a frickin pink house! WTF? We walked inside and my mom showed me my room. You have got to be kidding me! A pink bedroom? I have to sleep in a pink bedroom? A frickin pink bedroom! My mom saw the bewildered look on my face and she told me that we could paint it another color.

It was a tiny house measuring 924 square feet. Dude, I was like totally bummed out. My biggest concern was having to change schools which I refused to do so. I asked John if I could continue using his home address as my permanent residence. I wanted to finish up the sixth grade at Chase Street School rather than going to school at Burton Street Elementary. Neither he, nor my mom, had a problem with that. Although Burton Street Elementary was way closer to our new home, I couldn't stomach switching to a new school again. Dude, it would have pushed me over the edge. It would have been my fourth school in four years!

Our new neighborhood only had a few kids my age living on our block. It was morbidly depressing! Most of the houses were little dinkers so the people living in the neighborhood were either retired folks or young married couples. There was one good thing about living close to Burton Street School – it had a wide and sloping concrete walkway that started at the sidewalk and went all the way up to the front doors of the school. I enjoyed riding a skateboard that I had stolen from "Ralph's Five and Dime" and the ramp in front of the school was ideal for practicing tricks and stunts. I usually went over there right after school to get some exercise and be outdoors for a while. Afterwards, I would ride back home, do my homework and then eat dinner with my mom on TV trays while watching Walter Cronkite on CBS Evening News.

I would occasionally go back to my old neighborhood on weekends to visit with John and Sandy. John began drinking more heavily and I would often find him sipping on a Seagram's VO-7 Crown-Windsor Canadian whisky mixed with 7UP first thing in the morning.   John started his own construction company and bought a new one ton Chevy truck that consisted of a red cab and a frame. There was no box or flatbed on it so John built a heavy duty steel flatbed for it. He then built four locking wood tool boxes that he bolted to the bed leaving enough space between the driver side and passenger side boxes to use for hauling stuff.

One day, I walked over to Tony's house and he told me that his flaky dad ran out on his family. His mom, whose name was Irma, worked at the GM plant on Van Nuys Boulevard but she couldn't afford to pay the rent on the home they were living in. They ended up renting an apartment on Blythe Street which was located directly across from the GM plant. I didn't see much of Tony after that and my trips to my old neighborhood began to dwindle. Now my life was even more boring and isolated.

I tried to think of things to do that either got me outside or away from my pink room and my pink house. I bought a BB gun, set up a target and began practicing target shooting. My interest in pitching had not diminished so I set up some cans and practiced throwing a softball at them. Frequently, I would walk over to the Library and look through photography magazines and read articles in "Psychology Today", "Life", "Time", "Newsweek", and "Scientific American". I was particularly intrigued by "Scientific American" and was always able to find fascinating articles in them. My science teacher, Mr. Dempsey, gave us an assignment asking us to write an essay on: "What Does Science Mean to Me?"

After reading so many "Scientific American" articles, I knew that scientific research was extremely important in developing a greater understanding of medicine and space. That was one assignment that I spent a great deal of time thinking about and writing. Afterwards, I asked my brother Joe to review what I had written. He said it was a pretty good paper and suggested a few changes that would make the paper flow better and I incorporated those changes into my final draft. I even typed it all up. A few days after turning the assignment in, Mr. Dempsey asked if I would be willing to read my paper out loud at our next school assembly. Dude, I was so proud! I practiced reading that paper out loud over and over and over again. After reciting it at the assembly I got a huge round of applause from the audience and it solidified my nickname - "The Brain".

In January 1964 "The Beatles" released their debut album, "Meet The Beatles", in the US. All the girls in school were crazy about the music and they were all gaga over the four young British rock stars. Dude, it was driving me nuts not having this album so I stole a copy of it from the W.T. Grant

Company located on the corner of Van Nuys Boulevard and Chase Street. It was a monaural vinyl LP album. Stereo music was just being introduced in the US so hardly anyone had a stereo record player at home. The LP stood for "Long Playing" because they spun around a turn table at 33 1/3 RPM's as opposed to 45's which spun at 45 RPM's and were much smaller in diameter than the LP's. The 45's usually only had one song on each side whereas the LP's had several songs on each side.

We had an old portable record player that I played my first "Beatles" album on. It was definitely a new sound that was different from 1950's rock and roll. They had cool long hair, matching collarless suits, skinny little ties and black leather boots. These dudes were totally different and their music and lyrics were fantastic! After they appeared on the "Ed Sullivan Show" in February of 1964 they became an overnight success and all the girls were singing "Beatle" songs at school. They brought a new and refreshing change to the music scene that helped ease the pain of losing JFK in November of 1963.

In June of 1964, everyone was excited about graduating from elementary school. None of us had graduated from anything before and we were all ready and itching to move on to Junior High. It was a memorable day for all of us. The girls were decked out in dresses and nylons and they all were wearing makeup. Dude, the only extra effort I made was putting on a tie! Everyone's parents came to the ceremony and we all listened to speeches. During the entire time, I couldn't take my eyes off my female classmates.

Chapter 13

I was hiking in the mountains when I saw stairs leading downward into a tunnel. As I began walking down the steps, which were cut into the mountainside, I caught a glimpse of an enticing view at the end of the tunnel and I decided to check it out. After stepping through the tunnel and into the open, I had a magnificent overview of a beautiful valley. A meandering river was flowing through emerald green fields snaking along for miles and finally disappearing into the distance. Suddenly, I realized that the stairs I was standing on were dangling over a steep precipice. Fear gripped my throat and pulled me down onto my butt. Slowly, I began crab crawling my way back up the steps.

Robert Fulton Junior High had an orientation for seventh graders, aka "Scrubs". So, I was wondering, what's a Scrub? We were told that some of the older students may scrub us with lipstick on our first day of school. I mean how messed up is that? It brought back memories of Kindergarten and being made fun of by older children. When will it ever end? Why did the "big kids" always have to display their superior size and strength over their smaller and younger schoolmates? There's no frickin way I'm going to school on the first day!

The first kid I met at the orientation was Dimitri. I asked him if he knew where the room number was that had been assigned to me as my "homeroom". What the hell's a "homeroom" anyway? I already had a room at home. Dude, I didn't get it. Why didn't they just call it a "warm up room" where you can prepare yourself to be humiliated by other schoolmates? Anyway, Dimitri was a friendly guy and he said that he would show me where it was. I was astonished at how mature Dimitri was for a "Scrub". It looked like he already had a five o'clock shadow at nine o'clock in the morning and he was a good six inches taller than I was.

I thanked Dimitri for showing me where my "homeroom" was as I pulled open the solid wood door. Since, my eyesight wasn't the greatest, I always preferred sitting in the front row where I could actually see what the teacher was writing on the blackboard. Most of the time, I just listened to whatever teachers were saying rather than watching them write it down as they were saying it. Dude, that was totally redundant and since people could speak faster than they could write it was a huge waste of time. It was also B O R I N G!

Mrs. Johnson was the name of my "homeroom" teacher and she began explaining the purpose of a "homeroom": It was to gather together and warm up before we went out to be humiliated by older schoolmates. It was also a place to hear announcements and fill out paperwork for administrative purposes. A D M I N I S T R A T I V E was a big word and it took Mrs. Johnson a while to write it on the blackboard. She spoke in greater detail about the kind of stuff we would have to fill out and what it was used for. She also showed us how the school was laid out on an "overhead" projector. It was the first time I had ever seen an "overhead" projector and I didn't particularly like it. She placed an 8 ½ x 11 clear plastic sheet with a map of the school on it and the image was magnified and projected onto the wall. So, dude, this was modern technology back in 1964. Sheesh!

We were handed our class schedule that showed us which classes we had for each of our six periods. Oh yah, Mrs. Johnson explained what periods were. It was different than this: "……". She told us that we would be changing classrooms six times a day and we would have different teachers L E C T U R I N G on different subjects. I immediately liked this idea. If I didn't like a teacher, I would only see them for an hour a day. That's better than getting stuck with a single teacher you didn't like for a whole semester! Plus, we got to move around for six minutes between periods. How cool was that bro!

So, after explaining all that, we rotated around all our classes. The periods were way shorter than normal but we were able to meet all of our new teachers and get a feel for how much time it actually took to move from class to class. Our dry run was a bit chaotic but worthwhile. After the six periods were over we met up back in our homeroom. One of the kids asked Mrs. Johnson if we would have the same homeroom during the entire three years we would be attending Robert Fulton Junior High. She told us that we would. I was glad she was a nice teacher.

My mother agreed that I could skip the first day of school after I told her about the lipstick. I heard her mumbling something about "Crazy Americans". On the second day of school, I walked up Lanark to Van Nuys Boulevard and caught a bus at the corner. Dude, the bus was so frickin crowded I had to stand up. Fortunately, it was a short trip. I couldn't help listening to this kid named Jim who was telling the bus driver about his visit to the White House and his conversation with the President. WTF? Is this kid serious or seriously messed up in the brain? I continued listening to the kid's rambling story as he explained it in great detail to the bus driver. Before getting off the bus at Saticoy Street, I determined that the kid had some serious issues.

I got to school early and waited outside Mrs. Johnson's room with some of the other dudes in my homeroom and told them about the kid on the bus. One of the guys said that he was probably a "Special Ed" kid. WTF? What the hell was a "Special Ed" kid? The dude saw the confused look on my face and then told me that there was a special school for retarded kids at Fulton. Apparently they also had blind kids there as well.

One of the blind kids, Scott, was in my physical education class - we called them PE classes for short and we had them every school day. Scott was a cool dude who had long blonde hair and wore super dark sunglasses all the time. I asked him if he was born blind and he told me that he had a bad accident. He said that he took a can of "Drano", put some water in it, screwed the lid back on, shook it up and was getting ready to throw it when it blew up right next to his eyes. The chemicals literally burned his eyes out. I'll never forget him running the 50 yard dash as Mr. Dye, our PE teacher, blew a whistle so Scott could run toward the sound. Man, that dude wasn't holding anything back! I watched him flying to the 50 yard line imagining what it would feel like running that fast with my eyes shut. It was the most dramatic display of courage that I had ever seen in my entire life!

Ed was another kid I met at Fulton and one of the first things he told me was how he had sex with his sister. Dude, that is so frickin wrong! I wished that I had never heard that because it was so totally messed up that I didn't want to have anything to do with this dude. He didn't like me ignoring him. So, one day while I was passing him in a hallway, he slugged me in the arm as hard as he could. WTF? Did he really just do that? I couldn't believe it.

A couple of days later I was talking to my friend David when I spotted Ed standing a few yards away from us. So, I told David what the dude did and he asked me to point him out. We walked on over to where Ed was standing and I pointed my finger at him and I said that's the guy who just walked up to me and slugged me for no reason. David immediately started punching him while telling him to pick on someone his own size. Ed ran away as fast as he could, and I honestly can say that I never saw the kid again. Incidentally, my friend David became a police officer with the LAPD. The dude had a keen sense of justice at an early age.

Arturo and I were in Mrs. Pearlman's art class together. He had a heavy accent and spoke English poorly. I liked him and we hung out together outside of class. After a few weeks into the school year Arturo vanished. He didn't tell me he was moving or anything. He was just gone. Years later, I ran into him at a record store he was managing in Van Nuys and the dude recognized me! I asked him about his disappearance and he relayed his story to me.

He told me that the kid that sat in front of him in our art class was an asshole, so he cut a hole in the kid's shirt with a pair of scissors. He was accused of assaulting a student with a pair of scissors. He said it was a completely overblown interpretation of the facts. In my book, Arturo was being righteously creative! It was an art class after all. That's not the way the Vice Principal, Mr. TeMaat, saw it. After Arturo's parents came to school for a conference, they agreed to pull Arturo out of public school and enrolled him in a private school. Arturo told me that he was not at all happy about it and did not like the school his parents chose for him. But, that was all in the past. So, we talked about the record albums I was buying.

Mr. Hatch was my algebra teacher and a student named Bobby was in his class. The dude was a math genius! After being nicknamed "The Brain" at Chase Street Elementary, I had a hard time swallowing the fact that this dude was smarter than I was. He was also an arrogant SOB and nobody liked him. Sometime during that semester, he was hit in the head with a baseball bat in a PE class. I didn't know if it was intentional or not, but rumor had it that it was. After that episode, Bobby dialed down his arrogance. You've got to hand it to public schools for being the grand equalizer. But, just for the record, I felt sorry for Bobby. No dude should get hit in the head with a baseball bat just because he's an arrogant little prick.

Chapter 14

I became aware of a popularity spectrum beginning to form at Fulton. We were all like a bunch of ping pong balls in a bingo machine that were floating around bumping into each other and assigning numbers to all the other balls we bumped into. For example, if you were the biggest bully you would be assigned the category of bully with the designation of number one. So every time you saw that person your mind would shout out B – 1. If you were the most intelligent you would be labeled I -1, and if you were the nicest person you would be N – 1, the biggest goof off would be G -1 and the biggest odd ball would be labeled O – 1. B I N G O !

So, the cumulative results formed a "bell curve" with a few people at both ends of the spectrum rated the biggest or the least and the overwhelming majority of us falling somewhere in the middle. Of course there would be a moderate amount of differentiation in that middle ground. I became fascinated with the P category or "Popularity Quotient". What made one person more popular than another?

There was this dude named Craig in my class who was hugely popular so I began to study his behavior and interactions with other classmates. I observed that he was amiable, fairly calm, well groomed and good looking. That didn't give me nearly the amount of information that I needed to figure out "The Essence of Craig" so I invited him over to my house after school one day to play. We had a snack together and chatted amicably then went outside and rode our bikes around the neighborhood while carrying on our conversation. After a while, I realized that I was getting bored. Craig didn't have strong feelings about anything, he didn't think deeply about anything, he wasn't particularly bright, and he didn't seem to possess any giftedness other than being popular.

I know that my study of popularity was only based on a sample of one and clearly wouldn't hold water for a peer reviewed paper on the "Essence of Popularity", but my theory was this: The farther away you were from the middle of the bell curve, the less popular you would be. Dude, this discovery was totally righteous! There was one exception to the rule though and it was this: If you were the absolute best at something, you would gain superstar status and absolutely everyone would be in love with you. That's a pretty weird dichotomy bro.

Anyway, I felt good about my discovery and the new personal truth that evolved from it which was this: I was far more interested in people who were on the periphery of the popularity scale because they were far more interesting than those huddled in the middle. Of course, I gravitated to the positive end of the spectrum and preferred making friends with the best and brightest and most talented of my classmates. As far as assessing my own strengths? Dude, I was like 13 years old – give me a frickin break!

I became friends with a guy named Byron. I never met anyone with that name before or since. It sounded like a snobbish name, but Byron was at the opposite end of the spectrum from that. He was a regular dude, or as some would say "A Man's Man". Byron noticed that I walked to school every day because he saw me as his dad passed me by on their way to Fulton. They pulled over one day and gave me a ride. They offered to drive me to school every day as long as I walked over to Byron's house by 7:30 am. Dude, I totally agreed to that. His dad was a construction worker who drove a 1960's Ford Econoline van. He always wore Levi's and some heavy duty boots to work and he treated me well.

It didn't take long to drive to Fulton so we always got to school early. Byron and I would walk over to the covered cafeteria and buy a hot chocolate and a warm, buttery slice of French bread for eleven cents. We were usually the first kids sitting there savoring our simple meal. Slowly, kids started gathering around us and by the time class was ready to start we were surrounded by a mob of loud rambunctious teenagers. There was an open concrete plaza just below the cafeteria where kids would throw pennies and Jim, the dude who visited the President at the White House, ran around collecting them. He was so busy! Kids threw pennies around before school, during nutrition, aka recess, and lunchtime. Jim never tired of chasing after pennies!

Tom, was another dude I met at Fulton and he came from a Greek family. We hung out together after school on the days that Fulton had after school activities. Tom and I spent time lifting weights, playing ping-pong and checking out who could do the most sit ups. One Saturday, I rode my skateboard over to his apartment and we spent some time skateboarding together. We ran into a couple older and much bigger dudes blocking the sidewalk so we had to stop and get off our boards. The dudes pushed us aside and took our skateboards and started taunting us. Are you kidding me!

Having grown up around older brothers I understood how they operated. They did mean things to me to get a reaction out of me like yelling, fighting or crying. They would just laugh and continue teasing me until they got bored. I figured these guys were doing the same thing so I refused to react at all. Tom, on the other hand, was totally upset and talking back to the dudes and they kept egging him on. They didn't even know how to ride skateboards even though they kept trying. Tom kept getting angrier and I could tell the dudes were enjoying lording their superior size and strength over us. Finally, someone yelled at the dudes from an upstairs apartment unit facing the sidewalk. Their faces turned red as they begrudgingly returned our skateboards.

This incident turned out to be a life changing event for Tom. He soon signed up for Karate classes where he earned a black belt. His dream was to open up his own dojo someday. I had joined the Van Nuys YMCA and took some karate classes as well but I quickly grew bored kicking and punching the air. Tom wasn't the main reason I took karate though. A girl by the name of Lynette, who was in one of my classes, told me she took karate lessons at the YMCA and that's what motivated me. Watching the instructor being abusive to a dude with long hair really turned me off to the class so I stopped going. I did enjoy the Olympic sized pool and the trampolines that the Y provided.

My interest in the opposite sex started stirring sometime in the eighth grade and Tom and I both liked this girl in our typing class. Her name was Cathy and she was attractive and had long, straight blonde hair. One day Tom asked me if I was interested in following her home after school and I told him that I was. So, we met up later that day and hung around outside until we spotted her leaving Fulton. We stayed put while watching her to see which direction she was heading. We didn't want to be too obvious so we let her get way ahead of us before we started after her.

We ended up following her up Blythe Street where Tom saw her duck into an apartment complex. We started running fast to catch up with her. Cathy was just entering her upstairs apartment unit when we arrived so we began hunting for a stairwell. Slowly, we climbed the stairs and began walking over to her unit. I rang her doorbell with a great degree of trepidation and shortly afterwards Cathy opened the door. We stood there staring at one another for an awkward moment until Tom said "Fancy meeting her here!" She immediately slammed the door in our faces. Well, that ended our crush on Cathy rather abruptly!

Cathy hung out with Donna and Cindy at school and the three of them were in my math class. One Friday afternoon after class, I was copying down a homework assignment from the blackboard when the three girls surrounded my desk. Cindy asked me what I had in the brown paper bag sitting on the floor next to my desk. I told her that every Friday I took my gym clothes and stuffed them into my empty lunch bag and took them home to be washed. In an instant, Cindy kicked the bag shredding the sack and sending my dirty gym clothes into the air. As luck would have it, my dirty underwear ended up draped over one of the ceiling fixtures and the rest of my stuff was scattered randomly around the room. The three girls laughed their heads off and ran out of the room. I was certain that this was retribution for following Cathy home. Payback's a bitch bro!

This Jewish dude named Andy was in one of my classes and we were chatting together outside our English class taught by Mr. Stokes who was the only African American teacher I had at Fulton. Our English class was right after lunch and Andy was telling me that he spent his lunchtime walking around with his friend Larry who searched for girls with shapely rear ends. After selecting his target, Larry sped up and squeezed their butt as he walked passed them. Dude! Who does that in school? I asked him if I could hang out with them during lunch the next day and he said sure. Larry was tall and lanky while Andy was short making them an odd pair. Larry was immediately categorized as an L – 1. He was the most lecherous dude I had ever met in my entire life! Andy wasn't kidding me about Larry. I watched him leering at several girls as he walked around the school randomly selecting his victims and squeezing their butts as he passed them by. This was universally greeted with a loud shriek after the evil deed was done. Ah… Junior High!

Chapter 15

In ninth grade, I had Miss Liepshutz for French. She had black hair and beautiful long legs that she proudly displayed beneath tight fitting miniskirts. The class had an unusual desk arrangement with half of the desks facing the other half. There was a wide isle dividing the two halves and Miss Liepshutz, wearing her black six inch heals, would proudly strut her long and shapely legs in front of us during much of the class. It was like her fashion runway dude! She sat on a high stool at the end of this aisle and that stool happened to be parked right in front of my desk. She frequently crossed her legs while sitting on that stool which hiked her skirt up to her crotch. It was a tough situation for a fifteen year old whose hormones were racing out of control! I can't tell you how many times I just wanted to reach out and grab hold of her thigh!

I quickly learned that I sucked at French because I always rolled my R's, as in "RRRRuffles have RRRRidges", which was apparently a big no-no. I should have taken a Spanish class where the teacher wanted you to roll your R's. I quickly lost interest in the class. One day I was fiddling around with my Bic pen when I discovered that I could dismantle it. I pulled out the little blue plug at the top end of the pen and then removed the metal writing tip that had a plastic ink filled straw attached to it. Now, I was holding a miniature blowgun that could propel tiny spit wads clear across the room. The class suddenly became more interesting.

I could randomly target half of my classmates, sitting on the opposite side of the room, while Miss Liepshutz strutted her stuff. All the guys sitting on the other half of the room had their eyes glued to those incredibly wonderful legs When Miss Liepshutz climbed off her perch in front of my desk and began walking to the other end of the aisle, her back was turned to me. As she progressed, I watched all the dudes sitting across from me turning their heads as their eyes tracked her movements. By the time she was near the other end of the aisle the bros across from me had their heads turned at a 45 degree angle exposing their puffy, pink cheeks. Dude, a soft, round cheek provided a perfect target for a flying wet spit wad! Having their eyes averted allowed me to stealthily take aim and fire the contents of my blowgun at the center of an unsuspecting cheek. As the projectile found its mark, I had already concealed my weapon and folded my hands on the top of my desk and had an innocent and attentive look on my face as Miss Liepshutz quickly turned to see what the cause of the commotion was.

One day, in-between classes, this red haired freckled dude pushed me and quickly walked away. WTF? What was that all about? I just brushed it off at first but time and time again he would do the same thing. I repeatedly ignored this demon possessed fiend but that only emboldened him. Finally, he flat out attacked me and I totally lost it dude! I grabbed his shoulders, wrestled him to the ground and started punching the shit out of him while releasing a long stream of obscenities that could be heard halfway around the school.

This brutal reprisal drew a teacher, Mr. Hatch, out of his classroom as he meekly attempted to put a stop to our fight. Just as there was no stopping Ralfy in the movie "A Christmas Story" there was no stopping me until my own red haired freckled foe was completely vanquished. Afterwards, I quickly got up and walked away. Remarkably, I was never punished for this uncharacteristic display of violence. Word quickly spread to other teachers in the faculty lounge and a few days later Mr. Dye, my PE teacher, paired me up in a wrestling match with my red haired rival. We wrestled vigorously with lungs panting for breath, sweat pouring from our bodies, muscles exerting themselves and hearts pounding until the two minute whistle was blown. Neither of us were able to pin the other but we were both completely spent. Dude, wrestling was a lot of work! The red haired demon never bothered me again.

I had a health class taught by Mr. Horowitz who was quite a chatty fellow. He shared some life lessons with us and his most memorable talk revolved around our countenance. He told us that if we wore an angry or unfriendly face, people would shy away from us but if we displayed a cheerful face people would be drawn to us. It was a simple but helpful piece of advice that most of us had never thought about. I did find it odd that he took great pleasure in drawing the female reproductive organ on the blackboard while pointing out various parts like the fallopian tubes. All I kept seeing was a cow's head with horns.

It had been rumored that Mr. Horowitz occasionally performed gymnastic stunts in class. One of my classmates asked him if he would do a handstand for us. He complied. Mr. Horowitz grabbed a stool that he frequently sat on and set it front and center in his classroom. Grasping the round wooden seat with both hands he easily and effortlessly rose to a full and perfect handstand and held it for an incredibly long time. The entire class was absolutely quiet as we were hoping that no harm would come to him. There was a collective sigh of relief as he effortlessly and gracefully lowered himself back to the ground. The entire class was awestruck. Dude, it was the most amazing feat that I had ever seen in a classroom in my entire life!

Another interesting demonstration occurred in metal shop that was taught by Mr. Cavenagh. He was explaining to us that atmospheric pressure created a force equivalent to 14.7 pounds per square inch. To give us a visual example he took an empty, one gallon, metal paint thinner can and heated it up with a torch. As he did so, he went on to say that the air inside the can would expand as it was heated up and be forced out of the can. This would create a partial vacuum inside the can. After he got the metal can good and hot, he screwed the lid back on. He said that as the air cooled, the pressure inside the can would be less than the pressure outside the can causing the can to shrink. We watched as the air pressure outside of the can began to push against the can's sides. It was as though two invisible hands had grabbed the metal can and began squeezing it. By the time the pressure was equalized, the can had lost about 50% of its volume. It was awesome dude!

Chapter 16

In ninth grade, I decided to run for student council competing for the spot of B-9 representative. No, that wasn't a bingo number! Back in the day, classes were divided into A and B, so if you were in grade B -9 it meant that you were a first semester ninth grader. So, like half a century ago you could start school in either the fall or spring semester. You could enter grade B- 1 in either September or February. I guess it was just too complicated running a school system like that so the Los Angeles Public Schools changed that system in 1970. But we're getting ahead of ourselves here!

So, the basis for choosing a representative for your class was listening to their speech. Of course, popularity was a significant determinant as well. After listening to boring speeches for two years, I was determined to shake things up a bit. Humor was my strong suit so I decided to make everyone laugh as best as I could. Our speeches had to be approved by the school administration so it made writing something hilariously funny very difficult. They had the right to censor and edit anything that they found objectionable - thereby making all the speeches soooo boring bro. The trick was to write something that looked totally innocent on paper but could be delivered in such a way that it could be completely altered depending on how the sentence was delivered. And in comedy, delivery is everything!

I won't bore you with reproducing my speech in its entirety but I will let you read the first two sentences to illustrate my point. "Hi, I'm Sain, how are you? I'm running for B-9 representative and I feel myself capable of doing a good job." On paper, these were two totally innocuous sentences that none of the censors could object to. But stay tuned dude and see what I managed to do.

On judgment day, aka school election day, all the budding young politicos were gathered on stage to present their fully edited, censored and redacted speeches. When it was my turn to speak, I got up to the lectern and read my first sentence which drew a decent laugh. Then I spoke my next sentence: "I'm running for B-9 representative and I feel myself... (pause) ...capable of doing a good job." and the entire audience began laughing hysterically. When the laughter started to settle down I had a totally quizzical look on my face and then scratched my head like I was wondering what everyone was laughing at. That raised the roof again. Then I turned around to see if something funny was going on behind me and then nobody could stop laughing for the longest time. I just let it all go and stood there watching the faces of students, faculty and administrators laughing their heads off. Internally, I felt a deep sense of satisfaction. I totally brought the house down dude! Oh, and I won the election as well. ☺

One of the most interesting classes that I had in ninth grade was Mr. Phillips' advanced science class. We did so many cool things in that class! One day, we were measuring the focal point of different types of lenses which varied depending on the thickness of the lens and whether the lens were concave or convex. In order to carry out the experiment we set a yardstick on a couple of stands and on the yardstick we had a lens, a lit candle and a white index card. These were all attached onto metal clips that were designed to rest on the yardstick and slide back and forth. For the convex lenses we placed a lit candle on the left side of the yardstick, the lens in the middle and the white card on the right. We then had to move the lens and the card until the image of the candle was focused on the white card. It was important to make sure that the image of the flame was in sharp focus. We would then measure the distance between the lens and the white card and that would determine the focal point of the lens.

I made an unintended discovery as I was bent over my desk moving my lit candle. At one point a lock of my hair had strayed into the path of the lit candle and caught on fire. And that was when I discovered that burning hair smelled really bad dude! A classmate of mine, named Peter, also had a mishap that occurred during our experiment with lenses. His candle had apparently accumulated a great deal of melted wax just below the flame and he inadvertently knocked over the candle spreading fiery wax across the top of his desk. He screamed liked a little girl! Mr. Phillip's was on the ball and he quickly grabbed a fire extinguisher and put out the flames.

We also dissected a worm, a frog, a cow's eye and a baby pig in that class. Genetics was another topic we learned about. We studied dominant and recessive genes in human beings and learned how to determine the probability of inheriting different genetic traits from our parents. It was a fascinating class. We even bred fruit flies with different eye colors to determine which eye color was dominant or recessive. The other nice thing about the class was that it was quite small and we got a great deal of personal attention from Mr. Phillips.

Another favorite class of mine was U.S. History taught by Mr. Massey. He was so cool and he had a great sense of humor. While wearing a smirk on his face, he would repeatedly refer to us as "children" when he needed to get our attention or had something important to say. It was demeaning but humorous at the same time. It was effective and everyone went totally silent bro! Mr. Massey sparked a great desire in me to study history in his class. He not only made history come alive, he also showed us how frequently the borders of countries changed by having us draw maps of Europe during different periods of time. It made me realize that history wasn't stagnant and that we all play a part in it as well. Our actions, or inactions could change the course of history and as a result, it made me aware that it was important to pay attention to what was happening around the world. Dude, that's a heavy responsibility!

I had Mr. Kuhn for English and he required us to write a ten page term paper on: "The History and Origin of the English Language". We learned about "The Indo-European Language Family Tree" and spent a great deal of time studying etymology. It was a great class and it helped us learn about the interrelationships of different languages.

Chapter 17

Now that we were ninth graders and at the top of the food chain we began to engage in riskier activities. One of those activities occurred along a set of railroad tracks that ran parallel to Raymer Street near Kester Avenue. After school, many of us walked down Kester to Raymer Street on our way home. There were no barriers between Raymer and the railroad tracks so it was easy to cross over them. Many of us actually walked on the railroad ties or the rails. Dude, my balance sucked so I could never master walking on a rail.

Frequently, trains would hook up specially designed railcars that carried newly assembled automobiles at the nearby General Motors Plant. One day, some friends of mine and I decided to hop onto a slow moving train heading over to the GM Plant. It was a bit harder than it looked. There were steel ladders built onto the side of the boxcars that we ran alongside and then jumped onto. The bottom rungs of the ladder were so high that you had to pull yourself up a couple of rungs with just your arms before you could catch the bottom rung with your foot.

Well, there were some anonymous classmates of ours who reported us to the boy's Vice Principal, Mr. TeMaat, and he summoned us to his office the next day. He and a friend of mine named Gordon, were given a lecture about the dangers of jumping onto trains. Since corporal punishment had not been banned yet at public schools, we had become the next targets of such punishment. I watched Mr. TeMaat pulling out a long paddle from behind his desk. It had a long handle on it allowing him to hold it with both hands. Holes were drilled into it enabling air to pass through the paddle as he swung it. The holes would make it easier to increase the velocity and thereby the force of the "swat" as it was so affectionately called. This unholy design would also eliminate any air cushion from developing between the surface of the paddle and the buttocks.

So, dude, I was asked to bend over and grab my ankles. After what seemed like a long time, I heard the hissing of the paddle as air rushed through its many holes and then I heard a loud W-H-A-C-K as the paddle met its target. It felt like my butt was on fire dude! The pain was incredible. I was told to stand up and then was dismissed to go back to my class. There was no way to put out the fire on my backside bro. I had to live with it for the rest of the day.

The next weekend, I was telling my friend, Tony, about the swat I got for jumping onto the train after school. He said that he had a cousin that would sneak into one of the new GM cars that were loaded onto railcars for transport and ride in comfort as the train made its way across the country. We decided to give it a try on Sunday when the GM plant was closed. We got up early the next morning and walked over to the railroad tracks. There were tons of new cars loaded onto specialized railcars just waiting to be hooked up to a locomotive.

All the cars had canvas covers over them. We selected a car and pulled the covering over the hood and front windshield and rested it on top of the roof. Both the passenger and driver side doors were unlocked and the keys were left in the ignition. We turned the ignition on and fiddled around with the car's radio until we got a good radio station on and sat there talking to one another. After a while, we got bored and returned the tarp to its previous position and walked back home.

Aside from being street savvy, Tony was gifted with having some kind of sexual magnetism that girls couldn't resist. He always had a girlfriend while I hadn't even kissed a girl yet. I would ask him how he attracted so many girls and he would tell me what he did in a nonchalant matter like it was no big deal. I was totally jealous dude.

Tom, my other friend, was more on par with me in the magnetism department. He wanted to go to the "Teenage Fair" at the "Hollywood Palladium" and asked me if I was interested in going. Dude, of course I said yes. We got all dressed up and Tom's dad drove us over to the venue dropping us off with instructions on where and when to meet him at 10:00 pm that evening. It was so crowded bro! We wandered around getting an overview of everything while checking out good looking girls.

Finally, we both decided to try our hand at a paint booth where you placed a half sheet of sturdy paper on a special bracket that spun around while squirting paint onto it. The bracket had a large box around it so the paint wouldn't get on your clothes. After experimenting with different colors of paint, we made some cool designs and then moved onto your typical amusement park rides.

Around dinner time, we bought a couple of hot dogs and loaded them up with condiments. We walked around eating our dinner while trying to decide what ride to go on next. One ride attracted Tom's attention so we stood around and watched people riding on it and they all seemed to be having a good time. After chowing down our hotdogs, we got in line and were seated in a car that held two people. It took some time to get everyone buckled in before the ride finally started.

It was a circular ride where the cars rode along a banked metal track that carried us over several moderately sized hills. As you went over the hills the car would rise and tilt toward the center then level out again when you were at the bottom. It was a mild but pleasant ride. After going around several times, the ride stopped and the cars started to move in reverse. This produced an entirely different feel that didn't settle well with Tom. He began moaning so I turned and looked at him. Dude, his whole face was turning green! I couldn't stop looking at him bro. Never in my entire life had I seen someone turn green. The undulations weren't helping either because they mimicked the motion your body made while you were throwing up. And soon, Tom was doing just that.

Tiny, chunks of hot dog marinated in bile were rolling along the floor of our car. When the car went up hill the hot dog bits rolled toward Tom's side of the car and when the car was on the flat part of the track the chunks started rolling back to my side. Dude, it smelled so frickin nasty! I spent the rest of the ride holding my feet off the floor. Finally, the ride stopped and I managed to get out of the car without stepping on the mildly digested food chunks. Tom was not so fortunate and neither was the young couple hurrying past us and stepping into the car we had just vacated. Once they realized what they were standing in, a look of total disgust erased their smiling faces. Dude, I felt so bad for them. I also felt bad for Tom because he smelled like puke the rest of the night. I pretended not to notice but It wasn't easy.

Chapter 18

The teachers that ran the physical education classes at Fulton were the greatest PE teachers that I ever had. They were quite unusual because they were not only intelligent, they were also genuinely caring individuals. They introduced us to all the major sports that were played in America and some that weren't all that popular like soccer, gymnastics and weight lifting. I particularly liked a six week session of soccer that they had organized for us and I was quite good at it. Having spent most of my life running around outdoors and walking back and forth to school, I had developed extremely strong legs and a great cardiovascular system. I was also good with my feet from all the skateboarding tricks that I had practiced. I always preferred playing a sport rather than being a spectator.

Most sports involved moving a ball around and because of my poor vision, I sucked at baseball. It was played with a small ball on a large field. I used to volunteer to play in deep right field because there was hardly any action out there. The problem was, I had to play by the Braille method. I could not see the ball at home plate when I was playing 200 feet away from it so I had to listen for the whack of a ball coming in contact with a wooden bat. You could tell by the sound of the whack weather the hitter really connected with the ball or not. I loved the sound of a good solid hit but instead of searching futilely for where the ball was traveling, I just looked at all the other players on the field to see which direction they were all looking. Usually, that direction was in left field. I was so totally tankful for that dude.

Occasionally, I would hear that solid whack and notice that all the players were looking at me. Oh, shit! I hated it when that happened bro. I searched the sky for that frickin little sphere until I heard a dull thud instantly telling me where the ball had landed. At that moment, I ran as fast as I could to retrieve the ball, picked it up and fired it over to the closest infielder. I had a good arm and could throw well so I found some redemption in that.

The gym teachers also had us spend time weight lifting. I soon learned that I was stronger than most of the kids in my class. I could curl a 60 pound barbell with no problem. My friend Tom and I worked out together and competed against one another on lifts and pushups and pull ups. Pull ups were a bitch dude! The time we spent learning about gymnastics was fun as well. It gave me a great appreciation for the difficulty of some of the routines I saw while watching them on TV during the Olympics. The standout PE teachers were Mr. Fee and Mr. Dye.

We were taught to do calisthenics which became a daily routine. Here's a list of exercises we went through: Jumping jacks; Pushups; Sit ups; Toe touches; Burpees, Trunk twists; Arm rotations with both arms lifted level to the ground with our palms up rotating them in small circles going forward and then backward and repeating the same routine with are palms down; Running in place; Marching; and chain pulls. After that workout, our shirts would be drenched in sweat. Dude, as a result of all that daily exercise, there were only a handful of fat kids at our school!

My time spent in student government was rather boring. My biggest accomplishment was reporting that the wire mesh above the paddle ball (now called racquet ball) courts were broken and the balls were constantly going through to the other side which was a total drag. Repairing the mesh required a written report to the school administrators who had to review it and then approve or deny the request. I thought it was taking too long to make a determination, so I had to send another request asking for an update. The matter was approved and taken care of shortly after that. This taught me two great life lessons: Always follow up when you are trying to get something done and try to limit your involvement with any form of government agency. This was reiterated quite nicely by Obi-Wan Kenobi in "Star Wars" when it was released in 1977: "Let's just say we'd like to avoid any Imperial entanglements."

The most fun task in student council was making special announcements with a female classmate over the school's public address system. I scripted the announcements as though we were the lead stars of the TV program called "Get Smart". Maxwell Smart was agent 86 and his female counterpart was agent 99. I also reversed the two numbers so that I was agent 99 and she was agent 86. After all dude, the feminist movement was well underway by 1967!

"Star Trek", another one of my favorite TV shows, started airing in 1966 and ran through 1969. I found the multi-racial and multi-ethnic crew of the Starship Enterprise fascinating to watch. There had never been such a mixed cast acting together in any previous TV show. You had a Russian named "Chekov", an Asian American named "Sulu", a female African American named "Uhura" and a Scottish dude named "Scotty". Oh dude, let's not forget the pointy eared "Spock" who was half man and half alien.

Another TV series at the time was "Man From U.N.C.L.E." which aired from 1964 through 1968. It was a secret agent series with two main characters: "Napoleon Solo and Illya Kuryakin". Once again, the matchup of an American working with a Russian played well due to the continued high tension between our two countries taking place during the cold war era. Coming from a Slavic country and also having longish blonde hair, I totally identified with the character Illya. Illya frequently wore black turtleneck shirts which were fashionable at the time and I couldn't resist acquiring a couple of them myself. ☺

Chapter 19

One day, after school, I met Frank who was a semester behind me at Fulton. He noticed that I walked home from school every day and he asked me if I would like a ride. I accepted his invitation and learned that he lived a block up the street from me. Frank told me that his parents escaped from Hungary after the Hungarian Revolution that occurred in 1956. After realizing that both of our families had immigrated to the US, we quickly bonded. Frank was the oldest of six siblings and was born in Hungary and had three brothers and two sisters. From then on, Frank's parents always gave me a ride home.

Soon, I began hanging out at Frank's house. We talked about all kinds of things while playing chess. We always kept track of who won and ultimately realized that we were equally matched. Frank and his family spoke Hungarian at home just like my mother and I spoke Croatian. One day I heard his dad say "fakanal" and I thought it was a bad word. I asked Frank about it and he started laughing and told me that it just meant wooden spoon.

I also made friends with another guy from Fulton named Tim. He and I quickly became close friends and we started hanging out at each other's homes. His dad had a sporting goods store called "The California Sportsman" located next to the "International House of Pancakes" in Panorama City. Tim's mom worked at a dentist's office and he had a younger sister named Jill. Tim's parents had divorced and both had remarried. His stepdad was a Manager at Hughes Market. His folks had a real nice pool in their backyard and we made good use of it. Tim was also a master at playing caroms and he frequently beat the pants off me with great zest. Most of the time he lived at his mom's house but occasionally he spent time at his dad's home as well. From time to time we would have sleepover's at each other's homes.

One day at school I was hanging out with Tom when he started calling out to another classmate by the name of Pinky. Pinky came over and quickly told me that his name was Peter. It was the first time in my life that I met someone who had a lighter complexion than I did. He was a year and a half younger than we were, but we were all in the same ninth grade class. He told me that he skipped a grade and a half, and as it turned out he came from an immigrant family as well. His mother had been a physician in Switzerland, and his father had been an architect in Germany. Peter started hanging out with Tom and me after school and I got to know him better. The age difference was quite pronounced and we didn't become close friends until we started attending Monroe High School in Sepulveda.

In my last semester at Fulton, I decided to run for school president. This time around the school censors had gone through my prepared speech with a fine tooth comb. I couldn't get anything past them and ended up reworking my speech about four times until it was completely devoid of anything interesting. Dude, I felt like pulling out of the election in protest but went through with it anyway. This taught me two great lessons: Don't compromise your creativity and always follow your gut feeling. I should never have run because the speech I ended up with had no life to it whatsoever. Needless to say, my speech was mediocre at best and a fellow classmate named Dan won the election. I was elected as the A9 representative however and served on student council yet another semester.

I didn't mind having Dan as student body president, he was a cool dude and the only Asian kid in the entire school. He also played drums in a rock band and I saw him perform at one of our school's dances. I ended up getting through another rather boring semester of student government and after completing that semester, I vowed never to seek public office in any capacity whatsoever. As my three year stay at Fulton was coming to a close we were required to choose which high school we wanted to attend.

The neighborhood that I lived in allowed students to either go to Van Nuys High School or James Monroe High School. I had no clue as to which school offered the better education so I called my Cousin, Gordana, who taught Spanish at Monroe High and asked her which school would be the best choice. She had no qualms whatsoever about recommending Monroe so I took her advice. Monroe also offered a summer session so I signed up for a U.S. History class. The school was about three and a half miles from my home, so walking was not an option. I figured out which bus route was the best and I bought a student bus pass. It was called an RTD pass which stood for "Rapid Transit District" so I was all set to attend my new school.

The day I graduated from Fulton, in June of 1967, was sunny and bright. This transition was a big deal for me. My mom and my brother, John, attended the graduation ceremony which was held in the school's auditorium. I was totally stunned that this dude named Daryl, who was built like a stump and was a total jock, performed a beautiful piano piece that was executed perfectly. I was quite aware of his competency because I had been playing piano for five years. Watching this solidly built dude sitting down at a piano and playing a delicate piece of classical music with such feeling was totally mind blowing and inspiring at the same time. It taught me that judging people by what they looked like was wrong and it was a lesson that I remembered for the rest of my life bro.

After the ceremony, I hung around outside reminiscing with classmates and asking them which high school they were going to attend. We all promised to keep in touch with one another knowing full well that it was unlikely that any of us would see one another until summer vacation was over. As the crowd thinned out, the last guy I saw before leaving Fulton was

Dimitry. He was the first kid that I had met on my first day at Fulton. He was so tall and mature then but now I was staring down at him realizing that I was a foot taller than he was. I felt odd knowing that I had grown so much over the past three years both physically and intellectually. Dimitry provided me with the best bookends to mark my Robert Fulton Junior High School years.

Chapter 20

With school being out for the summer, Frank's mom would frequently drive us to the beach in Santa Monica. Dude, we had a great time body surfing, eating junk food and checking out all the babes sunning themselves on the beach. I had to wear a hat and a tee shirt when I was out of the water so that I wouldn't burn up completely under the intense rays of our California sun. Sunscreen was not available to us at the time and products like sun tanning lotion and baby oil only intensified the suns strength. I envied Frank because he tanned so easily and quickly. You might say that I had a severe case of pigment envy. ☺

On my first day of summer school, I spotted a cute young lady named Jackie sitting close to me in our U.S. History class. Dude, she was a cool looking brunette who was smart, quiet and petite. As we were walking home after school, I introduced myself to her and we chatted as we walked. She was walking in the opposite direction that I needed to go but sometimes a dude needs to make sacrifices right? It was a good class and I was appreciative of the quick pace of it – six weeks rather than a full semester. I nailed that class bro and got an A+. You are probably wondering how a righteous dude like me could pull an A+? My secret was this: I had a near photographic memory and could regurgitate a ton of facts on essay questions. As a result, I became quite a fan of essay tests.

One day after summer school, I was hanging out at Frank's house when a neighborhood kid knocked on Frank's door. His name was Steve and he lived a few houses away and across the street from Frank's place. He asked us if we wanted to play ping pong at his house. We both agreed and spent a long time playing in his backyard. Frank and I took turns playing Steve because he won nearly every game. He had an annoying style of play. It was nothing fancy, he just kept making sure he got the ball over the net and waited until we made a mistake trying to slam the ball, curve the ball or hit the ball to his weak side.

Steve also liked to play catch with a football, so the three of us would go out into the street and toss the ball around for long periods of time while chatting about whatever was on our minds. Sometimes one of Frank's brothers or a friend or relative of Steve's would join us and we would play a little two on two. So, the three of us whittled away at the remaining days of that summer playing chess, ping pong, football or going to the beach.

At home, my mom was growing more and more depressed. She was collecting aid to families with dependent children through the social security system at the time. It severely penalized recipients if they went to work by deducting one dollar of aid for every dollar that they earned. Dude, after factoring in all the additional costs of getting to and from work and after paying taxes on your earnings, it didn't make any sense to work at all. As a result, the US Government was creating a welfare class and my mom and I were a part of it.

My father was partially to blame for our dire financial situation by not planning for the future and setting aside some money and investing it. As a result of his insistence on my mom not working or learning to drive, life became difficult for both of us. She did earn some extra money babysitting for neighbors. Just running our household took up a good part of her day. She had to walk to the grocery store and could only purchase small quantities of food because she had to carry the groceries all the way back home.

So, shopping, cooking, washing clothes and gardening took up most of her time. She loved to garden and she planted fruit trees in our backyard and kept a vegetable garden going all year long. Dude, it was so much fun to walk into our backyard and pick fresh apricots, figs and some other weird fruit that I didn't even know the name of. An old Italian neighbor planted the weird fruit tree for my mom shortly after we moved into our home. All the trees produced an abundant crop so I developed a lifelong love of eating fresh fruit and vegetables.

My mom was a great cook and all the meals she prepared were made from scratch. She was a master chef working with an international cuisine. We ate German, Italian, Slavic, Middle Eastern, American and Mexican food. She didn't waste her money buying prepared foods, sodas or junk food. We drank water, orange juice, milk coffee and tea and that was it. As a result, I had no cavities, which amazed all my friends, and I grew healthy, strong and lean. Since there were just the two of us, we ate dinner on TV trays, that folded up for easy storage, while watching "CBS Evening News with Walter Cronkite".

My mom asked me to help her maintain our front and back yard by mowing the lawns with a push mower, raking up leaves, pulling weeds and watering. I would also figure out how to fix things that broke or weren't working properly around our house. She also asked me to help with larger projects like tree trimming. I loved climbing up trees and cutting down branches that she asked me to take down. After cutting down a big branch it would take me days to cut it up into smaller pieces. All I had to work with was an ax and a hand saw. I enjoyed being outdoors and working hard. It was satisfying and it made me happy to be able to help my mom.

Chapter 21

My first semester at James Monroe High, I had Mrs. Swan for Biology – and dude, I have to admit that she was a fine biological specimen! She was by far the most beautiful teacher that I ever had in my entire life! I was a little miffed, however, that we did many of the same things that I had already done in Junior High. Her classroom was in Nagoya Hall which was named after our sister city in Japan. She was a strict teacher and didn't waste time during class. We moved rapidly through our textbook and labs. At least we got to get up and move around a bit during our labs and that was refreshing.

My worst class that semester was a dumbbell English class taught by Mr. Bennett. Holy smokes dude, it was the most mind numbing class you could ever imagine. One of the worst things I had to deal with in that class was a guy who sat right in front of me. Holy shit, this dude was like the dumbest dude in class and he was always turning around in his chair laying his arm across my desk while chewing gum and asking me stupid questions. His face, with its black hair, brown eyes and pale complexion, left a lifelong indelible mark on my memory. I was, however, able to erase his name. To tell you the truth, I'm sorry I even mentioned him.

Mr. Bennett's class met in one of the bungalows on campus and they all had these incredibly tall, double hung, wood windows against one wall. There was no air conditioning in these buildings so the teachers always had the bottom half of the window opened all the way up. None of them had screens on them either. I sat in the row of desks positioned next to the windows which provided me with some distractions during my long days in class. Mr. Bennett had no control over the class whatsoever. The class was intolerable and verged on cruel and unusual punishment. On our first day, when the bell rang signaling the end of that period, the tormentor who sat in front of me bolted for the window and jumped through it. He was gone in an instant! Mr. Bennett and I just stared at each other as our jaws dropped. While frozen in a moment of disbelief, we were both thinking, "Did that really just happen?" Yep.

I had a geometry class that semester with Miss Black. Dude, I figured she was a Miss because she wasn't the easiest person to look at with her unkempt hair black horn rimmed glasses and her disheveled clothes. She did have nice legs though. I did enjoy her class and found out that I really liked geometry. It ended up being one of my easiest classes.

During lunch, I hung out with the twins, David and Daryl and one of Daryl's friends. We all felt a bit lost being the new kids in a school that was much bigger than Fulton Junior High. We had gone from being the oldest kids on campus to being the youngest kids on campus and that was a big adjustment. David was upset about something and he looked quite nervous so I asked him what was up. He asked me if I remembered that bully that he beat up after school one day when we were walking home from Chase Street School. I asked him if he meant the kid who started pushing me around and telling me to never walk in front of his house ever again? David said yeah and went on to explain that the kid's locker was right next to David's locker. He said that the kid kept looking at him but didn't seem to remember who he was. Apparently, the dude was huge and on the football team. David was worried that the big guy might eventually remember who he was.

As the school year progressed, nothing ever happened with the big football jock and my friend David but I also had an unpleasant encounter with the dude later in the semester. He stared at me for a long time and I could see the wheels in his brain turning slowly. I quickly faced the opposite direction and kept walking past him without looking back. The dude never bothered me so I figured he couldn't quite remember who I was either.

A few weeks into the semester I ran across a couple of other dudes from Chase Street Elementary - the needle piercing bullies Leslie and his sidekick Bill. I spotted them in the school library squirming in their seats while staring at me. I gave them a dirty look. I recognized them immediately and they quickly buried their heads in a pair of open books that were laying on the table in front of them. They kept giving me sideways glances while wondering what I was going to do to them. They were both easy to spot because they hadn't changed one bit, and I mean one bit dude - dressing the same, acting the same and also remaining the same height that they were in elementary school. They were absolutely frantic because I was now six feet tall and staring down at both of them. They were afraid that I was going to harm them in some way for past crimes and misdemeanors. Instead, I just kept walking by them without saying a word – it was a library after all. ☺

As soon as I passed by them, I heard a couple of books slam shut, chairs scooting and two pairs of footsteps beating their way to the exit. I have to give them credit for one thing bro – that was the first and last time I had ever seen them. They must have been rather adept at keeping their distance from former victims. As they say dude – "What goes around – comes around." I wouldn't be surprised if they both became undercover cops who had already honed their skills at making themselves invisible all throughout high school. It cracked me up just thinking about it.

Chapter 22

It was the winter of 1968. My mom had become more depressed and anxious and I didn't know what to do. She carried a small, red rubber ball in her hand most of the day and just kept squeezing it. At night, she couldn't sleep well and sometimes she just paced around the house. It was as though a dark cloud had descended upon our home making me feel sad and heavy.

David invited me to go tobogganing with Daryl and his friend Kerry. Their mom drove us up to the mountains in their old Ford station wagon. When we got there I asked David if he wanted to take a walk and check the place out. He said sure, so we walked up to the top of the groomed runs that went from short beginner runs to long steep runs for the more daring tobogganers. As we walked along the top of the runs, I noticed that a tree had lost big chunks of bark that were laying in a pile close to one of the toboggan runs. I told David that we should grab a couple pieces of bark and slide down one of the runs. He quickly agreed and we did so with great enthusiasm.

When we got to the bottom, some mean old man was yelling at us as he was walking towards us. He let us know that we weren't supposed to do that because our natural bark toboggans gouged out a huge groove in the middle of the run. What did we know? I had never been in the snow before so we both apologized and walked over to David's mom who was standing by a couple of toboggans that she had rented for us. She was several yards away from us and she just kept shaking her head as we slowly approached.

David and I had a blast that morning climbing up and sliding down the runs properly while the mean old man ran some kind of machine down the toboggan run that we had ruined. After a while, our legs were too tired to lug our toboggans up the hill again so we decided to have a snowball fight. I found a huge ball of snow, about four feet in diameter, that someone had made. I thought it would be terribly heavy but I tried to lift it anyway. To my amazement, it wasn't heavy at all. I carried it over to where Kerrie was standing and hoisted it over my head as I snuck up behind him and then threw it at him. It knocked him down, which also surprised me, and hurt him. I apologized and told him that I didn't mean to hurt him. It put a bit of a damper on things but he slowly recovered and we kept on having fun.

After a full day of tobogganing, David's mom dropped me off at my house and I was happy that we all had a wonderful day playing in the snow. After opening the front door, I noticed that our home was dark and quiet. It was early in the afternoon and all the drapes and curtains were pulled shut. This creeped me out because my mom liked to have them open during the day. At first, I thought she might have closed everything up and left. But, as I listened closely, I could hear her breathing rather strangely in her bedroom.

At first I figured that she was taking an afternoon nap which she did sometimes. When I went into the bathroom, I saw quite a bit of blood in the sink and then I noticed a red trail leading into her room. I flicked on the light and stood frozen staring at a wall at the head of my mom's bed that had blood smeared all over it. Her pillow was ripped to shreds and pieces of yellowish foam were all over her bed and floor. There was blood all over her carpet and bed as well. I walked to the side of her bed to see where the blood was coming from.

Her face had blood smeared all over it so I went into the bathroom and wet a washcloth to wipe the blood off of her to see if there was a wound there. After gently wiping her face, I realized she had no injuries there. I felt weird pulling down her covers to check her out more thoroughly so I called 911. After the dispatcher answered, I told her that my mom was in bed and bleeding badly. I was very calm about it and they said they would send an ambulance over.

I waited a long time and nothing happened. I called Sandy, my sister-in-law who lived a few blocks away, and she came right over. After looking into the bedroom she quickly ran to the phone and dialed 911. As soon as they answered, Sandy started yelling loudly and hysterically that her mother-in-law was hemorrhaging and they needed to rush an ambulance over as quickly as possible. Dude, I had no idea what the hell hemorrhaging meant but I knew it wasn't good. I also learned that you needed to scream loudly and sound half crazy when calling 911. I guess I was far to calm and quiet to be believed. Soon, I heard sirens in the distance and they grew louder as they approached our home. A couple of EMT's came in and checked out my mom then went out to retrieve a gurney. They strapped her to it and rolled her out to the ambulance and drove off while we followed behind them in Sandy's car.

It was a total bummer dude. I was in shock and unable to make sense of what was happening. What went wrong? I just couldn't put the pieces together. At the hospital, they wheeled my mom into the emergency room and one of the nurses started cutting the clothes off of her. Another nurse led Sandy and me to a waiting room where we sat and sat and sat. Finally, a doctor walked into the waiting room and called out Sandy's name. She popped out of her chair and rushed over to him and he quietly explained what happened. Afterwards, she broke the news to me. My mom had attempted suicide by slashing her wrist but she was going to be okay. I had never heard of such a thing. "Slashed her wrist?" "Attempted suicide?"

So, dude... What started out as a fun day playing in the snow, ended up in tragedy. An innocent day of sliding down toboggan runs ended in pain and suffering and shock. I had never known that people even did that – tried to take their own life. It was all hard news to digest. I felt like I was in a thick and dark fog. Why? That word just kept popping into my mind.

Why, why, why? There was no answer. All I could do was cry, and then cry some more.

My life was ripped apart and flat out torn to pieces dude. Where was I going to live? Who was going to take care of me? What was to become of my mom? More questions were swirling around in my brain. Sandy drove me to her place and when my brother John came home from work, she told John what happened. The two of them tried to comfort me. They fed me dinner and told me to stay at their place and watch some TV while they went back to my mom's house to clean things up and get some of my clothes and stuff. I ended up just crashing on the floor of their den. I was completely drained. Totally empty. It was January 27th 1968 – the same day that my father died in 1963. Was that why she did it? Sometimes there are just no answers bro.

After a couple of days, my mom was released from the hospital. In the meantime, I had learned that committing suicide was a crime. I was trying to figure that one out. Like do they arrest the dead person after they did it? What would be the point of that? Did it get recorded on the person's criminal record? None of this was making much sense to me and I tried not to think about it. I was just happy that my mom was alive and I could go back home. What I didn't realize was: My life would never be the same. My innocence was lost - never to be regained.

From that time onward, I realized that life could change in an instant. It was a sobering thought dude. Every time I came home from school I became more and more anxious about walking into my home. The closer I got to the front door the greater the anxiety grew within me. What would I find this time? This question haunted me every single day just before opening the front door of my home. What would I find this time?

My mom was required to undergo psychological observation and counseling for a period of 21 days at a psychiatric hospital. John and Sandra said that I could stay with them, but I chose to stay at home instead. They took care of paying the bills and giving me money to buy groceries. So, for the next year and a half, my mom was in and out of psychiatric hospitals while I continued going to high school and living alone.

Chapter 23

My PE class was much the same as the ones I had at Fulton except they were not as much fun. It seemed that my PE teacher never had any idea what to do with us and inevitably started the class by having us run laps. I tell you dude, there is nothing in life that I find more boring than running around in circles – especially little circles. But once again, we did what we were told to do. Eventually, our teacher would come up with a plan for us. After running laps, anything looked better and was more fun than what we had been doing.

One of my favorite activities throughout my high school years was playing chess at lunchtime. There weren't many students that showed up for this activity but those of us that did were quite consistent in our attendance. There were about six to eight games going on most days. We all brought our lunches and ate while we played. There were three guys, David, Paul and Bill, who were quite good chess players. They beat me most of the time but occasionally I would win a game. Bill had the most annoying strategy: He would capture pieces, even if it wasn't advantageous to do so, and clear the chess board of pieces as quickly as possible. Then, the first player to get a queen usually won the game. Many of these games simply ended in draws. I went to Paul's house once and he actually had a chessboard set up that he used to reenact Grand Master chess games. He was also reading a book on chess strategies. Dude, I just liked to play the game – not study it.

One time this airhead named Blake came in to play chess. I think he was angry that he lost a game and I made some sarcastic comment that really pissed him off. So, he waded up some papers that some student left behind at the desk that Blake was sitting at and he threw it at me. Well, that ticked me off bro so I grabbed my lunch bag and wadded it into a much larger ball and threw it at him. Now he was totally angry because he was older than I was and he must have felt more entitled to be angry than I was. So, he grabs a dictionary that was at the desk he was sitting at and flung it towards me. It ended up landing on the desk I was sitting at and totally knocked all the chess pieces onto the floor. I was winning that game against one of the better players so I was absolutely outraged. Without thinking, I picked up my desk and started walking toward him with the intention of crushing him with it. Dude, you should have seen how big Blake's eyes grew when he saw what I was intending to do. Reason got the better of me, fortunately, and I decided that I was definitely overreacting to the situation so I set the desk back down.

One of my favorite classes was drama and it was taught by Mrs. Rude. She was a great teacher and a lot of fun. I enjoyed improvisation the most. Life is improvised, or at least it should be. If you weren't good at improvising you weren't going to be good at life either. And I can tell you one thing dude, I excelled at improvising. What I hated, was memorizing lines. Memorizing and regurgitating words written by someone else did absolutely nothing for me. As a result, my drama career at Monroe was rather short lived. I could understand memorizing a speech and presenting it to an audience because a speech was something you wrote in your own words and it represented your own thoughts and beliefs and stories. Improvisation was similar in that it came from deep within you and it was experiential and emotional. Whoa dude, I'm getting too heavy...

I also had a beginning German class with Mrs. Hohman. After my utter failure trying to speak French properly at Fulton, I decided to start learning a different language. She was the youngest looking teacher that I had. She shared a funny story with us after we had returned from a fire drill one day. She told us about another fire drill that had occurred the previous year. She had marched her class to the gym, just like she did today, and once students were in the gym they were required to sit down. Well, a female gym teacher who had never met Mrs.

Hohman, because it was her first semester teaching at Monroe, started yelling at her to sit down. Mrs. Hohman said that she was a teacher but the PE teacher refused to believe her and kept yelling at her to sit down. Mrs. Hohman told the PE teacher that she had her roll call book with her and showed it to her. The female PE teacher still didn't believe her and told her to sit down once again or she was going to make her sit down. Mrs. Hohman said she was totally embarrassed and sat down just to defuse the situation. I enjoyed her class and was happy to have her the following semester as well.

I was glad that I survived my first semester English class at Monroe but I made sure that I would be in an AE, or academically enriched, English class my next term. My new English teacher was Mrs. Hecht and it became clear to me from day one that she was rather "highbrow" but I could deal with that. At least the class was respectful and quiet. This classroom had no desks but was set up with tables that sat two people next to each other. It took a little time getting used to sitting right next to a classmate – particularly one you didn't want to be sitting next to. I don't want to embarrass her, so I won't mention her name – actually I have forgotten it.

The biggest topic of discussion in Mrs. Hecht's class was the dress code. Students were lobbying for changes to the dress code which required young ladies to wear dresses and men to be clean shaven with hair that was not to hang over the collar of their shirt. It was 1968 and we were in the middle of a social revolution in the United States. One of the guys in our class, named Maurice, who sat directly behind me, was saying that he opposed the change in the dress code which would have allowed young ladies to wear jeans to school. Dude, I had to turn around just to make sure some alien from another planet hadn't taken residency in the chair behind me. Nope, it still looked like Maurice. All I could do was shake my head while turning around to face the front of the class once again. Was this guy for real?

Mrs. Hecht loved Shakespeare. Oh my goodness – don't ask me why. Maybe it had something to do with her pretentiousness. Anyway, I remember reading the play "Julius Caesar". She went around the room and made people read certain sections of the play. I hated reading aloud bro. The only quote I recall from the play was when Julius Caesar was being stabbed by his friend Brutus, and as Julius is dying he looks up and said, "Et tu Brute?" The only reason I remember those words was the result of eating lunch with one of the guys in the class. While we were chewing our sandwiches he leaned over and asked me what I thought Brutus had asked Caesar at the moment he stabbed him. I told the dude that I had no idea so he tells me that he thought Brutus asked Caesar how many hot dogs Caesar ate for lunch and Caesar replies: "Ate two Brute."

Mr. Waterman taught my second semester biology class and he was a great teacher. It took a little while to get used to his heavy Boston accent though. Here is the best way to imagine how he spoke. Just pretend that there was a little sheep that lived inside of his vocal chords and it only spoke when he tried to pronounce a "short A" sound. For example, he would say "I like driving my caa to the beach." He was hilarious. His class was one of the most fun and memorable classes that I ever had.

We spent a great deal of time studying cellular structure and genetics and the theory of evolution. I was so excited about biology as a result of his class that a couple of friends of mine and I went to listen to Dr. Watson speak at Cal Tech in Pasadena. His lecture was all about discovering the structure of DNA which he wrote about in a book entitled The Double Helix. It was a great lecture and a great book as well. It was also exciting to learn about the incredible complexity and inner workings of cells.

In our study of evolution, we learned about natural selection which basically showed that certain genetic variances in a particular species may prove to be more beneficial for survival than those without that particular variance. As a result, those with that particular trait would live to breed resulting in future generations having a higher percentage of individuals in that population that had that same trait. That made total sense to me. However, Darwin leaped to the conclusion that as a result of natural selection "transmutation" of species occurs and a completely different species is created. Sorry dude, but I couldn't take that leap with him when there was no clear fossil evidence to prove it. Darwin was saying that all these different species on earth sprung from one cell that somehow magically appeared one day.

Unfortunately dude, the fossil evidence shows us that there were far more species that existed in the past than exist today. And even in our own lifetime some species have become extinct or are threatened with extinction. So, there is no evidence that supports "transmutation" of species. The fossil evidence shows a decay of a multispecies system that continues to deteriorate and shrink in size over time – the complete opposite of what Darwin postulated. Those are the cold hard facts bro and don't let anybody convince you otherwise.

Chapter 24

My friend Tim, from Fulton, ended up going to Van Nuys High School but we still hung out together. I frequently walked over to his house where we spent time listening to music and talking. In the summer of 1968, after our first year in high school, Tim invited me to San Diego for a week. He said we would drive down to Mission Bay with his dad and stepmom. After a week, his parents would drive me to the airport in San Diego and fly me back to Burbank while they spent another week at Mission Bay. I couldn't believe it. Nobody ever extended such a generous offer to me in my entire life! Of course I accepted. His dad picked me up in a lime green Lincoln Continental. It was the same model JFK drove in when he was shot in the head while visiting Dallas. The coolest thing about the car was how the backdoors opened up in the opposite direction as the front doors making it easier to get in and out of the back seat.

Tim's parents had rented a beach house right on Mission Bay. Tim's dad was just beginning to sell sailing boats at his store, The California Sportsman, and he had been giving Tim sailing lessons. We spent a great deal of our time sailing around the bay in a sabot – a small sailboat that only had a main sail to control it. It was simple to sail. Tim showed me all the different positions of the main sail and how that helped determine the direction the boat would travel. He let me take the sabot out on my own one day but I was a bit nervous about doing it. I wasn't the greatest swimmer so I was real cautious while sailing it around the bay. We had a blast dude!

The week went by so fast! I was shuttled to the San Diego airport and flew back to Burbank where my brother John picked me up and took me home. I was glad to see that my brother, Joe, was staying at my mom's house. After graduating from UCLA, he had moved up to Berkeley with his friend John. Joe worked for the Teamsters union as a computer programmer and he seemed to like living in the Bay Area. He told me that he and John were volunteering to work on a mutual friend's election campaign in San Bernardino and that they would be coming and going all summer.

There was so much going on politically in 1968. Martin Luther King had been assassinated earlier that year sparking many riots across the US. In June, Robert Kennedy, who was running for President, was assassinated in Los Angeles after winning the California Democratic Primary. The Vietnam War was in full swing and waves of anti-war protests were occurring across the US. These three events were igniting a social revolution that was blazing across our country. I was personally upset about Kennedy's death and it was pushing me over the edge of complacency and prompting me to grow my hair long and participate in political and anti-war protests. I was 16 years old and would be eligible for the draft in two years. I was determined to avoid ending up in Vietnam.

My brother Joe's roommate, John, was a radical. You would never have guessed it by the way he looked. He had close cropped hair and dressed like an Ivy Leaguer. Hubert Humphrey was running for President in 1968 and after Kennedy's death, he was the leading candidate. Joe and John headed out to LAX one night during one of Humphrey's campaign stops intending to protest against him. They waited in a receiving line as Humphrey worked his way toward them shaking his supporter's hands. When Humphrey extended his hand to John, he took hold of it in a vicelike grip and proceeded yelling at Humphry calling him a political hack. Two US Secret Service agents immediately grabbed John and pulled him over a three foot high chain link fence and arrested him. He was released on bail and the next morning two FBI agents were parked in a car across the street from our home watching us. This went on for about a week bro.

Dude, it was hard for a high school kid to find work In the summer of 1968. The minimum wage at the time was $1.60 an hour. My brother John, a building contractor, needed some help so he hired me to work for him. He was only paying me $1.00 per hour but I was enjoying the physical aspect of the job and used the extra money to buy rock and roll records. Joe bought us a stereo system that summer and my mom and I totally enjoyed it. My mom liked listening to operas while I spent my time listening to the Beatles, the Stones, Steppenwolf, Janis Joplin and Jimi Hendrix. Dude, my favorite song from that year was "Born to Be Wild" by Steppenwolf.

By the time school started in September, my hair was getting long. Quite a few of my classmates turned 16 by then and they were driving to school. My friends, Frank and Steve, who lived up the street from me, both got their licenses. Frank's dad bought him a 1968 Ford Mustang and Steve's dad bought him a 1964 Ford Galaxie convertible. I frequently hitched rides with them that school year and was thankful not to have to take the bus to school every day.

Waiting for buses was a drag dude so I started hitchhiking at bus stops. Many times I would get lucky and someone would give me a ride. One day, I was hitchhiking to my allergist's office, located on Van Nuys Boulevard near the 101, to get my weekly shots. Some guy stopped to give me a ride so I hopped in his car and told him where I was going. The dude was a little strange. Every time we came to a red light he turned and stared at me. It made me uncomfortable dude.

I kept ignoring the guy until he told me that he was either getting bigger or his underwear was shrinking. Now, I was getting super uncomfortable. I told him that it just happens sometimes. As we were approaching my stop, he changed lanes and we were now in the far left lane. There was a red light coming up and he said that the traffic was so heavy that he didn't know if he could get back into the right lane to drop me off. When the car came to a stop, I opened the passenger door, hopped out and started making my way to the curb. When I reached it, I let out a huge sigh of relief.

Van Nuys Boulevard was not only where my allergist was located, it was also the most popular cruising strip in the San Fernando Valley. Occasionally, my friends and I would cruise up and down the street checking out the scene on a Wednesday night - the designated cruise night. I particularly liked the customized cars the Chicano dudes were parading around in. Some of them were lowered so close to the ground it was hard to believe they could even drive them. Most of the lowrider cars had cool paint jobs and custom wheels. Some had hydraulics that let the driver raise or lower the vehicle at will. Cruise nights were always interesting and fun. Afterwards, we usually ended up at Bob's Big Boy, located on the corner of Roscoe and Van Nuys, where everyone was devouring double hamburgers with French fries and milk shakes. Dude, it wasn't like we worked up a sweat driving around. We were all just starving teenagers.

Chapter 25

Richard Nixon, Hubert Humphrey and George Wallace were the three Presidential candidates to choose from on election day in November of 1968. When I read that Richard Nixon was going to speak in Panorama City, in the Robinson's parking lot, I was determined to protest the disappointing choices that Americans were being offered on election day. I had an idea that would get me very close to "Tricky Dick". His motto that year was: "Nixon's the One" so I created a sign with those words on it. I also created a protest sign that read: "Nixon? Humphrey? Wallace? America's Choice?" My plan was to hide my protest sign under my pro Nixon sign and work my way up to where he would be speaking.

My brother, Joe, was planning on going as well and he agreed to give me a ride to the event and then drop me off at school afterwards. Protesters were herded to a special area but I chose to weave my way through the Nixon supporters. I would show them my sign and tell them that I would really like Nixon to see my sign and they let me inch closer to the stage where he would be speaking. There were two Secret Service guys wearing green tinted sunglasses who quickly caught on to me and followed me through the crowd. They stood directly behind me – one to my right and the other to my left.

After inching as close as I could get, I just stood and waited until it was time for Nixon to speak. The two Secret Service dudes were talking to each other and saying things like check out the snipers on the roof of Robinsons. I, of course looked up and saw them with their rifles trained on the audience – one of them probably had a bead drawn on my head. They continued talking about the snipers in the helicopter hovering overhead and the ones that were standing on the roof of the International House of Pancakes. None of this bothered me because all I was armed with was a sign.

Finally, Richard Milhous Nixon made his appearance flashing his trademark victory sign, formed with his index finger and middle finger, with both arms held high above his head in another "V" formation. To the hippie generation, this was our peace sign. As everyone around me raised their placards, I tore off my pro Nixon sign and held up my protest sign approximately twenty feet in front of Nixon's face. I could actually see him reading my sign as his eyes swept the crowd. I left my sign up while everyone else lowered theirs.

This was turning out better than I had imagined. People behind me, however, were getting more and more irritated that I was still holding up my sign during Nixon's speech and many of them began shouting at me to lower my sign. After Nixon finished his speech, people began slowly dispersing. Several of them were now able to read my sign and they started giving me dirty looks and yelling at me and calling me names. Soon a large circle of angry grey and white haired people were surrounding me. They were vicious and their pink, pudgy little hands were forming into fists. Fortunately for me, the two Secret Service dudes started yelling at the crowd to break it up and move along. Standing by my side, they ushered me over to the protest area. I thanked them for their assistance. (A news photographer from the "Van Nuys News and Valley Green Sheet", which later shortened their name to "Valley News and Green Sheet" snapped a photo of my sign and it appeared on the front page of the paper the following morning.) By the way, Nixon won the election bro.

In my Junior year, hippies began blossoming around campus. Guys started growing their hair long and sprouting beards, mustaches and sideburns. A huge cluster of hippies met outside the main halls during breaks and soon became the dominant group on campus. I decided to give student government another shot so I registered to run for 11th grade class president. My campaign consisted of cutting and pasting provocative photos of partially clad women on poster board and peppering them with humorous "One-liners" outlined in talk bubbles. I made a point of cutting these images from magazines that were available for reading in our school library.

After producing about a dozen unique posters I taped them up around campus where I knew students congregated. Each day during recess and lunch I made a point of walking around campus checking on my posters making sure they were still prominently displayed. Students were usually huddled around them reading the talk bubbles and laughing. I considered it a successful campaign until we received our midterm report cards. I was astonished to find out that my algebra three teacher had given everyone in our class, except for two students, unsatisfactory grades in cooperation.

She was totally pissed off at us for not returning to class after coming back from a school field trip. Most of us figured that it wasn't worth going back to a class with only fifteen minutes left in that period. So, we went to our lockers and loitered around campus until the bell rang. Two of our classmates, Fred and Greg, thought it was totally appropriate to return to our math class to rat on the rest of us. I won't mention the algebra teacher's name, but not out of respect or politeness for the teacher. The truth is, I completely blotted out her name and face from my memory. Dude, the mind is a wonderful thing.

Anyway, as a result of this grave injustice, I was notified that I would not be participating in the campaign for student government. Apparently, it was written – who knows where – that students could not run for student government if they had received an unsatisfactory mark in cooperation. How ridiculous! In the real world of politics, no one cooperated. Everyone was out for themselves and did whatever they could to cut their opponent to shreds. Everyone knew that. In a few short years, Richard Nixon would be impeached for hiring people to burglarize Democratic offices in the Watergate office complex in Washington DC. Nobody told him he couldn't run for President.

I was told to take all my posters down. Having been labeled an "uncooperative" student, I decided to disregard this request. Instead, I decided to exercise my first amendment right allowing me the privilege to express myself freely. I bought a bright red marker and altered every single one of my posters. The phrase: "Vote for Richard Sain" was prominently displayed on each placard. I drew a red line through the words "Vote for" and inserted the words "Write-in" directly above the crossed out words. Afterwards, all my posters read: "Write-in Richard Sain for 11th grade class president. Dude, I was quite proud of myself.

Leaving the posters up for the duration of the campaign led to another run-in with school authorities: Mr. Foster - aka - "Boy's Vice Principal". I was summoned to his office by way of a pink slip of paper that was personally delivered to one of my teachers during class. After reading the note, my teacher looked up and called out my name. I automatically stood up and was told to proceed to the Boy's Vice Principal's office. Upon my arrival, Mr. Foster notified me that he was setting up a parent conference with my mom because of the provocative photos on my campaign posters. He handed me an envelope to give to my mom that stated the date and time of the conference.

On the appointed day, at the appointed time my mother, my oldest brother, Tony, and I were seated across from Mr. Foster. He went on and on about the inappropriateness of the photos that I plastered all over the school. I spoke up and told him that all those photos were cut out of magazines that were available for all the students to see in the school's library. Dude, Mr. Foster was pissed off that I even dared to stand up for myself as he glared at me with his angry eyes. My comment prompted my mom to ask Mr. Foster to show her the photos that he was talking about. He pulled the posters out from under his desk and showed them to her. My mom quietly looked at each and every one of them.

Mr. Foster had a smug look on his face completely unaware of the wrath that was awaiting him. After reviewing all the posters, my mother looked directly at him and she began speaking broken English in an angry voice, "You brought me in for this?" As she spoke those words she shook the stack of posters that were still in her hand. Mr. Foster was totally stunned and speechless. Once again, in a louder and angrier voice my mom repeated herself, "You brought me in for this? My son had to take time off of work to drive me here and for what? For this?" Again, she was shaking the stack of posters in front of Mr. Foster's face. Dude, inside my head I was yelling "Yeah mom, give it to him!" At this point, Mr. Foster looked totally embarrassed and his face was bright red. My mom shouted, "I don't see anything wrong with these posters!"

Mr. Foster was finally able to pull himself together and replied, "Well I do." He stretched his arms out and took the posters from my mom and set them down on the floor next to his chair. My mom stood up and told him that her son needed to get back to work and then turned around and started walking toward the door. As I stood up, I asked if I could have my posters back and Mr. Foster answered with a quick no. I quietly turned and followed my mom and my brother out of his office and that ended the parent conference.

Mr. Foster's embarrassing moment was never forgotten. Anytime I passed him in a hallway, he felt awkward and turned bright red. He always tried to put a smile on his face but was never successful at it. His expression was like that of a dental patient awaiting a root canal with no pain killers. Dude, it made me feel bad that I had that kind of effect on him. Incidentally... I won the write-in election. ☺

Chapter 26

About halfway through my German three class, taught by Mrs. Evers, a new student was assigned to sit at a desk directly in front of me. He looked too old to be a high school student but some kids were maturing early and looked more adult like than others. Anyway, the dude was never prepared for class and when the teacher called on him, he never knew how to answer her question. I was suddenly running into this dude around campus and many times I ran into him at the Panorama City Library where I went to do research for homework assignments – no internet back then dude! I would occasionally talk to him at the library and tell him that he needed to be better prepared for class. I knew that the school had undercover narcs around and I think this dude was one of them.

I had a dearth of interesting classes that semester. Aside from German and Algebra 3, I had chemistry with Mr. Carr, P.E with Mr. McKenna, another lousy English class and a guidance class. The guidance class was totally boring, but I did learn something from it. We took a barrage of aptitude tests in that class and it was supposed to show us what our strengths were. I remember getting the cumulative results of the various tests laid out in a bar graph depicting which percentile we were in. There were several categories represented such as: Verbal; Math; Science... As I went across the page I was happy to discover that all across the board I was in the 99th percentile except for one noticeable exception – mechanical aptitude. I am embarrassed to report that I was in the 20th percentile in this category. Well, becoming a mechanic was definitely not in the cards but pursuing any other career was clearly within my capabilities.

School became more interesting in the second semester of my sophomore year. By this time, there were several dudes circulating around campus with long hair and the PE teachers were conspiring to teach us all a lesson. They were dividing each PE class into two "squads" – a "long hair" squad and a squad comprising everyone else. The long haired "squad" would be spending all period running laps while everyone else did something more fun and interesting. Dude, I can't tell you how much I hate running around in circles. Something in my brain just wants to explode anytime I was forced to do it. So, I needed to figure out a way to skip PE that semester.

In a previous semester, I needed to make a change in my classes so I was familiar with the process. I went to the school office and asked for a change of class form and was given one. Changing classes required the permission of your teachers. I handed the form to Mr. McKenna, my PE teacher, and he checked me out of his class and signed the form. I was delighted. Now, that I was officially without a PE class, I simply skipped signing into another class and never returned the form to the school office.

Fortunately, my cousin, Gordana Katurich, was a Spanish teacher at Monroe and she agreed to allow me to sit in her class during that entire semester. I actually learned quite a bit of Spanish that term. When it came time for report cards, we were all required to hand carry our blank report cards to each of our classes and have them signed by our teachers. Since the school office still had me registered for Mr. KcKenna's PE class, I had to assign myself a grade and sign his name to it. Fortunately, I had a friend who also had Mr. McKenna and I asked him if I could take a look at his report card. He said sure and handed it to me. I studied Mr. McKenna's signature then handed it back to my friend. I quickly started walking over to an empty bench on campus where I forged Mr. McKenna's signature on my own report card.

I had Mr. Falatico for second semester chemistry and the most interesting thing about this class was Barbara who sat behind me. She was a beautiful young lady who was well developed and liked showing off her breasts by wearing very low cut dresses. I purposely walked into class as late as possible in order to catch a glimpse of Barbara's cleavage while taking me seat in front of her. It became the highlight of my day bro. My friend, Peter, was in the same class and he would often think of reasons to come and talk to me before or after class so he could gawk at Barbara's breasts while talking to me. Barbara didn't seem to mind and she and I would smile knowingly at each other as Peter's eyes peered down Barbara's top.

Peter was also in my Algebra four class taught by Mr. Anterasian. That was my most boring class that semester. Once again, one of the highlights of the class was sitting at the desk right in front of Mindy. She also favored low cut dresses that she filled out abundantly. Peter's desk was in the row next to me and he sat directly across from me. He would frequently turn to talk to me while staring at Mindy whenever she wasn't looking up. Mr. Anterasian often attempted to work out algebra problems on the board without much success. After trying to muddle through an equation, he would get a confused look on his face, check his teacher's guide, erase what he had written and then copy the example out of the book. This was a painful and tedious process that was repeated throughout the entire semester.

I knew that if I were to survive that class and maintain my sanity, I would have to find some creative way to make the class tolerable. I sat in a row of desks right next to an exterior wall with large double hung wood windows that always had the venetian blinds pulled all the way to the top in order to maximize the air flow in the classroom. This resulted in an incredibly long cord lying on the ground beneath each window. I had recently learned how to tie a "hangman's noose" so I practiced this during class on a daily basis. The cords were so long that I could usually tie four nooses on the cords that were within my reach.

None of the windows had screens on them and one day while Mr. Anterasian had his back to us puzzling through a math problem the school custodian came walking by. He saw me making nooses and he was mad. He stuck his head through the window while reaching inside and grabbing the venetian blind cord out of my hands and mumbling some unintelligible swear words at me. It disrupted the class and by the time Mr. Anterasian turned around to see what was going on, I was sitting innocently at my desk with my hands folded shrugging my shoulders with a bemused look on my face. By that time the custodian had already walked out of view. Mr. Anterasian looked more confused than he usually did.

On days when I was particularly bored, I would concentrate on Peter. I knew that Peter had this strange reflexive habit that occurred if you disturbed him when he was in a state of total concentration. If you flashed your hands in front of his face when he was in this zone, he would immediately jump up in his seat while his arms and his feet spasmodically jutted out in front of him while simultaneously letting out a loud scream. It was very disruptive to the entire class and Mr. Anterasian would always turn around and scold Peter for his outburst.

Once again, by the time Mr. Anterasian turned away from the blackboard to admonish Peter, I would be sitting innocently with my hands folded on my desk staring at the problem that Mr. Anterasian was unable to solve. Peter would always point an accusatory finger at me as if I were to blame, which of course was true, telling Mr. Anterasian that Richard caused the outburst. I simply shrugged my shoulders while sporting a dubious look on my face. Mr. Anterasian, once again, looked totally befuddled. This went on sporadically during the course of the semester until one day Mr. Anterasian was so fed up he moved Peter to an empty desk clear across the classroom. This was done as Peter continued protesting that it was Richard's fault. Mr. Anterasian wasn't buying it.

As the class dragged on that day, I began fiddling around with my pink pearl eraser which was about the size of my thumb. Being made of dense rubber it had a decent amount of heft to it. A thought suddenly came to me as I was staring across the columns of desks while studying Peter on the opposite side of the room. We were both sitting in the second row of desks near the front of the class and I could tell that Peter was in "the zone". I began wondering if I could lob my pink eraser clear across the room and hit Peter in the head with it.

I stuck my left arm out to the side of my desk testing the weight of the eraser while studying the dynamics of the room. There were three long rows of florescent lights hanging down from the acoustical ceiling. I began calculating the proper trajectory of the eraser and concluded that it needed to go up and over the middle row of florescent lights. The flight path needed to be a perfect arc that reached its high point as it traveled between the ceiling and the hanging light fixture in the middle of the room. I took my time raising and lowering my outstretched arm trying to determine the appropriate amount of thrust required to accomplish my goal. It was a complex problem in which every variable had to be calculated with great precision. I knew that I only had one chance at success.

Finally, I felt confident that I had calculated all the variables correctly and I let my pink eraser fly. I watched it take flight while holding my breath. The beginning of the arc looked correct. The eraser rose and sailed between the ceiling and hanging florescent fixture. It appeared to be right on course reaching its peak heighth at exactly the right moment. As it began its decent, I was beside myself with anticipation. Peter was totally in "the zone" and all system were go for a direct het. The pink eraser struck Peter directly in the side of his head. Voila! Peter produced his typical reaction totally disturbing the entire class with his spasmodic thrusting of arms and legs accompanied by a loud scream.

Mr. Anterasian was furious. He turned toward Peter and started yelling at him exclaiming that he knew that Peter was entirely to blame for all of the previous outbursts and told him to report to the boys vice principal's office immediately. Peter was vehemently protesting and was once again claiming that it was my fault. Mr. Anterasian was adamant and Peter reluctantly left the classroom. Dude, I was basking in my incredible success against insurmountable odds. It was the best day I ever had in that class.

Chapter 27

Another class I had that semester was an AE U.S. History class taught by Mr. Thomas who sported a buzz cut but seemed like a solid and interesting dude. I was assigned a desk directly across from Larry, who was purportedly the smartest kid in our class. Rumors circulated around school that Larry actually went through the dictionary memorizing the meanings of words. Like dude, could you imagine a more boring activity? Larry was also quite arrogant and not particularly popular either. He did make it onto the Monroe team that competed with other high schools for a shot at "The Knowledge Bowl" which was a televised event. The team was comprised of Larry, my friend Peter, Fred, one of the guys that caused me to get an unsatisfactory mark in my Algebra 3 class, and David who was one of my favorite chess opponents in chess club.

Anyway, one of our assignments in the class was to read a book from a list of four titles that we would be tested on via an essay exam. One of the books was The Prince by Machiavelli. It was the shortest book and the teacher forewarned the class that if we chose that particular title he would grade our essay answers more critically. After checking out all the offerings, I was totally drawn to The Prince because it was the most historically significant book on the list. I didn't care if the teacher was going to use a more stringent grading system.

I purchased a copy of it so that I could underline key phrases which would make it easier to review and jog my memory when studying to take our essay test. The night before the exam I reviewed the entire book and then reviewed it once again in the morning and again during our lunch break at school. After taking the exam, I knew that I had totally nailed it bro. I was pleased to see an A+ on the cover of my "Blue Book" when the teacher returned the graded exams a few days later. I proudly displayed my A+ paper on top of my desk for all my fellow students to see.

After looking at his test, Larry looked quite disappointed and concerned. He reviewed what the teacher had written and then slipped his test into his notebook. When he looked up, I caught him peeking at the grade that I had gotten and he looked totally dumbfounded. He opened his notebook again just to double check on the grade that he had received and slowly slid his exam back into the darkness of his notebook. He looked wounded and hurt and his face was frozen in an expression of sheer disbelief. Finally, he leaned over and asked me if he could take a look at what I had written for my answers to the exam questions and I happily turned the "Blue Book" over to him.

Mr. Thomas was lecturing and I was watching Larry out of the corner of my eye as he slowly and methodically read through my entire test. When the class was over, Larry handed my test back and with great wonder and admiration in his eyes told me that I had memorized the entire book. My response to him was, "Yeah, pretty much." Chalk one up for the hippie dude vs. the smartest kid in the school.

I also had a philosophy class taught by Mr. Kelly who was considered to be the coolest teacher on campus. Admittedly, he had some interesting life stories that he shared with the class and he relayed those tales with great enthusiasm delivered in quite an animated manner. As far as teaching, he was less than mediocre and as time progressed he proved himself to be quite a charlatan. He was chronically late to class and didn't show much respect for his students and I finally wrote him off completely. As his lectures became increasingly boring, I began setting the clock in the classroom ten minutes fast before he entered the room. He was as interested in ending the class as early as I was, and would dismiss the class as soon as the clock reported that the period had ended.

One day, the class became more and more discontent waiting for Mr. Kelly to arrive as his tardiness became more and more egregious. I set the clock ahead by twenty minutes just to see if he would let us out even earlier than normal and then walked up to the front of the room, grabbed some chalk and wrote the word "STONED" across the top of his black attaché case which was left open on his desk. This prompted other students to grab chalk and write things on the board and floors of the bungalow in which the class was held. Others grabbed trash out of the trash can and started throwing stuff around the room and rearranging desks and repositioning stuff hanging on the walls. Dude, it was pure pandemonium. When Mr. Kelly walked into his classroom that day, he was totally pissed off. He gave us a big lecture on respecting people's personal property as he sadly tried to remove the word "STONED" from the lid of his attaché case. I felt no remorse bro. The dude was a huge disappointment.

Mrs. Taksar was my German teacher and she told us stories about Nazi Germany and surviving in a concentration camp. Even though her experience was inexplicably horrible, her resilience was amazing to me and quite inspirational. She was a serious woman and a good teacher who was kind but stern and had complete control of her classroom. When I was applying to colleges in my senior year, she was gracious enough to write a letter of recommendation for me which I was absolutely grateful for.

Chapter 28

Steve was another student in my AE U.S. History class who sat in the very last desk in the row next to me. He had never been in any of my classes, but he decided that he wanted to be my friend. Steve drove a black VW bug that he had "customized" by flaring out the fenders and installing oversized wheels and tires on it. It was nice to have another friend who drove and we took quite a few fishing, camping and backpacking trips in that car.

One of the most memorable backpacking trips we took was in the Southern Sierra Nevada mountains. Steve's friend, who was a total stoner, came with us. His name was Charlie. We left the Valley early in the morning and hit the trail hard. It was a six mile hike with a significant elevation gain. I had strapped on my down sleeping bag and for some reason I had also strapped on an old cotton bag that one of my older brothers had given me. It was a warm day and I wasn't accustomed to hiking at higher elevations. So, when we arrived at our destination, I was totally exhausted. I immediately rolled out my sleeping bag and passed out. I was in a deep and heavy sleep when Steve shook me and started yelling "Fire, fire, you need to get up and help us."

I jumped up and started yelling "Fire, fire," as I watched Steve running away into the distance. Suddenly, I realized that I was too exhausted to even care so I laid back down and passed out.

Shortly after that, I woke up to the noise of a clanging aluminum frying pan that Steve was banging against my head while yelling "Wake up! Wake up! Charlie started a fire! You need to help us put it out!"

Once again, I stood up yelling "Fire, fire!" But this time Steve grabbed me and pulled me along to where the fire was. Apparently, Charlie had gone for a short walk and climbed up a dead tree that had been topped at about 30 feet. He had been sitting on the dead trunk with his feet dangling over its edge smoking a joint. Without thinking, he had dropped a match used to light his cigarette into the hollow core of the dead tree. As soon as he saw smoke rising from the tree, he stood up and urinated down the hole hoping it would put out the fire. Well, that didn't work so he quietly walked back to camp, picked up a six pack of beer that he had brought up the trail with him and headed back to the tree without saying a word. He climbed back up the tree and poured all six cans of beer down the hole but that didn't stop the fire either.

When I arrived, the entire top of the tree was engulfed in flames and burning embers were floating onto the forest floor igniting spot fires. A huge fir tree was within four feet of the burning trunk and it was smoking from the heat of the fire. If that tree caught on fire, the whole forest would go up in flames! Dude, adrenalin started to kick in and my brain went to work. The spot fires were the most immediate threat and they needed to be put out quickly before they spread to other trees. I heard water running close by. "How far is that creek?" I yelled out to Charlie.

"It's just down that hill!"

"Hang on, I'll be right back!"

I turned back toward our campsite and started flying through the underbrush. I unstrapped my old sleeping bag, carried it down to the creek and soaked it in the water. Dude, that frickin thing weighed a ton when it was all wet! I lugged the waterlogged bag back up the hill and told Charlie to grab the end of it and help me set it on top of the spot fire he was trying to put out. We moved rapidly smothering all the spot fires that were burning at the base of the fiery tree trunk. Steve decided to run back down the trail and get help from the forest rangers.

Charlie and I were managing to keep the spot fires under control while the tree was slowly burning down to the ground. It was like watching a giant wooden match burning its way down. We were working with our shirts off due to the heat and we were both covered in sweat and ash as we kept fighting spot fires for hours. I told Charlie that the tree was probably going to be burned all the way down to the ground before we got help. As time went on, both of us started worrying about Steve and wondering if he could have fallen and injured himself on the way down the trail.

The sun was nearing the horizon when we finally heard a helicopter approaching. The pilot found a good spot to land and two firefighters got out and unloaded their equipment. By the time they walked over to where the fire was, all that was left was a smoldering stump. I pointed up to the charred mark on the neighboring tree and told them that the smoldering stump had been that high when it first caught fire. The helicopter returned again and this time Steve stepped out of it and we were both glad to see that he was in good shape. A couple of weeks after we had returned home, we all got letters from the U.S. Forest Service notifying us that the cost of the fire to us, as taxpayers, was $1,000. We all gulped at that and wondered if they were going to make us pay for Charlie's lack of foresight. Fortunately for us, we never heard back from them.

During that same semester, Steve and I drove out to U.C. Riverside to participate in an anti-war demonstration featuring Mario Savio as the keynote speaker. As it turned out Mario Savio chose to sit directly behind us while he was waiting to be called up to speak. He appeared to be just another hippie dude in the audience hanging out for the main event. For a dude who was one of the leaders of the Berkeley Free Speech Movement and nationally known, he wasn't the least bit arrogant.

We were all wearing black armbands as a sign of respect for all the soldiers who had died in Vietnam and it became the most visible and controversial symbol for the peace movement. When we got back to the Valley we met up with another carload of classmates who had attended the rally and we all stopped to get a bite to eat at Sandy's Restaurant on Van Nuys boulevard in Panorama City. The hostess seated us and gave us water and menus. Most of the customers were quite old and several of them were staring at us as though we were aliens from another planet. We all tried to ignore their nasty looks and buried our heads in the menus.

Soon, a large, rotund dude with a buzz cut wearing a short sleeved shirt and tie came walking over to our table. As he stood there towering over us, I wondered WTF is this all about? After a prolonged silence, the dude announced in a loud voice that he was refusing to serve us because of the black armbands that we were wearing in his restaurant. My first thought was: Are you shitting me? Suddenly, everyone in the entire restaurant started applauding. We all looked up at him with utter disbelief registering on our faces. Finally, I said "You can't do that." After taking a long deep breath he said "Yes I can and I would like all of you to get up and leave my restaurant." So this was the big Kahuna! There was no greater authority in the restaurant to take our grievance to so we slowly got up and walked past all the gloating old faces.

This gave me a small glimpse into a much larger world of discrimination that was occurring in African American communities throughout the deep South at the time. It was completely humiliating bro. I had also noticed that police officers were pulling over my friends with greater frequency. It wasn't exactly racial profiling, but it was hippie profiling. I could easily take off a black armband and cut my hair but changing my skin color would be a bit more problematic. Why were so many light skinned people so prejudiced against darker skinned people? Was it a severe case of pigment envy? I can tell you

124

one thing bro, I would totally trade-in my pinkish white skin for a permanently deep tan any day.

As time went on that year, police were becoming more aggressive in breaking up anti-war demonstrations by wearing full riot gear and firing tear gas canisters into the crowds. Demonstrators quickly learned to retaliate by throwing the canisters back at the police. Quite a number of people who were being drafted into the army were heading into Canada. Some of my fellow classmates were already dropping out of school and heading up to the Pacific Northwest to live on communes. One of our friends by the name of Rodney told us that he was going up to Bellingham, Washington to join his brother, David, who was living in a commune up there. He asked us if we wanted to join him. Steve and I looked at each other and I told Rodney that I would think about it.

A seventeen year old kid in high school is not prepared to make such a life altering decision bro. But, Steve and I decided to drop out of high school and join David up in Bellingham. The trip was uneventful and we safely arrived at some person's home which was full of people our age. Several people were sleeping in an unimproved attic space where we were directed to roll out our sleeping bags for the night. I was totally exhausted and I didn't care where I slept.

The next morning, David showed us around Bellingham and told us that we were invited to go with him to a "Ballin' Jack" concert at the gym at Western Washington State College later that evening. We accepted the invitation and as we were walking to the concert, David pulled out some LSD and gave each of us a tablet. The old adage, "When in Rome, do as the Romans do," came to mind so I swallowed the tab of acid.

By the time we walked over to the campus I was starting to feel the effects of the LSD. As we approached the gym, it appeared as though the building took on a life of its own. The walls were expanding and contracting like a huge lung. As I walked across the gym, I felt like I was walking on the moon. A huge cloth was covering the entire gym floor protecting the wood finish. The material slid underneath us with every step that we took. It was totally disorienting.

We found a place to sit on the floor and I began having audio hallucinations. I was hearing the sound of deep breathing that was synchronized with the walls breathing in and out. The band finally began to play and they were great. I was totally enjoying the music. As the band played on, I began hallucinating that everyone was taking off their clothes and I started doing the same. Except, in reality, I was the only one removing his clothes.

This created quite a commotion around me and some football jock started yelling at me and telling me to quit looking at his girlfriend. At this point I was totally gone and my hands were not responding to what my brain was telling them to do. Steve and Rodney helped me up and walked me outside the gym. Steve became aggressive and started punching me in the gut and yelling at me to zip my pants up and fasten my belt. My hands went down there and I thought they were doing what I wanted them to do but they weren't. Finally, Steve fastened my belt and we walked over to his car and Rodney was directing us to another place to stay for the night.

I was totally pissed off that Steve had been punching me and decided to grab the steering wheel of the car and steer the VW into an oncoming car. Steve quickly regained control of the car and slammed his fist backhanded into my chest. He pulled the car over to the side of the road and then started strangling me. There was nothing I could do to defend myself because I was totally out of it. The last thing I remembered was Rodney coming to my rescue from the backseat. He leaned forward and started fighting Steve and yelling "Stop it, you're going to kill him." Those were the last words I heard before I passed out.

When I woke up, the LSD had worn off but I was still dazed and confused. It was totally dark when I opened my eyes. I could not see anything. It was pitch black. I knew I was lying on a bed and that I was inside a house. There were other people in the room who were breathing deeply, but I couldn't tell how many. I sat up in bed and dangled my feet over the side of it but I couldn't feel any floor under my feet. So, I just sat there trying to collect my wits and figure out where I was and what happened to me. My first thought was that maybe I was strangled to death and I woke up in hell – not a pleasant thought.

Steve heard me moving around and he must have sensed that I was sitting up in bed. He got up and turned the light on in the room. We were in a bedroom with two bunkbeds in it. I was on a top bunk and Rodney was on the bunk below mine. Steve and some random dude were sleeping on the other bunkbed. Steve was afraid I was going to create more problems and he gave me a Darvon which was a pain reliever that he used because he had broken his pelvis. After my experience with the LSD, I was reluctant to ingest anything else, so I pulled the red and white capsule apart and spilled the contents on the floor. He was rather annoyed but was no longer behaving in a violent manner.

Now that I knew where I was and who I was with, I got back under the covers, turned my back to Steve and fell asleep. The next morning the sun was shining through the bedroom curtains and we all got up and ate some oatmeal in the kitchen of a farm house. After breakfast, Steve and I stepped outside and walked around a bit. The fresh air felt good in my lungs and the bucolic setting with dark green pastures and wooded hillsides had a calming effect. Steve looked agitated and asked me if I wanted to stay where we were or go back to the San Fernando Valley.

My brain still couldn't figure out what the hell had happened to it. Everything was still foggy. I tried to decide if it would be safe traveling back to the Valley with Steve. I finally asked Steve what he wanted to do. He said that he didn't want to stay where we were at and he wanted to head back home. That sounded like the best solution so I agreed to go back with him. We packed up the black VW, said our goodbyes and started heading back home. Needless to say, traveling with a guy who nearly strangled me to death was an awkward situation.

At first, I said very little. I was enjoying the scenery while sitting back in the passenger seat letting time drift by. After a long while of silence, Steve began coaxing me to talk and making jokes about being high school drop outs for a week. He was also wondering what we were going to tell our classmates when we went back to school. After thinking about it, I told him that I would just say it didn't work out for us up in Bellingham.

Chapter 29

My mother was ecstatic when I returned home. Psychologically, she was doing much better and she told me that she was starting to look for work. I told her that I thought it was a good idea and said that she would be a lot happier getting out of the house, being productive and earning an income. It would be less than a year before I turned 18 years old and her social security checks would stop coming. My checks, on the other hand, would continue for another four years if I attended college fulltime. That sounded good to me – it would also give me a "student deferment" that would keep me out of the military draft.

When I returned to school, my friends welcomed me back excitedly while asking me why I came home so soon and I told them that it just didn't work out for me in Bellingham. I didn't want to spend my lunchtime with Steve for obvious reasons. So, I started hanging out with a schoolmate named Joe who had just broken his leg and was hobbling around on crutches. He was in my English class which was the period right before lunch. I saw him struggling on his crutches and I held a door open for him and we walked outside the building together. Joe stopped at the first bench he came to and wanted to show off his prowess on crutches by swinging both feet off the ground and trying to land his cast on the bench. He miscalculated and caught the bottom of the cast on the bench and ended up tumbling over onto a concrete walkway.

I helped him back up and we both sat down and started eating our lunch together. He started telling me that his dad owned a funeral home and Joe had the perfect way of promoting his father's business. He said he wanted to hire a helicopter and load a dead body onto it and fly the corpse over the parking lot at Ralph's grocery store in Panorama City. He would then push the dead body out of the copter and immediately afterwards start throwing out handfuls of leaflets advertising his father's funeral home. A couple of Joe's friends sat down next to me and introduced themselves as Mike and Willy. Mike wore glasses and was a bit on the quiet side but Willy was an enthusiastic and smiling hippie dude who you couldn't help but like.

There weren't too many weeks left in my junior year and I ended up hanging out with these guys during lunchtime for the remainder of the semester. I grew fond of Willy and on the last day of school he asked me if I wanted a ride home and I accepted. Little did I know that Willy rode a Honda 160 motorcycle to school. After he kick started his bike, I hopped on the back of it and confirmed that I was good to go. Willy opened the throttle up all the way and we started accelerating faster than I thought was possible. He pointed the bike between to steel posts that were sunk into the asphalt parking lot that prevented cars from driving into the section of the lot that was reserved for motorcycles. I pulled my knees close to the seat just as two solid steel post went flying be me. Dude, they were only inches away from me! Holy shit! What did I get myself into? When we finally reached my home, I was grateful to be alive.

We got off Willy's bike and chatted for a long time about our plans for the summer and we decided that we would hang out together. Willy moved to the Valley with his parents when he was around twelve years old. They had been living in a rural area in Indiana and he said that he did quite a bit of dirt bike riding when he lived there. His parents owned and operated Sepulveda Health Food Store located on Sepulveda Boulevard near Parthenia Street. It was one of the first health food stores in the Valley and provided his family with a good income.

I hung around Willy's house a great deal and his parents were very kind and friendly to me and occasionally they would ask me to stay for dinner. I was astonished to see how many nutritional supplements his mother gave to him in a mini-paper cup. There were eight to ten tablets and capsules of different shapes, sizes and colors. One night when I was there after dinner, they asked me if I wanted to sample a B3 supplement to see what would happen after I swallowed it. I said sure. Everyone at the table took one and swallowed it. Both of Willy's grandmothers took a tablet as well. They were in their 80's and they both lived with Willy's family. Shortly after taking the tablet, my skin started feeling warm and slowly started to turn red as did everyone else's. They all thought it was hysterically funny and started laughing as we all sat around the table with very bright red faces. Apparently, niacin enhances the blood flow into your capillaries which causes your skin to turn bright red.

Willy was quite mechanically inclined and he told me that he had rebuilt his motorcycle engine recently. He said that he threw all the pieces in a big box then put everything back together again but ended up with a few extra parts. After he was done, he started the motorcycle and it worked perfectly without the extra parts. Willy's dad was an antique car collector and he had some cool old Fords that were built in the early 1900's. Willy's mom was super nice to me and she was always upbeat and cheery.

A new kid on the block moved into a home up the street from me that summer. He lived in a house directly across the street from Frank's house. His name was Mike and the two of us quickly became friends. Mike's father had passed away and he had moved into his older brother's home. Mike didn't drive either, so he and I ended up hitchhiking to Hollywood and hanging out there many times that summer. Sometimes, we hitched rides to Griffith Park and hiked around the hills. While hiking there one day, we ran across the remains of an old, abandoned zoo that still had big steel cages randomly scattered around in a huge open area. It was a fun place to explore and hang out. Sometimes we would head over to the park's Merry

Go Round. It was a beautiful old carousel that we occasionally rode. It seemed that every time we caught a ride that summer, the song "Aquarius/Let the Sunshine In" by the 5th Dimension would be playing on the radio. It was written for the hit musical "Hair" and was one of the top 10 pop songs in 1969. Later that summer, Mike's older brother got a job as a firefighter in Lancaster and they all moved.

I had been hanging up posters and artwork on the walls of my bedroom and my mother was embarrassed by the messiness of it. She told me that she wanted to paint my room and didn't want me to put anything back up on the walls. I asked her if I could hang stuff up in our garage and paint a mural on one of the walls and she said that it would be fine with her. I transferred everything out of my bedroom into the garage. Afterwards, I helped my mom paint my bedroom white leaving behind a bed, a desk and a chair to furnish it. I also left the shade off of the ceiling fixture because I was shooting for the décor of a prison cell. The dim light cast by a single low wattage bulb was the coup de grace.

The only thing adorning the windows of my room were a couple of roll up shades. Shortly after we were done with the room, I decided to apply some black electrical tape, the width of prison bars, to both of the windows in my room. It provided the last decorative element of the prison theme. When my mom came home that day, she was livid and demanded that I take the tape off immediately. I reluctantly complied.

My mom found a full time job that summer working for a small manufacturing outfit by the name of Vacuum Metalizing located just off Roscoe Boulevard. She only had to walk a couple of blocks to hop on a bus to Orion Avenue, which was right next to the 405 freeway, and just walk a block and a half to her job. She liked the work and quickly made friends with her coworkers.

Meanwhile, I was having a blast creating new artwork, sculptures, and murals. I even built a strobe light by mounting an old fan motor onto the inside of a cardboard box leaving the rotating spline poking outside. Afterwards, I popped a drop light with a low wattage bulb into the box and taped up the flaps. After searching around the garage, I found an old LP that I had scavenged from the dump where my brother John and I had unloaded a truckload of construction debris. I got some matches and melted a two inch diameter hole near the edge of the record. The hole in the center of the LP fit tightly over the spline sticking out of the box. After cutting a hole in the box that was the same size as the hole in the record, I made sure the two holes were perfectly aligned. With each rotation of the record, the two holes overlapped. That night, I invited friends over to check out the new strobe light that I created and we had a blast watching each other jumping around while the strobe light was flashing. It was totally cool bro!

My favorite creation was a dummy I made by stuffing wadded up newspapers into some old jeans and a long sleeved flannel shirt. I cut the image of a warrior's face out of a "Life" magazine and tapped it to his head. He was prominently displayed sitting on a wooden chair that I had also found at the dump. On Halloween night that year, my friends and I took the dummy and placed him face down in the middle of our street. We picked safe places to hide so we could watch the reactions of people who drove by that night. Most of them stopped, got out of their cars, walked over to our dummy and knelt beside him to check his pulse. After a deep sigh of relief they typically yelled, "It's just a dummy."

Once I had covered all the walls with artwork, I had the idea of creating a completely different black light environment. I bought a bunch of fluorescent paint that I wove throughout the garage. I even painted several fluorescent green dots on a shop light hanging in the garage. After staring at the four foot fluorescent fixture for a while, I would have after images of the green dots when I looked away from the bright light.

This gave me a great idea. I started painting green dots very subtlety all over the garage so that they just blended into the mix of colors and shapes on the walls. When I invited friends over I would ask them if they wanted to see something cool and of course they would say yes. So, I would turn on the shop light while telling them to stare at it for a while. After about ten seconds of staring, I would tell them not to look at the light too long because they would start seeing green dots everywhere. They would quickly avert their gaze from the fixture and begin looking around the garage with a totally freaked out look on their face as they started seeing green dots everywhere! Dude, it was totally hilarious! It freaked everybody out. Working creatively with my hands that summer, was a great catharsis and it provided me with some self-confidence and lots of fun times.

Chapter 30

The Fall semester of my senior year at Monroe was the most fun semester that I ever had in high school. To a great degree, it was due to my physics class taught by Mr. McMillan. He was a great teacher who introduced us to lasers, video tape recorders, meteorology and astronomy. For anyone interested in astronomy, he gave us extra credit for attending a series of six evening lectures held at Griffith Park Observatory. Once a week, several of us carpooled to Glendale to listen to Dr. William Kaufman, an astrophysicist, who was a tremendous lecturer. He talked about quasars, pulsars, black holes and worm holes with illustrations projected onto the planetarium ceiling. It was a fantastic opportunity and a great learning experience.

Four of us drove with Willy and his newly acquired Ford Falcon. We took the back road off of Forest Lawn Drive following Mount Hollywood Drive up and over a steep mountain. It was a terribly windy and narrow road that went through a cool tunnel near the top. Willy drove reasonably well on the way up to the observatory but on the way down he inevitably tested out his driving skills by racing down the mountain. We were all being buffeted about mercilessly as he accelerated around tight turns with all four wheels screeching. These were insanely scary rides where you just had to go with the flow and hope for the best. Fortunately, we all survived the six trips over the mountain without getting involved in a serious accident. However, the Falcon was totaled on the 405 with Willy at the wheel a short time after the lecture series ended.

One day at school, Mr. McMillan pulled out a laser and had us go into the hallway to see if we could bounce the laser beam around the building using mirrors. He sent four students out to stand at four designated spots to hold mirrors up so that the laser light would bounce and hit the mirror of the student next to them. It was amazing to watch the beam bouncing all the way around the building and ending up shining on a piece of construction paper that Mr. McMillan was holding in his hands. He told us to notice how thin the beam was coming out of the laser and how much the diameter of the beam had increased over the distance that it had traveled. He told us that a more powerful laser would maintain the same diameter. (A student by the name of Paul, who sat directly behind me in class, would go on to get a PhD in chemistry and start his own company growing crystal rods for high powered lasers.)

Another day in our physics class, Mr. McMillan broke out a video camera and had us set up a mock "Divorce Court" episode. "Divorce Court" was a popular TV program playing at the time. None of the girls in the class wanted to volunteer for one of the leading roles so someone in class suggested that I play the role of a woman getting a divorce. Since I had long blonde hair and blue eyes I guess I was the obvious substitute for the female role. Being the good natured dude that I am, I agreed to do so. I called myself Mrs. Sweetwater and during the trial I referred to my husband as a "Crumb". The cross examination was conducted by Randy, a mutual friend of Willy and mine, and it got pretty heated. The episode ended when I became so angry at Randy that I stood up in the witness stand, pointed my finger at Randy and yelled, "You're a crumb too!" The students in class were roaring with laughter throughout the entire filming of our episode of "Divorce Court."

Some of the students in our class were totally out of control. One day, a dude pulled a rubber supply hose, leading to a Bunsen burner, off of a gas supply valve. He lit a match in front of the valve and then turned the gas on full blast. Yellow and blue flames came shooting out about two feet from the gas valve. It looked like the back end of a rocket being launched! Another day, a dude named Fred held onto an opened bobby pin with a piece of folded cardboard that he used as an insulator and stuck it into an electrical outlet at his desk. We all heard an incredibly loud bang as the bobby pin shorted out all the electrical circuits in the entire building! Dude, this was totally a righteous class.

Mr. Aisenstadt taught my senior composition class. He was over six feet tall, had a buzz cut and always wore a black suit and tie. He spoke with a deep voice and exuded a sense of authority without being overbearing. He was a great teacher who had an off-color sense of humor and related well to high school seniors. His teaching style was low key and he had a great reading list for us to work through. One of the first things he had us do was purchase a copy of The Elements of Style which was a short, succinct and informative book on writing. To me, this book was like the "Rosetta Stone" of the English language.

One of the most powerful books that I read in his class was The Jungle by Upton Sinclair. It was a great read and I wrote a great composition about it. I quoted a line in the book that I thought Mr. Aisenstadt would like describing a vicious fight that the protagonist was involved in. In the book the protagonist had just bitten a chunk of his opponent's cheek and as he was being pulled away from the fight the author wrote: "He had ribbons of flesh hanging from his teeth." When I got my paper back, I was thrilled to have received an A+ on it. Once all the papers were distributed, Mr. Aisenstadt asked me to get up in front of the class and read my paper. When I read the line: "He had ribbons of flesh hanging from his teeth" the entire class let out a long moan. Mr. Aisenstadt quickly said, "Oh, that's good stuff. Read that again." Dude, if I had to vote for the best teacher that I ever had at Monroe, it would definitely be Mr. Aisenstadt.

I turned seventeen and a half that semester and was able to apply for a learner's permit at the DMV in Van Nuys. I received a carbon copy of a typewritten ID and stuck it in my wallet. My friend Tim, from Fulton, spent a great deal of time teaching me how to drive in his step dad's old Ford sedan.

Another dude, named Nathan, also let me drive his folks car around several times. Nathan, who had the biggest Afro on campus, hung out with the hippie crowd and he had a girlfriend named Diane. He suggested that we go out on double dates and I told him that I would love to. I invited a classmate named Ruth out for our first double date and we all got along well and had a great time. We went to several parties together as well and it was at these parties that I discovered how much I liked Jose Cuervo Gold Tequila.

In high school, it was always tough to find someone to buy booze for you so I broke out my learner's permit and erased the 52 from my date of birth and replaced it with 48. Instantly, I was over 21 years of age! Even though I didn't look anywhere near 21, I surmised that liquor store owners would only care that I had the appropriate documentation stating that I was the appropriate age to purchase booze. They couldn't be held responsible if I had fraudulently altered my age on my learner's permit. From that point on, I always had a fifth of Cuervo Gold sitting in my room just waiting to be taken out to a party!

At one of the parties I went to, someone was passing around a joint that, unbeknownst to us, had been laced with angel dust. When I noticed that everything I was looking at was becoming warped and everything I was hearing was becoming distorted, I told myself to ride it out. I hated the feeling and the experience so much that I walked out into the backyard to catch a breath of fresh air. It was peaceful outside. There was no place to sit outdoors so I climbed a six foot cinderblock fence and sat on top of it taking in deep breathes and enjoying the night sky.

After a while, I started coming down from the warped high and just as I was about to jump down from the fence a large group of party goers opened the sliding door and walked outside. A full moon was to my back and one of the partiers pointed to me and asked "What is that?' Someone said that it was a sculpture and someone else said let's check it out. I played along with their perception and sat perfectly still. I was sure that they were still wired and their eyes had not adjusted to the darkness so all they could see was my silhouette. They were all huddled together and walked tentatively toward me. When they got close to me I slowly raised up my arms like two giant wings lifting them high above my head while slowly leaning forward. When I got to the point of nearly falling forward, I pushed off with my heals against the cinderblock fence, flapped my arms down and lunged toward the small crowd of stoned party goers. Their faces were all lit up by the moon. I will never forget the looks of absolute terror that fell upon all those faces as I came sailing down from my perch screaming like a pterodactyl.

Chapter 31

The hippie revolution was exploding in 1969. On June 20th, 21st and 22nd some of the greatest rock stars like: Jimi Hendrix; Creedence Clearwater; Steppenwolf; Jethro Tull; The Rascals; Marvin Gaye and Booker T. and the MG's performed at Devonshire Downs. "Easy Rider" was released in July and the theatrical performance "Hair" was playing across the U.S. "The Beatles" also released their last album, "Abbey Road", in September of 1969.

Things really ignited on February 25th 1970 when a bunch of surfer dudes from UC Santa Barbara burned down a branch of Bank of America in Isla Vista. On May 4th of that year, National Guardsmen shot four students protesting against the Vietnam War adding millions more to the long haired revolt.

In my last semester at Monroe, I had more than enough units and classes to meet my requirements for graduation so I decided to only take morning classes allowing me to leave school at lunchtime. Since I had extra time in the afternoon, I decided to walk home from school. I took a part time job washing dishes in the cafeteria at the Robinsons Department store but I quit after six weeks. I was happy to have the extra spending money though.

The most memorable class I had that semester was a "Current History" class which amounted to reading Time Magazine and discussing the news in class. It was one of the easiest classes that I had ever taken. The teacher, whose name I won't mention, always showed up drunk. His slurred speech and flushed face was a total give away dude. It was a fun class though and we did have some good discussions on some controversial news stories. The Charles Manson murders was one of the biggest news stories that semester and the news media went crazy photographing the long haired dude and implying that all people with long hair were crazy murderers. I was so disgusted with the media that I cut off my long hair. The students in my class were astonished that I had done so but my mom was happy about it. I figured I could grow my hair back after the Manson murder trial was history.

My classmates were anxious to be done with school that semester. They were all looking forward to the prom, graduation and the all night grad party at Disneyland which was scheduled immediately after our graduation ceremony. The ceremony was rather painful. It took a long time to call out over 1,200 names, even though they were calling out four students at a time. Watching all those people walking up to receive their diplomas was totally boring dude. We were all ready to take off our caps and gowns and get on a bus heading to Anaheim for an evening of fun.

Disneyland was filled with high school grads who were so happy to be done with high school forever. Forever dude! That was a long time. We were walking past a huge dance floor just outside a restaurant when a section, right in the middle of the dance floor, started rising out of the ground. WTF? We were startled as B.J Thomas and his band came rising out of the ground on a round stage performing one of his hit songs. It was a great night of entertainment rides and food.

Afterwards, several of us drove over to Kim's house where we all had breakfast together. Kim was a gracious host and an incredibly good friend to me. She had set me up with her friend, Gail, and she set Peter up with her friend, Judy, so we all had dates to Disneyland. We all chatted about where we were going to college and our plans for the summer. I told several people that I had been accepted to UC Berkeley and decided to take an English 101 class at San Fernando Valley State College over the summer in order to get a head start on my degree.

Willy was at Kim's place and he said that he was going to be working full time for a small auto parts wholesaling company that was expanding. Jay was the owner's name and he had designed a flex fan that did a superb job cooling the water in a car's radiator. This was his biggest selling product but he also wholesaled transmission coolers and many other automotive parts as well. Peter and I said that we were looking for summer work and Willy told us to show up for work on Monday. I did all kinds of odd jobs for Jay that summer including driving his big ass Cadillac to a Sears store to have a set of four tires installed on his car. I was thrilled to be working part time.

Later that summer, Peter and I drove out to the Ventura County Line with Kim and her friend Judy. LA county didn't allow fires on their beaches so "County Line", as it was called, was a favorite destination point for LA residents who wanted to sit around a campfire at the beach. I had told my friend, Frank, that we were heading out that way and he asked if he could bring his date, Nancy, and meet up with us. I said sure.

We arrived at the beach around dinner time and started a small fire inside a ring of stones where we heated up some hot dogs on skewers. We were all having a pleasant conversation in between bites of hot dogs and enjoying each other's company. Frank and Nancy joined us after we were all done with our simple dinner and getting ready to roast some marshmallows over the campfire. They both sat down close to the fire but neither of them wanted to join in the ritual burning of marshmallows. Nancy sat next to Peter who was sitting next to me. She was wearing a tight fitting pair of white pants which I thought was a poor choice for hanging around a campfire at the beach.

After a while, I was growing bored and began teasing Peter by grabbing a pinch of sand and slowly moving it toward Peter's marshmallow as he was roasting it over the fire. He would merely move his skewer away from me as I repeatedly tried to pour sand on his ever drooping marshmallow. I decided it was time to trick Peter so I grabbed another pinch of sand,

142

and quickly moved it over to his dangling marshmallow. Peter flicked his skewer away so fast that the melting marshmallow was sent flying toward Nancy's white pants where it landed on her inner thigh! The burning hot marshmallow was like napalm and Nancy screamed and shot up like a rocket smacking her inner thigh trying to remove the hot and sticky marshmallow from her white pants. Frank and Nancy were both pissed off and quickly hiked back up to the highway where they had parked Frank's Mustang. Frank was forever angry at us and he blamed us for Nancy breaking up with him. He carried that grudge with him for a long time. Nancy ended up marrying my identical twin friend, David, and she ended up walking out on him as well. Some women are just hard to please bro.

Chapter 32

As the summer of 1970 was drawing to a close, I was wondering how I was going to move my stuff up to UC Berkeley and wondering where I was going to stay. In late August, I flew up to Oakland where my brother Joe picked me up and took me to his apartment in Berkeley. I had some time to scope out the campus and the residential areas close to it. North Berkeley was the most appealing to me so I secured a one room studio attached to a home that had a private entrance in the landlady's backyard. It was just off of Euclid Avenue near the Berkeley Rose Garden. I had a wonderful view of a beautifully landscaped back yard which included a duck pond. I was totally stoked dude!

In September, my oldest brother, Tony, volunteered to drive me up to Berkeley in his orange square back VW station wagon. The trip was uneventful but I was surprised at how friendly Tony was to female students. I had no idea he was such a flirt. He began striking up conversations with several of the female students on campus. We unpacked my stull after spending the night in a cheap motel and he turned around and drove back to LA. I liked the solitude of my studio but Joe thought that I was too isolated from campus and should move into one of the dorms. Dude, what did I know? He kept pressuring me to move, so I finally did.

I didn't like the old dorms that were being used as "overflow" dorms and I didn't like having to be bussed to the high rise dorms located closer to campus for our meals. I was assigned a room with a roommate in Oldenburg Hall. After living at home in my own room for the past six years, it was difficult for me to be in a situation where I not only was sharing a room but also sharing a bathroom and showers with a bunch of guys I never met before. Dude, I was traumatized. I should have stuck to my guns and stayed in my private room with a private bath on the north side of campus.

One night, soon after classes started, my roommate's dad showed up to spend the night in our dorm room. WTF? This wasn't a frickin hotel room! What is this guy's old man doing sleeping in our room? It was odd dude and I barely slept at all that night. I hadn't been sleeping much the prior nights either and as a result, I was starting to hallucinate due to lack of sleep. Everyone on the bus heading for breakfast that morning had bright blue faces and hands. It was beautiful but quite disturbing for me. I couldn't concentrate on anything my professors were saying in class and at the end of the day I was so exhausted I passed out on my bed as soon as I got back to my room. The only saving grace was having a piano downstairs in a common area that no one ever used. I spent a great deal of time playing that piano and it provided me with an excellent emotional outlet.

Walking to class on Telegraph Avenue was like time traveling back to the middle ages. Homeless people doing drugs, beggars asking for "spare change" and vendors selling handcrafted items lined the sidewalks making them nearly impassable. One weekend there was an antiwar rally at Sproul Plaza on campus. The police were out in full force and helicopters were buzzing overhead. Things got out of hand and police started shooting teargas canisters into the crowd and I beat it out of there. Dude, I wasn't ready for all of this. I was used to a very peaceful and quiet life. So, I decided that Berkeley was not a good fit for me and I dropped out after my first quarter.

When I told my mom that I wasn't going back, she supported my decision. I immediately signed up for classes at Valley College which only cost me $10. I was determined to graduate in four years bro and once I decided to do something I had the self-discipline to make it happen. The first thing I did was talk to Willy about helping me get some wheels. He told me that he just happened to have a motorcycle, a Honda 65, sitting in his garage that he would sell to me for $50. The price was right so I bought it and immediately took it over to Ralph's parking lot and practiced riding it around. I can't tell you how much fun I had with that little bike.

After riding the Honda 65 in traffic, I decided that it just didn't have the oomph I needed so I started looking for a bigger bike. About a week before Christmas, I went to take a look at a Honda 175 that some dude had for sale for $295.. He looked like a family man who probably was a bit short on cash for Christmas presents. I took the bike for a ride and was totally impressed with its acceleration and nimbleness. I told the dude I would buy it, but all I had was $225 in cash. He looked really disappointed, hung his head down and replied in a mournful voice "I'll take it."

On February 9th 1971, shortly after starting my semester at Valley College, I was rudely awakened by violent shaking and a thunderous noise. Holly shit dude, it was a frickin earthquake! I jumped out of bed, wearing only a tee shirt and underpants, and ran to our front door while all kinds of shit on my mom's shelves came crashing down and breaking on our floor. My mom started yelling that she couldn't move so I ran into her bedroom, grabbed her by the arm and helped her get to the front door and outside into our front yard. It was like some huge monster had picked up our house and was shaking it violently. Dude, it was the scariest thing that I had ever experienced in my entire life!

Fortunately, the earthquake didn't last long, but as the day progressed there were several aftershocks. I talked to my friend Frank, who was stocking shelves at Ralph's Grocery Store when the earthquake hit. He said tons of bottles and jars flew off the shelves and exploded as they crashed onto the store's concrete floor. The power went out and Frank was standing in total darkness during the entire quake. He told me that he thought World War III had started. The next morning, the "Van Nuys News and Valley Green Sheet" had a front page photo of some poor dude's pickup truck that was smashed by a section of the 210 overpass that had collapsed during the earthquake. The section of freeway had fallen directly over the dude's cab and it was totally flattened bro! The box of the truck was sticking out from under the concrete slab. Sheesh, what a way to go!

That same evening, Willy and I rode our motorcycles up to Griffith Park Observatory to watch a total eclipse of the moon. We were in the planetarium watching a show when a big aftershock struck and they evacuated everyone outdoors. There were a bunch of dudes with telescopes focused on the moon in front of the observatory that evening. Willy and I just laid on the grass and watched the moon slipping into the earth's shadow while the earth shook intermittently below us. It was the eeriest feeling that I ever had in my entire life!

A few weeks after the Spring semester started, a friend of mine told me that the school had a placement office where I could look for a part time job. I checked it out and found a part time job working for Columbia Wholesale Supply located in North Hollywood. The company was a wholesaler of travel postcards, souvenirs and knickknacks that were sold to gift shops around the U.S. I worked in the warehouse pulling orders and placing them on roll carts. When I was done with the orders, I would wheel them over to the shipping area where they were boxed, addressed and weighed for shipment via UPS. When the UPS truck arrived, it was my job to toss the boxes up to the UPS driver who neatly stacked them in his truck.

An old Italian guy, named Tony, was my supervisor and he took his seriously. He taught me how to bundle certain products together and secure them with twine and he showed me how to keep my utility knife sharp by rubbing it against a sharpening stone. He even showed me how to clean the toilet that we all used. I worked there 20 hours a week and was earning $1.60 an hour which was the minimum wage at the time.

I had saved up enough money from my job to buy my first car so I asked Willy for his advice. He told me to find a car that had bald tires on it because nobody wanted to buy a used car with bald tires. Willy told me that he knew of a place where I could find nearly new tires that were being thrown into a dumpster at a tire store on Sepulveda Boulevard. The store specialized in selling Michelin radial tires to people who wanted to upgrade their standard issue tires for top end Michelin's. The shop owner was just throwing away the nearly new tires that were being replaced.

Armed with this information, I was on a quest to find a used car - with bald tires. I ran across an old Austin A 40, with bald tires, that a guy was trying to sell for $250. I took the car for a test drive and it seemed to be in decent shape. I told him that I would have to buy new tires for the car and could only offer him $200 for it. He looked annoyed but took the deal. After buying the car, Willy showed me where the tire store was and I started checking out the trash every evening after dinner. Sometimes I found a couple of good tires and other times I found a set of four which I would throw into my car and take home. I finally acquired a set of four tires that were the right size for my car and I had them all mounted at a local gas station.

The owner of Columbia Wholesale Supply was a kindly old gentleman by the name of Mr. Horn who drove a beautiful blue Mercedes SL convertible with white leather interior. Dude, it was a totally cool ride. One day he received some boxes of merchandise that had suffered a great deal of breakage. After being compensated by his insurance company for the damaged freight, he made a deal with me and told me that he would split the proceeds from the sale of any of the merchandise that I could salvage from the broken pieces.

The boxes contained candle lanterns that had four pieces of colored glass held in place by a sheet metal frame that was painted bright colors. The glass plates could be pulled out easily so, after removing all the broken glass, I was able to replace them with unbroken pieces from other units. When I was all done, I had salvaged half of the merchandise. I repacked the candle lanterns in their original boxes and planned to sell them at the Saugus Swap meet that took place on the weekends at a drive –in movie theater.

There was another guy who pulled orders full time in the warehouse who was originally from Georgia. I told him about the owner's deal with me and he told me to let him know the next time I was going out to Saugus because he had some stuff he wanted me to sell for him. I took him up on his offer and the dude came over to my home and unloaded boxes and boxes of knickknacks. He told me how much he wanted for the stuff and he said that he would split the proceeds with me 50 / 50.

I got up early one Saturday morning and drove a carload of merchandise to Saugus. After setting out my merchandise, I was surprised at how many people bought all the cute little products that I was selling for a dollar or less. I made a profit of $75 for a few hours of work. Since the minimum wage at the time was only $1.60 an hour, my take was equivalent to working for 46 hours! Dude, I was loving it. On my next trip to the swap meet I threw in a couple of the best used tires that I had and took them along as well. I sold the two tires for $25 along with all the other merchandise. I made four trips to Saugus before I sold all my stuff.

I used the extra money I had saved up and went to Pep Boys on Van Nuys Boulevard to buy some chrome "baby Moon" hubcaps and trim rings for my Austin A 40. I painted the wheels black and installed the new wheel coverings and was pleased at the transformation. I went back and bought some rubbing compound, car wax and some Armor All and totally detailed out the car. Dude, it looked really sharp. The interior needed some help too, so I tie dyed a couple of pillow cases to use as seat covers and repainted the metal faceplate on the dash. I also bought some nice floor mats. The car looked so good I decided to put a "For Sale" sign on the rear driver side window for $325 and sold it within a few weeks. I quickly ran across a good deal on a 67 Ford Falcon with four brand new tires and snapped it up for $400. I was coming up in the world bro!

Chapter 33

Willy bought a used Honda 600 coupe which was introduced in America in 1969. I saw it for the first time shortly after ringing Willy's doorbell. As I was standing on his front porch, I heard this horrific screeching of car wheels and turned around just in time to see Willy approaching. He was driving insanely fast. As he was pulling into his driveway, he nearly flipped the car over as he slammed on the brakes and skidded to a stop! The car teetered on the driver's side front wheel for a moment and then fell back to earth pounding the three airborne tires into the pavement. I had never seen a car with three of its four wheels completely in the air. Willy got out of the car after it stopped bouncing around.

One of the new features on the Honda 600 was power front disc brakes. As anyone who has ridden a motorcycle with front disc brakes can tell you: "Hit the rear brake first and then gently apply the front disc brake." You may ask, why? If you jam on the front disc brake by itself, chances are your bike is going to do a cartwheel and send you flying into the air like a catapult. Willy's 1969 Honda 600 was trying to do the same thing as he was hitting his brakes hard. Fortunately, the car didn't completely roll over.

Willy's friend, Randy, asked us to help him out. He was putting together a pit crew for a college buddy who was competing in the "Mint 500". It was a cross country race for dirt bikes. It began in Barstow and ended in Las Vegas. Willy and I agreed and we drove the Honda to UC Riverside where Randy and his motorcycle buddy were attending college. From there, we carpooled to Barstow to watch the start of the race. I had never seen so many dirt bikes congregated in one spot in my entire life! When the starting gun went off the motorcycles were quickly engulfed in a massive cloud of sand. The roar of all those two stroke engines was deafening!

We all jumped into our car and headed over to our designated pit stop carrying all the supplies that our rider might need. It was a beautiful warm day with blue skies and very little wind but it didn't help us fight the boredom as we waited at our designated spot. By the time the first bike came screaming past us, the crowded group of riders were spaced out and traveling in their very own little dust cloud. For a long while, there was a constant stream of bikers followed by some stragglers followed by those who had mechanical problems or flat tires. It was late afternoon by the time our rider showed up with a flat. He was done. We loaded up his bike and headed back to UC Riverside. We grabbed a bite to eat on the way back and then got out and congregated in the common area of Randy's dorm.

We sat around drinking beer hoping to drown out the excesses of the day: Too much sun; Too much noise; Too much dust; Too much tiredness. Willy and I were trying to decide whether to crash at Randy's place or head back to the Valley. I told Willy that it was his call. When we were nearly done with our beer, Willy said he wanted to head back home. That was fine with me. We lingered at Randy's place for a while longer while we finished our beers.

Dude, as I was sitting there, I had one of the most bizarre experiences ever. The best way to describe it was like getting an instant message – except instant messaging wasn't even invented in 1971. It wasn't a voice that I heard, or words that I saw it was a complete thought that suddenly exploded in my brain. And this was the thought: "On your way home, get into the backseat of the car, lay down with your feet against the driver's side and put your sleeping bag behind your head. The car is going to roll over."

My first thought was WTF? Where did that come from? It certainly wasn't the familiar inner voice that I heard when I was thinking things over. It wasn't an audible voice. It was simply an urgent message planted in my brain by some anonymous source. What should I do? Should I pay attention to it? Should I tell Willy about it? The strange thing about the message was that it was so matter of fact but completely calm. As puzzling as it all was, I decided to do what I had been directed to do. After all, what harm could come from following the explicit directions? When Willy stood up to leave, I told him that I was totally beat and was going to crash in his back seat. Dude, that pun was totally intended. ☺

I followed my orders and got into the backseat of the car with both feet pressing against the driver's side of the car while wedging my sleeping bag behind my head against the passenger side. Willy took off while I laid quietly awaiting my fate in the backseat. We hadn't traveled very far when I heard the driver's side tires rolling over gravel. Uh oh! Willy began steering the car to the right but the car started sliding sideways. Suddenly, the car went airborne, rolling over, crashing down on its roof, bouncing once and landing on all four tires so violently that it shattered the rear window.

After the car rocked a few times on its suspension, I began to assess my situation. I was laying on the backseat looking out the rear window that once had glass in it. A streetlight provided me with enough light to see small shards of glass covering me from head to toe. I started brushing glass off my face and checking my hands afterwards to see if my face was bleeding. It wasn't. In the meantime, Willy had gotten out of the driver's seat and circled around the car to check out the damage. I crawled out of the car through the rear window and shook off the remaining splinters of glass. As I looked at the damage done to the car, I felt like I was hit by a tsunami. My jaw dropped when I saw the roof. It was completely crushed directly over the passenger seat! Anyone sitting in that seat would have been killed instantly.

Willy and I pushed the car off the road and parked it next to the curb. We walked over to a gas station that had a phone booth out in front. We called Randy. Afterwards, Willy phoned his dad to make arrangements to have him haul the Honda and our asses back to the Valley the next morning. We were both shaken up and I began experiencing "anxiety attacks" for the first time in my life. They occurred randomly and suddenly. The phrase "gripped with fear" is about the best way to describe one of these "panic attacks". Your heartrate skyrockets, it's hard to breathe, your throat chokes up, and you are nearly paralyzed with fear. These anxiety attacks were absolutely debilitating. Somehow, they had the nasty habit of showing up while I was out in public and surrounded by people going about their daily lives.

During Easter break, Willy and I decided to check out a new amusement park, Magic Mountain, that had just been built in Newhall. We rode our motorcycles up to the park one night and hid them in a grass field next to a chain link fence surrounding the park. We climbed over the fence and started exploring all of the newly built attractions. When we walked around a corner of a building we nearly bumped into a security guard patrolling the area. Just off in the distance, a small group was getting a guided tour of the project. The security guard asked us what we were doing. Willy told him that we were with the group of people getting a tour and we both started boldly walking toward them. When we caught up with them we just started following them around.

The security guard didn't trust us, so he walked up to the tour leader and asked him if we were a part of his group. The dude, who was wearing a fine looking suit and tie, looked at us like –who the fuck are you? Willy and I just gave him a big smile and a twinkle appeared in the man's eyes as he told the security guard, "Oh yeah, they're with us." A slight smile appeared on his face as he directed us through the remainder of the tour. The tour ended in the man's office where a huge map of the park hung on his wall. We lingered as everyone else in the group left his office and we thanked the man for his kindness. He even chatted with us a while longer and answered some questions that we had. The entire experience restored my faith in humanity.

Chapter 34

I signed up for an Economics 101 class taught by an extremely enthusiastic student teacher that spring. When I first heard the word "entrepreneur" and learned what it meant I fell in love with the idea of becoming one and immediately decided to get a degree in business. I also knew that I needed to nurture my creative side. So, I signed up for an art class as well. I was carrying 15 units - four academic classes, an art class and a volleyball class.

The art class was held in the evening and I was surprised to see Ruth, who was a friend of Kim's, taking the same class. We got to talking and I found out that she was taking the bus to class so I told her that I would be happy to drive her home. The class only met once a week. Afterwards, we stopped at a "Winchell's Donuts" and bought a couple of old fashioned glazed donuts. We enjoyed each other's company and spent some time hanging out together. When she told me her father owned his own company making, selling and renting portable, wooden dance floors, I told her that I would love to meet him and see his shop. One night, after class, we drove over to meet her dad, whose name was Bob, and see his product. He had designed a round dance floor that was built in sections and secured by a cable around the circumference. It was totally cool bro.

Being a full time student and working part time kept me busy. But, it didn't keep me from going out on Friday and Saturday nights! I loved to dance. So, I started hanging out at Dirty Pierre's on Sepulveda Boulevard which was a popular club in the Valley. They booked some great rock bands and they had a decent dance floor. The cover charge was only a buck and the beers were reasonably priced. Most guys didn't like to dance so I had a whole roomful of women to choose from. Dude, I ended up dancing with 15 to 20 different women every night! It was a total ego boost bro.

In the summer of 1971 I was out in my front yard detailing my Ford Falcon and wrapping the hard plastic steering wheel with an insulated fabric that kept me from burning my hands. A hippie dude, named Howard, saw me as he was walking by and he stopped to chat. Howard went to Monroe High but he was a year behind me and had just graduated. We had some mutual friends who moved up to Bellingham Washington to attend Western Washington College. Howard told me that he would be joining them in September. We ended up hanging out together that summer spending most of our time going to "The Paradise Ballroom" in Hollywood or grabbing a bite to eat at "Barney's Beanery" on Santa Monica Boulevard.

In my Fall semester, I arranged my schedule so my classes ended by noon. One of the classes started at 7:00 a.m. and I also had a Spanish class that met in the evening. My schedule allowed me to continue working at Columbia Wholesale Supply in the afternoons. I took an Accounting 101 class that term and was totally frustrated with it. Sometimes I couldn't balance all the books and would be off by a few cents. I ended up wasting hours trying to find my mistake and as a result, I knew that I would never want to be an accountant. I also had a symbolic logic class that term and discovered that I had an extremely analytical and logical mind. Most students in the class had a hard time understanding the material but I found it to be a piece of cake.

I kept my afternoons free in my Spring 1972 semester and scheduled another 7:00 a.m. class. Riding my Honda 175 to college was a breeze that time of the morning. The traffic lights in the Valley were all timed for 30 MPH. I thought it was too slow. There were hardly any cars on the road at that time in the morning. So, one morning, I had forgotten to set my alarm clock and I was running late. I blew through my neighborhood with ease, but the timed lights were going to do me in so I decided to do something different. I gunned my bike until I was doing 60 MPH and was pleased to find out that I was hitting all the traffic signals on green. Dude, I was ecstatic! Every morning after that, I got to my class twice as fast without hitting a red light or getting a ticket!

I loved my motorcycle and I ended up doing even crazier things than driving fast. When traffic was heavy on Woodman Avenue during peak commute times, and two cars were driving side by side in front of me, I simply kicked the bike down a gear, cranked the accelerator wide open and blew between the two cars in less than a second! This became my standard operating procedure. I didn't ride my bike when it rained though. The streets in the Valley were way too slick after a rainfall.

The most interesting class that I had in my last semester at Valley College was a geology 101 class. I had always harbored a lifelong interest in the hard sciences so this class appealed to me. The teacher was a geological consultant on the side and he helped design a tall tower at Magic Mountain. He told us that it withstood the 1971 Sylmar earthquake. He was quite proud of that.

One day, I got my midterm geology exam back and I was disappointed that I had only gotten a "B" on it, but after reviewing it, I realized that I had scored high points on all of the essay questions. It didn't make sense that I got a "B" so I totaled up all the answers and sure enough they were added incorrectly. After class, I proudly walked up to my professor, set my test on his desk and announced that whoever graded my test needed a refresher course in arithmetic. He looked at me with a totally angry and annoyed look on his face and told me that he had graded my paper. Dude, talk about sticking your frickin foot in your mouth!

I also had a business law class that term and realized that I had a natural ability to understand the "rule of law" that applied to many case studies that we went over throughout the semester. At the end of the term, I was actually contemplating becoming an attorney. As I was reflecting on the past three semesters, I realized how much I enjoyed the mix of students on campus. Most of the people attending classes were recent high school graduates but there were also returning Vietnam Vets and retired people taking classes as well. I was looking forward to attending California State University at Northridge which had just changed its name from San Fernando Valley State College, but I didn't think the students there would be as diverse as the ones attending Valley College..

Chapter 35

In the summer of 1972, some of the top songs I liked were: American Pie; The Lion Sleeps Tonight; Nights in White Satin; Rocket Man; Morning Has Broken; I Can See Clearly Now and Hold Your Head Up. I worked full time at Columbia Wholesale Supply through July when I quit to take a one month trip up to British Columbia across to Alberta via Banff and Jasper National Parks and back down through Montana and Wyoming via Glacier National Park and Yellowstone National Park.

There was an oil embargo going on that summer and gas prices were rising like crazy. In 1970, gas prices were hovering around 20 cents a gallon. In the summer of 1972, the price was around $1.75. So, gas was costing nine times more than it cost in 1970. California had restrictions in place that required people with an even numbered license plate to purchase gas on even numbered days and those with odd numbers to purchase on odd numbered days. There were huge lines at all the gas stations.

On my first day of traveling, I stopped at Yosemite National Park. All the regular campsites were taken so I ended up in an overflow site for 25 cents. It was a huge open field with no demarcations so people were sleeping nearly shoulder to shoulder. I rolled my sleeping bag out under the cover of a huge stand of fir trees. They had a row of portable toilets lined up on the back end of the camping area and there were no lights.

There were about five dudes right next to me that decided to start a campfire. One dude started pouring Coleman lantern fuel into a metal cup and tossing it into the fire. Flames shot up ten feet into the air and there was a significant heat flash accompanying the monstrous flames. They did this repeatedly. Next, the dude started squirting fuel directly from the can into the fire. Bad idea bro! The fire instantly climbed up the stream of fuel right into the dudes hands. He freaked out and tossed the can – in my direction – which landed on its side and was continuing pouring out fire and instantly creating another significant fire right next to me.

Some big ass dude, who was camping at the foot of my bag, jumped up and quickly started kicking dirt onto the fire. He was totally pissed off and started yelling at the five dudes next to us, "Who's the dumb mother fucker who keeps throwing fuel on the fire?" There was no response so the dude repeated himself three times. He started calming down after he successfully smothered the fire. He ended his tirade by saying, "If I see one of you mother fuckers throwing fuel in the fire again I'm going to blow your fucking head off!"

As he turned to head back to his camping area, his girlfriend started yelling, "Shoot 'em Tom… shoot 'em Tom!" Needless to say, there was no more fuel being thrown into the fire that night. I finally got some sleep.

Around 3:00 am the next morning, I woke up needing to go to the bathroom. After opening my eyes, I couldn't see a thing and I didn't have a flashlight. Fortunately, I was camped at the edge of the campground so I wasn't worried about stepping on anyone as I made my way to the portable toilets. There was no moon and the towering firs produced a huge canopy that blocked out any starlight from filtering to the ground. Holding my hands out in front of me, I slowly and carefully began feeling my way through a thick stand of trees that stood between me and my destination. After my hands fell upon a smooth fiberglass surface, I was relieved. ☺

The next day, I drove over Tioga Pass and checked out Mono Lake on the eastern side of the Sierras and then headed up to South Lake Tahoe where I met a young lady named Lynn. We hung out together talking and swimming in the hot afternoon sun. She was from Lethbridge, Alberta and was camping with her parents who were leaving bright and early the next morning. I told her that I was on my way up to Canada and said that I could stop by and visit her if she wanted me to. She was excited about that possibility and willingly gave me her address and phone number.

The next day, I camped at Lassen National Park. In the evening, I went to listen to a U.S. Forest Ranger talk about the wildlife living around our campground. He said we were most likely to see deer or elk. He cautioned us to be extremely careful around the bucks because their horns could rip you apart. Walking back in the dark, without a flashlight, was easy. Most campers had gas lanterns burning brightly on their picnic tables. When I reached my campsite, I couldn't believe what I was seeing. I stood face to face with a huge Elk. He was standing next to my sleeping bag just waiting to tear me to shreds with the biggest set of antlers that I had ever seen in my entire life! I walked over to a dude camping next to me and asked him if he could help me get rid of a huge elk standing in my campsite. By the time he found his flashlight and walked back to my campsite, the beast was gone. We neither heard nor saw any sign of it. It was eerie. The dude looked at me like I was some bullshitting little asshole. I thanked him for his help anyway.

The next morning, I started driving to Lava Beds National Monument and picked up a dude and his girlfriend hitchhiking alongside the highway. The girl climbed into the back as the dude slid into the passenger seat. The first words out of his mouth were, "Do you know anybody who wants to buy a pistol? The Sherriff took us to jail last night because we were carrying it in our backpack."

The dude was dumber than dirt. I quickly responded in a casual manner, "No shit!" That put us on the same level and let him know that I was neither sacred nor intimidated by what he said. Meanwhile, his girlfriend was riffling through her backpack in the back seat. I was expecting her to pull out a pistol. I imagined her pressing a loaded gun to my head while I was having an unintelligent conversation with her beau. After hours of mind numbing conversation, I began pulling into a turnout at the entrance of Lava Beds explaining that I was getting off the main road and heading into the park to camp.

I quickly opened my door, walked to the back of my car and opened the trunk where I had access to an ax and a large collapsible plastic container filled with fresh water. I stood back there fiddling around while watching the hitchhikers through the gap between the trunk and the bottom of the trunk lid. They slowly pulled their stuff out of the car and set their packs on the dusty ground and when they were all done, I picked up the water container and walked over to them and filled up their canteens.

Afterwards, I drove into the park and stopped at the Ranger's station. Inside, I began chatting with a female Ranger who was friendly and helpful. I told her that I was only going to spend one night there and asked here which cave would be the most interesting to explore. She walked over to a large map on the wall and pointed out one of the "must see" caves. She said it was the longest and the tallest cave in the park. Afterwards, she handed me a hardhat and a lantern to use.

I drove over to the cave, put on my hardhat and lit up my lantern. It was huge inside. The cave was much cooler than the temperature outside and the ceiling was well above my head. I slowly walked through the cavern as it gently meandered downward and to the left and right. I stopped several times to look at interesting rock formations. It seemed like the cave was endless. At one point there was a long, straight section that looked like someone had chiseled a bench into the wall. As I got closer to it, I realized that someone was sleeping on it! He was an older dude with long black hair that went well below his shoulders.

The light of my lantern woke him up and he greeted me with a friendly hello as he shifted into a sitting position. He said

163

that he found it quite peaceful to lay in the cool dark and silent cave. He also said that his lantern ran out of fuel. I told him that I had explored enough of the cave and would be happy to walk him back out with a lantern that had plenty of fuel remaining in it. He accepted my offer and we had a pleasant conversation as we retraced our steps back to the entrance of the cave.

As it turned out, he was a professor at a junior college who was enjoying touring the country on his BMW motorcycle. He invited me to camp with him and I accepted. As evening approached, he showed me his method of starting a campfire. He began by placing two short twigs on the ground. They were about ten inches long and laid parallel to each other about six inches apart. The next two twigs were set perpendicularly on top of the first two twigs. He kept repeating this pattern with progressively thicker twigs. When his structure was about a foot tall, he lit it on fire. After the towering twigs were completely in flames, he began leaning even thicker branches against his burning structure forming a tee pee. I was so impressed with his method that I adopted it as my own. Once we had a good and steady campfire, we cooked our dinner over it and chatted until nightfall.

The next morning, I got an early start and drove up to Crater Lake. It began raining steadily shortly after crossing into Oregon. Welcome to the Pacific Northwest! After stopping to take a look at Crater Lake, I headed to the Oregon coast. Raccoons and rain kept me inside my car day and night as I traveled north along the Pacific coast until reaching Vancouver, British Columbia. At that point, I headed east along the Trans-Canada Highway stopping to explore Banff and Jasper.

The weather got better once I reached Alberta. I spent time in Lethbridge visiting Lynn - the girl that I met in Lake Tahoe. I had a wonderful time getting a guided tour of Lethbridge College and the surrounding community as we spent a couple of days getting to know one another. Afterwards, I was growing homesick and the remainder of the trip was rather uneventful. Coming home felt great. I could really appreciate having my own room, a comfortable bed and a hot shower. After settling in at home, I met up with Willy and Randy and Tim and shared my adventures with them. They thought that it was cool that I went on such a long trip on my own.

I wanted to get a sportier car before starting my sophomore year at CSUN. I mentioned it to Randy and he said that he had a friend who wanted to sell his Volvo 544. He said it was in good shape and a real steal. I ended up buying it. I put my Falcon on the market and a couple of dudes showed up and told me they really wanted to buy my car. They were preparing to film a television advertisement for Uniroyal Tires and they needed my car so they could practice driving it on two wheels. They said that my Falcon had the same specs as the new cars they were using in the ad and they didn't want to damage the new vehicles while practicing for the shoot. They offered me full price which made me happy. I ended up seeing their ad running on TV shortly afterwards showing three white cars driving on two wheels around a racetrack with the words "Uni" "Roy" and "Al" painted on the roofs which were tilting toward the camera. It's amazing how some people make a living bro.

Chapter 36

I registered for my Fall classes at CSUN a week before school started. There was no computer registration at the time and I ended up waiting in the line marked: Last names starting with P-S. This was a slow and boring process but I signed up for four upper division business classes, an art class, and a weight lifting class. The tuition was only $95 per term and there were approximately 28,000 students attending the commuter campus sarcastically called "Drive Thru U".

One of the first things I did was head to the campus placement office where I secured a part time job working at "Accent on Nutrition" located on Ventura Blvd. The manager was a long haired dude named Dan and he was totally cool. I worked there three mornings a week and on Saturdays. The first day on the job, Dan threw a paperback book at me and told me I had to read it if I wanted to work at his store. I caught it and read the title - Let's Eat Right to Keep Fit, written by Adelle Davis. "Sure, no problem," I reassured him. Adelle Davis held a master's degree in biochemistry from USC and was the most prominent nutritionist in the US at the time. It was the most helpful book that I had ever read in my entire life! Well, at least in the field of nutrition. Actually dude, it was the only book I ever read on nutrition. After reading the book, I began my lifelong habit of taking nutritional supplements on a daily basis and making sure that I ate healthy and nutritious foods. It served me well bro... That was a pun, did you catch it?

My tasks at "Accent on Nutrition" were varied starting with vacuuming the floors and bringing in all the fresh produce, delivered on Monday, Wednesday and Friday mornings, and setting it all out on the display case in the store's produce section. Afterwards, I stocked shelves, broke up boxes and made fresh orange juice in the backroom. Dude, I have to admit that the fresh orange juice was so delicious I drank a half gallon of it every time I made it. On Saturdays, Dan would sometimes ask me to deliver groceries to their best customers. Sometimes, Dan was a jokester, and when he told me that he needed me to make a grocery delivery to Jane Fonda's home I was certain that he was pulling my leg. "Oh sure, right," I said.

"No, really the groceries are for Jane Fonda – here's the address." The home I needed to drive to was up in the hills, south of Ventura Boulevard, and off of Laurel Canyon Boulevard. I parked my old Volvo 544 at the top of a concrete driveway that rose steeply and curved to the right. I grabbed two bags of groceries, walked to the front door and rang the doorbell with my thumb. The doorbell didn't sound any different than those I heard multiple times in the homes of middle class Los Angelinos. I was standing there for a while and then rang the bell again. This time, I heard steps thumping on hardwood floors as someone started walking towards the door. As the door opened, I saw some dude holding onto an old rotary phone attached to a 20 foot cord. One hand was holding the receiver while the other held onto the body of the phone.

Dude, I was thinking, not even a hello? After entering the home, he motioned to me with the phone in his hand and gave me a head nod toward the kitchen. As I walked into the kitchen, I saw a woman, wearing a powder blue nightie, sitting at a round wooden table with her head bent down scribbling some notes on blue lined paper in a spiral notebook. Bro, it was like 5:00 o'clock in the afternoon and she's still in her nightie?

As I was standing in the middle of the frickin kitchen with both arms full of groceries watching a woman in her nightie, I was beginning to think that none of this was normal. This is the second person in the house who hasn't said a word to me while I was trying to figure out where to put the groceries. Finally, I asked "Where would you like me to set your groceries?" The woman at the table looked up at me and I suddenly realized that it really was Jane Fonda! Not the glamorous Jane Fonda of the big screen but the little, plain Jane who was hiding in her kitchen not even aware of who or what was going on in her own home. Dude, it made me feel bad for her.

"Just set them there," she said using her pen to point at a tiled counter that had things strewn all over it. I set the edges of both bags down on some ceramic tiles and slowly pushed them forward using them as bulldozers scooping up miscellaneous prescription drug bottles, spoons, forks and opened spice containers and listening to the sounds of falling glass containers, bouncing plastic pill bottles and tinkling cutlery. Once the bags were securely seated on the countertop, I slowly removed my hands while making sure the bags were balanced well enough to stay on the counter top without falling over and spilling onto the vinyl floor.

When I turned around to face plain Jane, all I was holding was the register tape pressed between my index finger and my thumb, which I had been holding onto the entire time that I was maneuvering groceries from my car to the kitchen counter. After not saying hello, not acknowledging my existence, not being helpful, not letting me know where to set the groceries and not caring about me whatsoever, I was somehow not surprised that she was not offering to pay for the groceries either! All I could see of plain Jane was a tangle of brown hair, a blue nightie and a pen randomly moving as it spread ink over white paper.

I walked slowly toward the round wooden table, set the receipt onto it next to the hand that was not holding a pen and kept my index finger on it pointing to the balance due. Once again, there was not a response so I started tapping my fingertip on the receipt. She tilted her head to one side as she looked at where I was tapping and pointing then simply said "Oh." She immediately picked up the receipt, turned it over, signed it "Jane Fonda" and then returned to her writing. Now, I was confused. Did she think I wanted her autograph? Is this how she normally handled the payment? There was only one thing I was certain of – I was definitely NOT receiving a tip. I slipped the autographed receipt into my pocket, saw myself to the door and did NOT bother to say goodbye.

At the top of the driveway in front of plain Jane's home, there was a large concrete apron that could accommodate three cars parked side by side. Although the driveway was steep and curved to the right, the top of the apron only had a slight slope to it. I had parked on the far left which was the closest to the house, and didn't particularly want to back down a steep curving driveway. So, I figured that I had just enough room to execute a U-turn at the top of the apron and then head down the driveway going forward instead of in reverse. Since the driveway and apron were both slopping downhill, the property owners had built a tall curb along the edge of the driveway so that rainwater would not erode their front yard. As I was finishing my U-turn, I knew that my left front wheel was very close to the concrete curb but I thought I had just enough room to make the turn. Unfortunately, the wheel hit the curb and wouldn't go any further.

At this point, the front end of my car was tipping forward and to the left with most of its weight concentrated on the driver's side front wheel. As a result, when I put the car into reverse and gave the car some gas the rear wheels started spinning without moving the car backwards. I was stuck in Jane Fonda's frickin driveway! I refused to believe it so I tried in vain to get the car moving in reverse a few more times. Oh, shit! I had to go back and knock on the front door again and ask for some assistance. But what was I going to ask for specifically? After a few moments of thought, I decided to see if they had a winch.

I approached the front door with great trepidation and embarrassment. Once again, I rang the doorbell, heard a pattering of footsteps approaching the front door and saw the same dude as he opened the door. A rather curious expression spread across his face communicating "WTF?" I asked the dude if they, by any chance, had a winch? He replied into the receiver of the phone "Just a minute." Now, I had his full attention as he was staring right into my eyes and asked "What?"

"I said, do you, by any chance, have a winch?"

"A winch?"

"Yes, a winch."

"For what?"

"My car, it's stuck in your driveway."

He stepped outside to take a look and said, "Oh, Tom Hayden did the same thing last week in his VW." Looking at me once again he said, "We don't have a winch and you can't leave your car there because we are having dinner guests arriving soon." With that, he turned around and shut the door in my face! Well, that went about as well as I thought it would. What was I supposed to do? As I stood there scratching my head and wondering how I was going to solve my problem some dude walked up the driveway. After explaining the situation to him, other people started arriving and he explained the situation to them. Soon, there were five people standing at the top of the driveway trying to figure out a solution to my problem.

Finally, I thought of a solution and asked hesitantly, "If all of you get in front of my car and push, I might be able to back it up." They immediately responded putting their hands on various parts of my car and started pushing my Volvo. I started up the car giving it some gas and slowly letting up on the clutch and the car backed up! Bro, I was so thankful. I repositioned my car, looked out my open window and saw five faces staring at me all conveying the same thought: Boy, this dude's an idiot. I smiled at them and said, "Yeah, I feel like an

170

idiot too." They all busted up laughing. When they settled down, I thanked them profusely, waved and drove away slowly.

Chapter 37

On Monday, Wednesday and Friday, I started work at 8:00 am, got off at 12:00 pm, jumped into my car and got on the 101 heading west. I had a 1:00 o'clock class so I ate my lunch while driving on the freeway. At that time of day, all the close in parking spots at CSUN were taken so I had to park in the farthest lot from campus which was a dirt lot. I really had to hustle to get to my class on time. After such a hectic morning, sitting down felt great.

I wasn't too far into my semester when I realized that the business department at CSUN was not a good fit for me. Their entire focus was preparing students to enter the corporate world and I had no interest in becoming a small cog in a big wheel. I just wanted to be the big wheel! I was determined to work for myself! It was a disappointing situation and I began thumbing through a CSUN catalogue trying to figure out what to change my major to. I still wanted to graduate on time because my social security checks would stop coming at the end of four years. Happily, I discovered that I could get a degree in economics, which had the same lower division requirements as a business degree, and get a minor in business without taking any longer to graduate.

That semester, my friend Tim talked me into moving out with him and a friend of his named Henry. Tim and Henry had both dropped out of college and were working fulltime. Tim was working as a store manager for a new branch of California Sportsman that his dad had opened up in the newly built Northridge Mall. Henry worked for a steel wholesaler. We rented a three bedroom house in Canoga Park on Bassett Street that was located a couple of houses off of Topanga Canyon Boulevard. Canoga Park High School was a short walk from our rental and it was a totally cool older school with huge Greek columns facing Topanga Canyon. Topanga Plaza, which had been the premier mall in the Valley for years, was just a bit south of the high school.

Both of the dudes I was living with were into smoking hash and they included me in this activity. It was a lot more powerful than the pot I had grown in my backyard and I was not accustomed to getting so stoned. Sometimes I would have audio and visual hallucinations that were rather bizarre. This distracted me from my studies. The extra time it took to shop, prepare food, clean up and do my own laundry also was cutting into my study time. My roommates also stayed up late and, as time went on, I was having a hard time balancing school, work and living on my own with two roommates.

I had been taking an Anthropology 101 class that term to satisfy a social science requirement and the professor was constantly talking about the transmutation of species which was a totally bogus concept as far as I was concerned. There was a student named Richard in my class who frequently spoke out against the idea of transmutation of species and one day the professor asked him if he would like to teach the class. He said sure and walked right up to the blackboard and started lecturing. It was totally amusing dude. After the class was over, I approached my classmate and told him that I thought it was quite brave of him to challenge our professor.

Richard turned out to be quite friendly and he invited me to a "fellowship" dinner at his house that night and I accepted. I had no idea what the hell a "fellowship" dinner was but I figured it would give me a break from cooking. There were about a dozen people at Richard's place that night and I enjoyed the potluck dinner that was laid out on his table. I was feeling tired and stressed out about living on my own and Richard picked up on it. He asked me if I had ever read the Bible and I told him that I had not so he gave me his own copy of the King James version of the Bible. He told me to start reading the New Testament that began with Matthew. There was something quite different about Richard and his friends. They were all extremely sincere and I could tell they cared about me and my welfare. I had never met such a nice and friendly group of people who were all taking a genuine interest in me. I thanked Richard for giving me his Bible as I was leaving.

As the end of the semester approached, I was becoming more and more depressed and stressed out. My boss at work was having financial problems and "Accent on Nutrition" ended up closing down. I was having difficulty sleeping because I was worrying too much about my finances and finishing up my semester. I ended up going on long walks at night just to calm down enough to fall asleep. I was starting to become more paranoid and not feeling like my normal self. Finally, I told my roommates that I couldn't afford to keep paying the rent because of losing my job. We all agreed to move back into our parents' homes.

After moving back home, I was still depressed and suffering from insomnia. I continued my long nocturnal walks. One night, I was totally pissed off at my situation and I started punching holes in newspaper vending machines when I came across them. I pulled down flags advertising apartments for rent and chucked them into the street like javelins. I pulled up water meter lids and threw them into the street as well.

I was walking down Roscoe Boulevard, across the street from Budweiser brewery, at the hight of my anger, when some dudes pulled over in a VW bug and asked me if I needed any help. I started screaming my head off at them and they quickly beat it back into their car and drove off. The screaming felt good so I kept it up as I headed east on Roscoe toward Haskell Avenue. When I reached Haskell, I jumped up and grabbed the Haskell street sign and it started to give a little so I started rocking the sign back and forth until it broke off and landed in the street.

By this time, I had been walking for hours and I had worked up an appetite. Fortunately, there was a Tommy's Hamburgers about 50 steps farther down Roscoe. Tommy's only had a walk up window and as I walked toward it I noticed that there was a spigot on the side of the building so I turned it on and started washing my hands. I had shoulder length blond hair and was wearing a bright orange, tie dyed, Mexican peasant shirt and cutoff jeans. I was barefoot and noticed that my feet and legs were absolutely filthy. It was about 3:30 in the morning and a bunch of workers from Budweiser were crossing Roscoe and lining up to get food. A warm breeze was blowing through my hair as I stood up and heard some dude behind me laughing and pointing me out to his buddy by saying, "Hey, look at that weirdo."

I was physically spent at that time, and I didn't want any trouble from a couple of creeps, so I started walking away without even turning around to see what the dudes looked like. As I got to the sidewalk, I heard a couple of guys walking behind me and I was expecting one of them to grab my shoulder, spin me around and punch me in the face. I had been jumped before and didn't want to get punched again so I quickly came up with a plan. If the dude grabbed me and started yanking me around, I was going to pivot on the ball of my foot. Using the momentum of the spin, I was going to jump up and kick the dude in the chest.

Sure enough, there was a firm hand on my shoulder pulling me around with great force which I used to my advantage as I turned, jumped and kicked the dude in the chest. It all happened in a split second. I was totally surprised to discover that the dude that I had just kicked was a member of the Los Angeles Police Department! He was about six foot two and 225 pounds. I was still in the air as he started going down. I noticed that I left a dusty imprint of my bare foot directly over his sternum and it contrasted nicely with his dark uniform. I also noticed that his partner was going for his gun.

175

Holy shit! I couldn't believe my eyes. Was this really happening to me? The felled officer managed to grab my tie dyed orange Mexican peasant shirt with a hand that was about the size of a large skillet and pulled me down with him. I immediately went completely limp. The cop rolled me over and got me in a choke hold while I provided no resistance. I was laying there wondering how long he would choke a completely limp body before he realized I was not going to harm him any more. It took him longer than I would have thought.

He jumped up, grabbed his cuffs and hooked my lifeless limbs behind my back. I began apologizing immediately, "I am so sorry, I didn't know you were police officers. You should have identified yourselves before grabbing me." I repeated these same words several times as we drove to the police station in Van Nuys. I was booked for a battery against a police officer which was a felony. I was assigned a public defender the next morning and pled no contest to a battery misdemeanor and was sentenced to two years of probation. Dude, I was already suffering from depression and anxiety attacks, I was stressed out, had insomnia and now I had a criminal record. Sometimes, life totally sucks bro!

Somehow, I finished up my semester – with the worst grades that I ever had in my entire life! This didn't help me feel any better psychologically and I continued slipping into a deep dark funk that was leading me further into darkness. Paranoia began creeping into my life and I was becoming certain that the LAPD and the FBI were following me around. On one of my epic evening walks I felt like jumping off a bridge that I was crossing. I sat on the railing with my legs dangling over the edge staring into a concrete wash. Soon a couple of LAPD officers approached me and started chatting with me. "You know, it's not far enough down there to kill yourself if that's what you're thinking," one of them said as he leaned over the railing.

"He's right," said his partner as he looked at me. "You probably would just break a leg."

I just sat there not responding immediately but I was thankful that they took the time to talk to me. I didn't feel totally alone in the world anyway. After a while, I said, "You guys are probably right, I would just injure myself and make my life even worse." Slowly, I swung a leg over the railing and then the other and jumped back down on the sidewalk.

"Are you going to be all right?"

"Yeah. I'll be okay. I just need to get home and get some sleep. Thanks for taking the time to talk to me. I really appreciate it."

"Don't mention it. Take care of yourself." They both turned and headed back to their black and white. I started walking over the bridge and I saw a little dachshund approaching me. The sight of its prolonged body and short stubby legs moving rapidly across the sidewalk, made me laugh. The dog looked directly at me and I heard a female voice saying, "I can't help the way I look." As the dog passed by me, my first thought was WTF? Did that really happen? As I turned to watch the dog as it moved away from me, I began thinking about what a strange encounter that was. I needed to get home and get some sleep because I was definitely losing it bro.

My insomnia, paranoia and total exhaustion came to a peak one night when my mom was out babysitting. I couldn't sleep because I was convinced that FBI agents were outside my home getting ready to break in and shoot me. I remember what my classmate, Richard, told me when he handed me his Bible. "If you ever are in need, just ask Jesus to help you." Well, I decided that I was in need so I asked Jesus for help. I told him that I couldn't go on living like this anymore and that I made a total mess out of my life. I asked him to come into my life and give me the strength, courage and wisdom that I needed to change things. Immediately after my prayer, I saw a brilliant white light in my mind's eye and felt a wave of peace wash over me as I drifted off to sleep.

When I woke up the next morning, I was a changed man. I felt strong and invigorated. My head was completely clear and I felt like a heavy dark veil had been lifted. The world around me appeared more vivid and colorful. When I stepped out of bed, I was actually happy and energetic. I felt great and decided that the first thing I was going to do was totally give up drugs and start reading the Bible that Richard gave me.

Chapter 38

In the summer of 1973 I joined Willy, Randy and another friend of ours named Kyle on a camping trip to San Simeon State Beach. We loaded up Randy's 1968 Studebaker Lark with our food and camping gear and spent most of the day driving up the Pacific Coast Highway. It was a beautiful drive and we all had fun stopping at vista points along the way to admire the views of the ocean and beaches. We had a great time joking and laughing with one another and sharing interesting tidbits of our lives. We had the radio going full time and some of the biggest hits being played were: Elton John's "Crocodile Rock"; Stevie Wonder's "You are the Sunshine of My Life"; The O'Jays' "Love Train"; The Doobie Brothers' "Long Train Runnin'".

When we got to San Simeon, evening was quickly approaching. We unloaded our gear and set up camp and then started taking a walk along the beach. A full moon was hanging above the ocean lighting up the sandy beach and some bluffs rising up from the high water mark. We spotted a steep trail cut into the side of the cliff and we started heading toward it. After climbing to the top of the plateau, we discovered a big empty field filled with knee high grass that was stiff and brown. As we were tromping through the field, we started horsing around and wrestling with each other until we were all out of breath.

It was completely dark when we turned around to head back to our camp. The moonlight was reflecting on the inky black ocean where choppy waves were splintering it into a thousand shards of light dancing upon the water. The ever changing patterns of light were providing us with a dazzling display of nature's beauty. Directly above us, the sky was black with pinpricks of white light shimmering in the darkness and creating their own patterns.

We were all quiet as we were retracing our steps back to our campsite while watching the nightscape unfold before us.

Shuffling through the sand was slow going. By the time we worked our way back to our campsite, we were all hungry and exhausted. I opened up a can of tuna and started eating it while Willy took the cap off of a jug of "Red Mountain" wine and passed it around. We each took a couple of gulps and handed the jug to the person next to us until it had gone around the circle several times. Afterwards, I opened up a huge bag of Oreo cookies and started passing it around for desert and it kept going around until the jumbo pack was completely empty. Afterwards, we all crawled into our sleeping bags for the night.

Just as I was adjusting my pillow and getting it into a comfortable position, Randy was busy taking off his jeans and frantically searching through his pockets. "Shit! I lost my wallet! It must have fallen out somewhere along our hike!"

Suddenly, I sprang to my feet and these words came spilling out of my mouth: "Don't worry Randy, I'll find it for you." WTF? Where did that come from? I was taken aback with what just happened. It was like my body and the words coming out of it were being remotely controlled by someone else! This was an interesting experience and I decided to go along with it. As my body began retracing its steps, I heard Randy calling out to me "Thanks Richard! I think I lost it up on the bluffs where we were horsing around."

All that came out of my mouth was, "Okay Randy." As some mystical force guided my steps, I passively watched were we were going. After a while, my body veered to the right leaving the hard packed sand and pointing me in the direction of the bluffs. We hiked up the bluff and into the field with tall grass and trudged through it until my body stopped. I received an "instant message" directing me to bend over and reach out my hands. Now, under my own will, I bent over and reached out into the tall weeds where my hands fell directly upon Randy's wallet! Holly shit, I thought. This is freakin incredible! I stood up holding his lost wallet. I was totally awestruck. I didn't even bother to look inside the wallet because I had no doubt that it was Randy's. I solemnly walked back to our campsite, handed the wallet to Randy, slipped back into my sleeping bag and passed out.

Later that summer, Willy, Randy and I – along with another friend named Mike – started out on another camping trip to Agua Caliente Hot Springs. Once again, we loaded up Randy's old Studebaker with our camping gear and headed to the desert. We stopped in Julian to get some dinner and then continued on our journey over the coastal range. As we drove down the eastern side of the coastal range, we had some great views of the Sonora Desert stretching out before us. The sun was setting by the time we hit the desert floor and Randy cranked up his eight track stereo cassette player as we sped along two lanes of blacktop. The road ran perfectly straight for miles and disappeared into a vanishing point along the horizon.

Mike and I were riding in the back seat listening to "Born to Be Wild" on a set of auxiliary speakers that Randy jerry-rigged with extra-long wires so we could take them outside of the car and listen to music at our campsite. We all had our windows rolled down so I decided to crawl thru my open window and sit on the door while holding onto the door frame. Mike did the same thing except he grabbed one of the auxiliary speakers and set it on top of the roof. I thought that was an excellent idea so I went back inside the car, grabbed the other speaker and set it on the roof as well. We drove for miles listening to rock music blaring as we were crossing the desert floor. As twilight fell upon us, we were mesmerized by the changing colors of the sky. The pastel blues, pinks and purples were slowly being sucked to the horizon as the sun slowly disappeared from sight. Afterwards, we were driving beneath a canopy of brilliant white points of light that had traveled light-years across the universe before lighting up the night sky. It felt good to be alive bro.

Willy, who was driving the car, suddenly started slowing down and pulling the Studebaker into a turnout. He parked next to a large "Caterpillar" WTF? We got out of the car and watched him heading over to the CAT. We followed along behind him as he climbed into the cab. We asked him what he was looking for. He told us that workers would sometimes leave a key in the cab when their shift was over just in case another worker needed to use the equipment. Willy found the key and he seemed quite proud of himself.

After a bit of trial and error, Willy was able to start the engine and was soon handling the equipment like a pro. He started racing around the desert checking out the top speed of the machine and then began exploring the controls trying to figure out how to manipulate the huge front loader. Soon he was attacking sand dunes and moving scooper loads of sand from one place to another. After reshaping some of the desert landscape, he asked us if we wanted to give it a try. So, one by one, we got a tutorial from Willy and got our turn operating the "Cat". We fiddled around well into the night and when we were all done, Willy climbed in and turned the ignition switch off. Unfortunately, the engine kept running.

Now what? After spending a long time searching for a kill switch, Willy changed tactics and decided to see if he could stall the engine. He turned on all the lights, plowed the front loader bucket into a sand dune and shifted it into second gear. As he slowly pulled out the clutch and gave the machine more gas you could hear the engine lugging and trying to move forward but failing. Willy kept at it by tilting the bucket down and lifting the front end up off the ground. Again, he tried moving forward in second and this time, after a great deal of chugging he was able to kill the engine. He put the key back where he found it and we all piled back into the car.

Our next trip that summer was to Sespe Hot Springs. Randy wanted to stencil "*U.S. Navy Exploratory Vehicle*" onto the doors of his powder blue Studebaker before taking off. I helped him do It. It didn't take us long to reach Fillmore where we pulled off the main road and onto an unmaintained dirt road leading into the Sespe Condor Sanctuary. After crossing Sespe Creek a few times, we made it into the back country where the hot springs were located. It was a rugged road and most of the vehicles moving along it had four wheel drives. We got stuck in one of the creek crossings but a dude with a winch pulled us out.

The hot springs were totally cool dude! Nearly everyone was skinny dipping in the hot thermal pools which were lined up in series. The hottest pools were the ones located closest to the source. As the spring trickled down the mountain the temperature dropped in each successive pool. We tested the water starting at the lowest point and worked our way up toward the source. After soaking our way uphill, we finally ended up in a pool that was just too hot for any of us. After piling out of the last pond, we all had horribly red skin bro!

Later that summer, Randy wanted to drive up San Francisquito Canyon Road and check out a dam that had failed in 1928 killing over 400 people. When we reached the broken dam, we walked around the remains climbing over huge chunks of concrete. We checked out both ends of the dam and could see where it had been anchored to the canyon walls. It was an amazing sight. After exploring the ruins, we started heading back home and came across a grass fire on one of the hillsides. We raced back up the canyon to a remote fire station and reported it to a dude who was on duty up there. We turned around and by the time we passed the fire again, it had grown into an enormous blaze.

Randy wanted to take one last trip that summer so we went to San Felipe. It was a small Mexican fishing village located on the gulf coast of Baja California - about 350 miles south of Tijuana. He was concerned about getting flat tires so he bolted two spare tires to the top of his trunk lid. We left the Valley before the sun came up and arrived in San Felipe late in the afternoon. It was incredibly hot and incredibly humid when we arrived. We all got out of the car and immediately started heading to the beach hoping to cool off in the gulf water. As we took our first steps into the Sea of Cortez, all our hearts sank when we realized that the temperature of the water had to be in the 90's. Dude, the last thing you wanted to do when you were hot and sweaty was step into a hot bath!

As we stood sweating in the hot water we saw a ton of flying fish. It was totally amazing bro. I had never seen so many fish in the air at one time in my entire life! The small silvery fish were like tiny flying mirrors reflecting sunlight randomly as they flew across the sky. As we were standing there, we saw a fishing boat heading directly towards us and we were trying to figure out where this thing was going. There were no docks on the beach but the boat kept moving toward us. WTF? Was the captain going to land the boat on shore? It was a good sized vessel and we all decided it would be better to watch the boat while standing on the shore.

When we were at a safe distance, we turned around and watched the boat continuing its journey toward the beach. The seafloor dropped off gradually and we were sure the captain was going to run aground soon. We were completely baffled when we saw the boat slowly rising out of the water! WTF? What the hell was going on here? Suddenly I yelled, "It's an amphibious duck!" And sure enough, the closer the duck got to the beach the higher it rose out of the water until it came rolling up onto the sandy beach! I had never seen anything like it dude.

The temperature was so unforgivingly hot, humid and uncomfortable that we all agreed to cut our trip short. The next day, as we took our place in a long line of cars waiting to cross back into the U.S., we decided to play Arlo Guthrie's "Coming

184

into Los Angeles" on Randy's eight track stereo. Fellow travelers within earshot of the loud music smiled at the four long haired freaks taunting Border Patrol Officers with a song about smuggling marijuana into Los Angeles.

The first thing the Border Patrol Officer did was ask us all to step out of the vehicle. He searched the entire interior, while the music was still playing, checked the underside of the car, checked out all our gear in the trunk and then pulled out a hammer and started hitting the two tires that were bolted on the car's trunk lid. We all stood there with big smiles on our faces as the dude was doing his job. He didn't know what to make of us, but finally waved us through. Willy, Randy and I also took some motorcycle trips that summer including jaunts to - Death Valley, Ballarat – for a rock festival that took place on a huge alkali flat, Vasquez Rocks, Joshua Tree, Big and Little Tajunga Canyon and Santa Susana Pass. It was the best summer I ever had and it slipped away all too fast.

Chapter 39

In my senior year at CSUN, I needed 17.5 units in both my Fall and Spring semesters in order to graduate on time. I decided to take out a student loan for my last year of college instead of working part time. I felt like I needed to concentrate on all my classes and focus on graduating. My probation officer was nice to me and she told me that the judge would probably waive my second year of probation if I showed him proof that I graduated from college.

In my spare time, I began reading the King James version of the "New Testament" that my classmate had given me. It took me a while to get into the flow of 17th century English but, as I did, I found the writing to be quite beautiful. More importantly, I was surprised to discover that human nature had not changed over the past 2,000 years. There were murderers and adulterers, thieves and armed robbers, there were lots of judgmental people, there were tax collectors and fishermen, carpenters and merchants and religious leaders who held themselves in high esteem. There were hypocrites and handicapped people and beggars. There was wine and money and prostitution and greed.

The "New Testament" was filled with a ton of wisdom dude. It talks about the ever present battle of good versus evil, it tells you about God's love for you and me, and it introduces us to the greatest role model who ever walked the earth – Jesus Christ. Little by little, the words that Jesus spoke 2,000 years ago have seeped deeply into my mind, my heart and my soul. The lessons in the "New Testament" are so profound that it is impossible to convey in words how life altering they are.

Many of the verses have been deeply embedded into my very being. Here are a few of the things that Jesus has told us: "I am the way and the truth and the life. No one comes to the Father except through me." "But small is the gate and narrow the road that leads to life, and only a few find it." "But seek first his kingdom and his righteousness, and all these things will be given to you as well." "The time has come," he said. "The kingdom of God has come near. Repent and believe the good news!" "So I say to you: Ask and it will be given to you; seek and you will find; knock and the door will be opened to you." "Here I am! I stand at the door and knock. If anyone hears my voice and opens the door, I will come in and eat with that person, and they with me." "But whoever drinks the water I give them will never thirst. Indeed, the water I give them will become in them a spring of water welling up to eternal life." "Love the Lord your God with all your heart and with all your soul and with all your mind and with all your strength. Love your neighbor as yourself. There is no commandment greater than these." "There is no greater love than to lay down one's life for one's friends."

The more I read, the happier I became. And when I completed reading it, I had a rather unexpected emotional response: I was totally angry dude! Why didn't someone give this book to me when I was younger? My life would have been far easier and more fulfilling! But, I guess it's never too late bro!

Early that Fall, I blew a piston while I was riding my Honda 175. I bought a shop manual and tore apart the engine in my garage. I asked my mom not to come inside because I had neatly stacked all the engine parts in sequence as I took it apart. I bought a new piston and rings and had the cylinder honed out and then reassemble it. My friend Mike helped me replace the timing chain because it was the most difficult part of the rebuild. When it was totally complete, I rolled the bike outside, turned the ignition on and gave it a good kick start. The bike started up on my first attempt and I was totally ecstatic! I actually rebuilt an entire engine! The weather in September was still good so I decided to sell my bike and buy a new one right before Christmas. Once again, I got a sweet deal on a newer Honda 450 that went from 0 to 60 in under 5 seconds!

Dude, buying a car with that kind of performed would have cost me tens of thousands of dollars! The Honda 450 only cost me of a few hundred bucks. It was a poor man's high performance, convertible sport's car. Aside from the enhanced acceleration, the Honda 450 was more comfortable to ride but wasn't as nimble as my Honda 175. I guess there are always tradeoffs in life bro.

One of the most interesting classes that I had during my Fall semester was Engineering 101 – which fulfilled a science requirement that I needed to graduate. It was taught by an Asian dude and he was totally cool. I was surprised to discover that I was actually interested in Engineering and its many different classifications. I had no idea that engineers worked in so many different fields.

With the extra time I had, because I wasn't working at a part time job, I was able to read more books like: The Electric Kool-Aid Acid Test; Slaughterhouse Five; Cat's Cradle; Player Piano; God Bless You, Mr. Rosewater; On the Road; The Teaching of Don Juan; and A Separate Reality. I also developed an interest in movies and spent more time watching a wider spectrum of films including classics such as: "Metropolis"; "Modern Times"; "The Great Dictator"; and "King of Hearts".

I was also able to go clubbing more often and added "The Rock Corporation", located on Burbank Boulevard in Van Nuys, to my weekend dance marathons. They had some great bands playing there and the cover charge was just a buck. I got tired of listening to their "house band", who played there frequently. As a result, I started calling ahead to see who was performing before heading over there. The phone conversation went something like this: "Who's playing there tonight? Not "Van Halen" again!" That's right bro, I had seen Van Halen perform more times than anyone left alive today! One night, when they were playing at the club, some record producer or talent scout, was trying to convince another dude representing some record company to sign a recording agreement with "Van Halen". That was the last night I ever saw "Van Halen" performing at the "Rock Corporation". Soon afterwards, they were performing at the Anaheim Convention Center to sold out crowds for $60 a pop! Dude, I was totally relieved knowing that I would never have to see Eddie Van Halen playing guitar with his shirt off again! They did have a cool drummer though.

One night, I ran into an old high school friend who was performing with his band at a club in the Valley. His name was Jacey and he played the electric bass. We reconnected during one of the band's breaks and started hanging out together. At the time, Jacey was going to CSUN as well and he invited me to a party near campus that his band was going to be playing at. Of course I accepted. It was a kegger and I had a great time. Jacey invited me to jam with his band at a house they rented close to campus. I played piano and I had a great time practicing with them. It was the first time I ever worked with professional musicians.

I started dating more than I ever had before with women in my classes and young ladies that I met at rock clubs. It was fun but also expensive. When I was working and going to school, I didn't have much time for dating but I was saving money. Now that I wasn't working, I had plenty of time to date but I was depleting my savings! Well, I decided that it was for a good cause so I continued going out.

Jacey talked me into signing up for a piano class during my last semester at CSUN and I was glad that I did. One of the coolest things about taking music classes was having access to practice rooms. These small rooms had acoustical tiles on all the walls and ceilings and they were just big enough for a piano and a bench. It was wonderful to play music in rooms with exceptional sound quality and I spent many hours practicing in them. My music professor was a wonderful older woman who loved having a man in her class and I loved being surrounded by women! My classmate, Leslie, was the most outstanding pianist in the class. She played with great feeling, and she had a wonderful sense of timing. She also had the most beautiful and dazzling blue eyes that I had ever seen in my entire life bro! At the end of the semester, I asked Leslie if she would like to get together with me over the summer. Her face lit up and a huge smile appeared as she told me that she would love to do that.

Chapter 40

Dude, all my life, people were telling me that I needed to go to college and get a degree and when I graduated all these doors of opportunity would be opened up to me. Well, in June of 1974, I graduated from college and all those doors were slammed shut in my face. Why? This trifecta of bad luck struck me down: 1. The U.S. went off the gold standard in 1973. The U.S. dollar became a "floating" currency and its value was determined by foreign exchange markets; 2. The U.S. fell into a deep recession in 1973 and the term "corporate downsizing" was coined; 3. The Arab oil embargo against the U.S. went into effect in 1973 resulting in the price of a barrel of oil going from $3 per barrel to $12 per barrel.

As a result of all this economic turmoil – pun intended there bro – no companies were hiring anyone, and all companies were firing someone. It totally sucked dude. So what was a 22 year old, unemployed college graduate to do? That was the big question. I was one of the few grads that actually had $3,000 in savings resulting from my part time jobs and entrepreneurial skills. I certainly didn't want to spend time sitting around my mom's house waiting for the economy to turn around so I decided that it was a great time to travel. Unfortunately, I was still on probation. My one year probation hearing wasn't until September. As a result, I had to hang out until then.

Well, I didn't want to hang out by myself so I called Leslie, the young lady in my piano class, and she was happy to hear from me. We made arrangements to go see a movie. I picked her up at her apartment and we drove into Westwood Village to watch a newly released film. Afterwards, she invited me upstairs to her apartment. She put on an album of piano music composed by Erik Satie, and offered me a glass of wine. We were sitting on some pillows on her floor, talking and laughing and sipping some red wine while falling in love. Leslie and I saw a great deal of each other during that summer.

Since no one was hiring, I started running a classified ad advertising my hauling and moving services. I had an old, candy apple red Chevy pickup truck and I started getting odd jobs right away. I worked through most of August 1974 when my friend Frank, from up the street, introduced me to a relative of his from New Zealand. His name was Steve and he had an accent that I found amusing. He wanted to buy a motorcycle and take a trip through Yosemite and Kings Canyon. He asked me if I might be interested in joining him and I told him that I would think it over and let him know. I called my probation officer and asked her if I could leave Los Angeles County for a couple of weeks to go camping and she said that it would be fine. I got back to Steve and told him that I would travel with him once he got himself a motorcycle and was all set to go. About a week later, Steve came riding up our driveway on a used Honda 350 and we decided to take off on our road trip the following weekend. That gave me enough time to figure out what to take on our camping adventure.

We had a great time cruising through the National Parks and hanging out together. One of his favorite expressions totally cracked me up when I first heard it. We were walking past a customized motorcycle that was totally cool and he looks at me and said, "Shit hot, man!" I just couldn't stop laughing and a smile came to my face every time he would say it. As we were riding out of Kings Canyon we pulled over at one of the vista points looking down into one of the steepest canyons in North America. It was a totally amazing sight dude! This gnarly, narrow canyon had cut its way down to a depth of 8,200 feet through solid granite and it was absolutely stunning. Every variation of grey known to man was spreading out before me. It was a sight to behold bro!

Steve noticed that his rear tire was low so he pulled out a container of "tire in a can" to reflate it and hopefully patch the leak. Afterwards, he felt satisfied with the fix and we both took off and hit the road again. It was a beautiful summer day with blue skies and warm temperatures as we were winding our way down some incredibly steep hills with tight turns. It was midmorning and the temperature started getting warmer as we dropped down to lower elevations. The road gradually became less windy and the terrain was shifting from granite walls to pines and scrub brush.

We had been riding for a while so I began shortening the distance between me and Steve. I wanted to take a look at his rear tire to see how it was holding up. There was a straight stretch of road up ahead so I began accelerating. As I approached his motorcycle, I saw a vehicle coming towards us and traveling in our lane. It was passing another car while they were both crossing over a narrow bridge. Steve hit his brakes to give the idiot driver some extra time to pass because it looked like he was going to run right into us!

The moment Steve hit his brakes, his rear tire blew out and he was suddenly sideways in my lane! A huge surge of adrenaline began pumping into my body and everything instantly shifted into slow motion. If I kept going, I would have hit Steve broadside. I couldn't swerve into the oncoming lane because I would crash head on into a car that was accelerating towards us as it cut off the driver it had just passed. My lane was quite narrow and there was no shoulder that I could pull onto. I executed the only maneuver I had. I hit the rear brake hard while leaning the bike over to the right causing the bike to skid into a brodie. I was now sideways in my lane, just like Steve, and slowing down as quickly as possible by leaning my bike more radically to my right. I needed to pull my right leg out from under my motorcycle before my bike was completely on its side! I was a bit late and ended up banging my shin on the motorcycle frame as I whipped my leg out from under the bike.

Once my leg was free, I turned 90 degrees to my left. Now, I was facing oncoming traffic while sitting on the side of my motorcycle as it began grinding grooves into the hot pavement. ☹

Meanwhile, Steve was able to regain some control of his bike and began pulling it over to the right. I could see that he was trying to maneuver it onto a dirt road just ahead of him. Thankfully, he made it and was no longer in my lane. As I was sliding sideways, both of my tires started grabbing pavement causing my motorcycle to shudder. Suddenly, I was catapulted into the air as my bike flipped over. Fortunately, I was in an ideal sitting position as I went airborne with my feet out in front of me. I landed on my boots, butt and gloved hands. The asphalt immediately shredded my jeans and underwear. A millisecond later, it was chewing my ass off. Somehow, I managed to pop up onto my boots. Unfortunately, as I was skidding down the road in a standing position, I was heading directly into oncoming traffic!

I began shuffling and sidestepping my way toward the right aiming for the same dirt road that Steve was on. Finally, I slowed down enough to tuck and roll off the highway. When I came to a stop, I stood up and saw that my motorcycle was lying on its side in the middle of the oncoming traffic lane. It was completely blocking traffic and a line of cars were stopped behind it. I ran over, lifted it up and pushed it onto the dirt road. A woman waiting in the line of cars climbed out of her vehicle and started shouting, "That was the most amazing thing I have ever seen in my entire life!"

When I got back home, I called my probation officer to let her know that I was back in L.A. She told me that I had a court hearing coming up in a few weeks. Now, I had to decide where I wanted to travel. I spoke to Howard, who was now living up in Bellingham, and he said that he had traveled around Ecuador on $5.00 per day. That sounded appealing to me so I came up with a plan. I would withdraw $1,100 in traveler's checks from my savings account at Gibraltar Savings on Roscoe Boulevard and purchase a Greyhound Bus ticket to San Ysidro, California. I would then walk across the Mexican border and see how long I could live in Latin America before my money ran out.

I started listening to a Mexican radio station to brush up on my Spanish. It had been three years since I had taken Spanish in college and I was a bit rusty. It was an easy language to learn and the vocabulary words were coming back to me as I listened to the radio. I sold my pickup and motorcycle and obtained my passport and international driver's license. I also bought some new boots and camping gear at an army surplus store on Van Nuys Boulevard. Afterwards, I got out my trusty backpack and began planning what to take along with me on my trip. When my day in court came, I stood before the Judge with short hair and conservative clothes. After respectfully answering all his questions, he congratulated me on completing college and he terminated my probation. My criminal record was expunged and I was a free man. It was a good day bro!

Chapter 41

Soon, I was shuttling down the highway on a "scenic cruiser" with a running dog painted on its side. I was riding high in the saddle looking over all the cars and trucks heading south on the 405 but a thick layer of grey smog was muting all the colors and making everything look dismal and depressing as I left the Valley. About four hours later, I stepped off the bus in San Ysidro under clear blue skies and retrieved my backpack which had been unceremoniously tossed on the ground. The pack was off its frame and everything that I had tied onto it was completely messed up. It took me about fifteen minutes to get everything secured properly. I picked up my pack and got it adjusted so that it was riding comfortably on my back and began walking over the border.

As soon as I stepped onto Mexican soil, I was surrounded by a small crowd of Mexicans yelling, "Taxi Meester?" I shook my head and just kept walking until I was close to a Mexican bus station where I was suddenly surrounded by a band of children yelling, "Shine Meester?" Once again, I shook my head and just kept walking as their enthusiastic smiles turned into frowns of disappointment. I bought a ticket to Ensenada and was soon traveling south once again. I found an inexpensive motel close to the bus depot and decided to call it a day.

The next morning, I was on a bus heading south again on the Baja California Highway which had just been completed in 1973. There were several major dips in the road that crossed over large gullies. I couldn't believe that they hadn't elevate the roadway by building it over some big culverts to handle the flash floods that had obviously caused the huge ditches in the first place. (About a year later, I read that massive flash floods washed away several sections of the highway.) My destination that day was La Paz. I sat next to a dude named Hector who was a Puerto Rican from New York and he spoke fluent Spanish.

By the time we got to La Paz, I felt comfortable enough to ask Hector if he wanted to share a motel room. He agreed and we found a cheap place close to the beach.

The room had a bare concrete floor and a shower was stuck in a corner. There were two other motel guests lounging on the floor near the shower. They were rather large and black and utterly naked! As a matter of fact, they were the biggest cockroaches I had ever seen in my entire life bro! It was immediately apparent that I would be using this room for showering and sleeping only. All of my spare time would be spent away from it. Hector and I changed into some shorts and headed over to a beautiful sandy beach where I laid on a towel and took a nap.

Later that Friday afternoon, as we headed back to our divinely appointed room, we saw two police officers rolling a portable traffic signal into position at the town's busiest intersection. Hector said that people who lived in the surrounding area would be flooding into town later that night. After showering, we went out to dinner where we bumped into a couple of surfer dudes who had driven their VW bus down from San Diego. They asked us if we wanted to hang out together and take a ride over to "El Ranchito" to meet some girls and we agreed.

El Ranchito was located at the outskirts of town and it didn't take long to drive there. We parked in front of a large auditorium that was surrounded by several small motel rooms. As soon as we opened the van's doors, we heard a Mariachi band playing. We walked in, sat at a table and ordered some drinks. We were in a long narrow hall with tall ceilings and a large dancefloor where young ladies were lined up against a wall sitting on chairs wearing formals. It reminded me of some of the school dances I went to at Monroe High School.

After having a couple of drinks, the surfer dudes walked over to the lineup of women and picked out a couple girls to dance with. After the dance was over, the young ladies escorted their "dates" to their rooms located just outside the main auditorium. Hector and I just chatted with some of the locals who came to join us at our table after the surfer dudes disappeared. Eventually, the surfer dudes returned and they were ready to head back.

The next morning, Hector and I caught a bus to Cabo San Lucas where we were going to catch a ferry to Puerto Vallarta. In 1974, Cabo San Lucas consisted of a dock and a Mexican equivalent of a 7-Eleven. That was it! The bus dropped us off in front of the primitive 7-Eleven and we went inside to inquire about tickets for the ferry. The cashier explained that the ferry was leaving right now so we bought two tickets and hustled over to the dock. Just as we arrived, the ferry was pulling away from the dock and two crew members motioned for us to jump on board. We leapt off the dock and the crew grabbed our arms and helped pull us onto the ship! Dude, talk about barely making it!

The ship was new and impressive. We chatted with a fellow American as we sailed across the Sea of Cortez under blue skies and calm waters. At dinnertime, I bought myself a meal and sat with Hector who said he wasn't hungry yet. He kept eyeing other passengers studying them so closely that it made me feel a bit uncomfortable. As passengers cleared out of the dining room, Hector walked over to where they had been sitting, grabbed their plates, carried them back to our table and began eating the scraps that were left behind. He looked up at me and told me he was on a tight budget. We spent the night sleeping on deck chairs and pulled into Puerto Vallarta about midmorning the next day.

Hector told me he was heading to Bucerias - a small fishing village just north of Puerto Vallarta on highway 200. We grabbed our gear and walked over to the highway where we hitched a ride with a farmer hauling a load of hay to Mezcales which was about halfway to our destination. After hopping off the pile of hay, we walked over to a small restaurant and ordered some chicken soup which was brought to our table immediately. I was presented with a decent sized bowl containing a whole drumstick drowning in chicken broth accompanied by a floating peppercorn. After eating the chicken leg and half the broth, the peppercorn decided to swim across my bowl! Holy shit! It was a fly practicing the backstroke in my soup. I mmediately lost my appetite and nearly gave up my lunch as well. I was left with a bad feeling that lasted the rest of the day.

Rooms in Bucerias were quite cheap and quite small so Hector and I rented separate quarters – each room came equipped with a shower, a toilet, a sink and a twin bed. I spent the late afternoon walking along the beach where fisherman cleaned the guts out of their daily catch and just dumped the entrails in a huge heap on the beach. The smell was absolutely putrid and it didn't help my queasy stomach or my general unease. I went to bed early that evening and woke up in the middle of the night with a bad case of nausea. It was a good thing the toilet was close by.

I woke up feeling weak but mentally refreshed. I was sure that I would feel better as the day progressed. The first order of business was gathering my things together and leaving this wretched little town behind me. I caught an early bus to Puerto Vallarta and checked into a fine old hotel that felt like the Ritz-Carlton after my most recent experiences. I left my stuff in my room and headed back outside and began checking out the city. The old quarter of town was delightful with cobblestone roads and Spanish architecture. I walked down to the beach and watched an old man collecting stones and loading them onto a small burrow. The sea breeze felt good and the air felt clean and refreshing. I headed over to the central "Mercado" and bought a pair of "huaraches" and a cool tee shirt made out of a flour sack.

After making my purchases, I walked over to the newer section of town where most of the tourists were hanging out on a beautiful beach. I did some sun bathing and then went into the water to cool off. A beautiful young woman came into the water right next to me and we started chatting. She was very nice and had a very peaceful aura about her and before leaving the beach we made plans to meet for dinner at a Restaurant she suggested. I went back to my room where I took a siesta and then showered and got dressed for dinner.

I walked to the restaurant and met the young woman and her girlfriend for dinner and dancing afterwards. Shortly after eating dinner, Hector randomly showed up at our table so I introduced him to my companions. He was a pushy dude and invited himself to our table and wouldn't leave us alone for the remainder of the evening. One of the gals was completely turned off by him and we ended up heading back to our separate rooms shortly before midnight.

Chapter 42

The next day, I bought a bus ticket to Guadalajara where I spent my afternoon walking around admiring the beautiful architecture of the city and the beautiful women as well. The next morning, I traveled to Mexico City. My first challenge was crossing the Reforma which was a huge six lane boulevard where cars were zooming along at 60 MPH. There were no crosswalks and I watched other pedestrians crossing the road one or two lanes at a time and then standing in traffic until the next lane or two became free. That looked too dangerous for me, so I took my time until there was a huge opening across all six lanes. The only car on the road was in the lane closest to the curb. As I stepped off the curb, I nearly fell flat on my face because the curb was unusually high. I quickly recovered and began my journey across a huge asphalt sea. As soon as I cleared the first lane, I noticed that the only car on the road changed lanes with me. The same thing happened after crossing the third and subsequent lanes. Shit! This dude was trying to run me over! I ran across the last three lanes and the moment my feet hit the far curb the car came flying by me at about 90 MPH! Welcome to Mexico City Gringo!

After a long bus ride and an exciting introduction to Ciudad de Mexico, I found a cheap motel and decided to take a long shower, grab some dinner and hit the sack early. The next morning, I bumped into a couple of Americans in the motel lobby and asked them if they knew of a good place to eat breakfast. They said they were heading over to their favorite café and invited me to join them. I ordered a café con leche, pancakes, eggs and bacon. I was totally famished dude! When my meal came, I dove in with great enthusiasm until I bit into something crunchy in one of my pancakes. I immediately spit it into my napkin and began dissecting the pancake to determine what that crunchy nugget was. Dude, it was a frickin cockroach! Even though I was still hungry, I couldn't eat another bite.

In Ciudad de Mexico, no one bothered to slow down before making a right hand turn! Diesel fumes from busses and trucks invaded my lungs, my eyes stung and everyone was honking their horns. Nobody seemed to be aware that they were driving around with either a rusted out muffler or no muffler at all. City busses didn't come to a complete stop when dropping people off or picking them up. As drivers were approaching a bus stop, they began opening their doors and pulling close to the curb slowing down to five miles per hour allowing people to either jump on or off the bus. It was a madhouse bro!

There were three places that I was determined to see in Mexico City: The National Museum of Anthropology; Ancient Aztec ruins at Teotihuacan, which was located about 30 miles outside of Mexico City; And, the University of Mexico. The museum was filled with ancient artifacts contained within the walls of a modern building designed with clean lines and an open floorplan. The Aztec ruins were a treat to see and walk around. I particularly enjoyed seeing the rectangular stadium where Aztec athletes played a sport outdoors that involved placing a ball through hoops mounted on the two longest walls. The hoops weren't mounted parallel to the ground as they are in Basketball, they were mounted perpendicular to the ground and were much larger and made of stone. At the University, I totally enjoyed the colorful murals that adorned the exterior walls of the buildings on campus.

After spending five days in Mexico City, it was time for me to move on. I took a train to Veracruz, located on the Gulf of Mexico, where I spent some time enjoying marimba bands playing on the city streets. I was also amazed to see a huge Soviet freighter docked in the port. The U.S. was still locked in a cold war with the USSR and I was shocked to see that Mexico was doing business with the Soviets.

My next destination was the Mayan ruins in Palenque which I reached by train. I spent the night in a small motel located close to the ruins, and after breakfast the next morning, I headed out to see the archeological site. It wasn't far from where I was staying, so I decided to walk. After 15 minutes, I heard a car coming my direction so I turned around and stuck out my thumb. A beat up old 1962 Chevy II came around a corner and stopped to pick me up. The car was a wreck and it had a bad muffler. I hesitated to climb in for a moment until the driver said, "Well, get in... get in" in an exasperated voice as he motioned to me with his hand. He had a British accent and I quickly learned that he was a pig farmer from British Columbia who was traveling through Mexico to nurse a broken leg. His name was Dick and I told him that I was planning on traveling through the Yucatan and then down through Central America. Dick had traveled through both Mexico and Central America many times and he asked me if I would like to travel with him. He seemed like a decent guy so I told him that would be great.

Dick was knowledgeable about Mexico's history and the Mayans. As we walked through the ruins he pointed out features to me that had been carved in stone. There were several carvings of what appeared to be elephant heads. He said that there were never any elephants in Mexico and postulated that the ancient Mayans migrated here from Asia. Dick, wearing shorts, a white dress shirt and a straw hat hobbled along using a cane. He had a dark tan and light brown hair with streaks of blond running through it.

After checking out the ruins, I was surprised to see him pulling out a blackened teapot from his trunk and filling it up with water. Apparently, it was tea time. After gathering some wood and dried grass and carefully placing them in a pile, he took out a box of matches and set it all on fire. We sat down on a log bordering the parking lot and Dick used his cane to dangle the teapot over the little campfire that he built. Soon, we were both sipping tea as he began telling me that there was a greater degree of freedom in Latin America compared to the U.S. and Canada. He said that you could start a fire anywhere and camp anywhere without obtaining any kind of permits. I found this guy to be totally amazing bro.

Chapter 43

Dick asked me if I had ever seen the Caribbean and I told him that I hadn't. He went on to tell me that it was the most beautiful place he had ever been. He wanted to show me a beach in Tulum and said that we needed to pick up supplies in Merida. We bought beans, rice, cheese and some miscellaneous jars and cans of food and I picked out a beautiful string hammock to sleep on. Afterwards, we headed over to Cancun where a huge hotel was being built right on the beach. It was odd to see a massive, multi-story, concrete shell sitting on an empty beach with absolutely nothing around it. WTF? Seriously? Well, I think I was the first American tourist to ever string a hammock between two palm trees and spend the night on the beach at this embryonic resort.

On the way to Tulum, we took a couple of side trips to Isla Mujeres and Cozumel. When we finally reached our destination, we pulled off the road and made camp under the shade of some coconut trees. I was amazed at the whiteness of the sand and the powdery nature of it. It wasn't as gritty as the sand on the beaches in Southern California. After setting up camp, we walked to the beach and my jaw nearly dropped to the ground dude! What a totally bitchin beach. It was absolutely gorgeous and the color and clarity of the water was incredible. Dick and I parked ourselves on that beach for two weeks.

We ran into a couple of surfer dudes in a VW bus who were camping close by and they told us that they had been there for two months. These dudes were cool. They both had Hawaiian slings which were made out of six foot steel rods with sharpened points on one end and surgical tubing tied to the other. They were basically crude harpoons. They placed the loop of surgical tubing between their thumb and index finger of one hand, and then pulled the end of the spear with the other hand stretching the surgical tubing out like a heavy duty rubber band. Once the tubing was stretched to its capacity they grasped the spear with the hand that was holding the stretched tubing. Once they found whatever they were fishing for, they simply released their grasp on the spear and the stretched tubing would propel the spear forward.

Dick decided to drive to the nearest town and buy a steel rod and whatever type of heavy duty rubber tubing or band he could find. He spent an entire day buying the materials and fashioning a point on the tip of a steel rod. The process began by sticking the rod into our campfire then smashing the red hot tip with a hand held rock while holding the rod against a much larger stone. He also used a hand held stone to help shape and sharpen the tip. After attaching a heavy duty elastic band to the opposite end of the spear, Dick marched out into the ocean like Hemingway's The Old Man and the Sea. And just like the Old Man, he returned to the beach victoriously with a decent sized fish dangling on the end of his spear.

For the remainder of our time at the beach, we ate fresh grilled fish with rice and beans boiled up with fresh vegetables. For breakfast and lunch we ate bananas, oranges, coconut milk and coconut meat. One day, Dick had the idea of making coconut oil to use on our skin. We were camping in a huge grove of coconut trees so we walked around collecting several coconuts that had fallen on the ground and carried them back to our camp. We used our machetes to husk the coconuts and crack open the nut. Then we switched to using our pocket knives to separate the coconut meat from the shell. We tossed the white chunks into Dick's pressure cooker, poured water into it and set it on our campfire overnight. In the morning, Dick opened up the lid and we skimmed off the congealed coconut oil and stored it in a couple empty peanut butter jars that we had saved. The fresh oil felt wonderful as we spread it on our dry skin.

Dick became quite good at spear fishing and I was growing more curious about it. One morning, Dick let me borrow his spear and I went into the water and began searching for something to catch. It was like fishing inside an aquarium. The fish were incredibly colorful and they swam close to you. I made several attempts to spear something but returned empty handed. I decided to get some advice about catching lobsters from our resident spear fishermen. They told me that lobsters liked to bury themselves on the seafloor and they said I should look for their tentacles which would be poking out of the sand.

I went back out to sea with my snorkel and mask clutching Dick's spear in my hand while swimming around face down looking for tentacles. I finally spotted a tentacle and I began circling around to see if I could spot the second one but I had no success. After swimming around in a circle again, I decided that the second tentacle must be buried under the sand. I came up for air and took several deep breaths. Clutching my spear with both hands, I dove down to the bottom of the seafloor and drove that spear into the head of my lobster. Dude, I was totally surprised that the lobster was strong enough to pull that spear out of my hands. Suddenly, the seafloor began to rise. Holy shit! There was a huge cloud of sand coming at me. I frantically kicked and worked my way back to the surface. I took a couple of deep breaths, stuck my face back into the water and watched a huge manta ray swimming away with Dick's spear stuck in its back!

Manta rays typically swam parallel to the seafloor, but when they had a six foot spear stuck in their spine, they swam perpendicular to the seafloor. I chased after it as fast as I could but it was clearly a much better swimmer than I was - even with a spear stuck in it! Dick would be pissed if I returned without his spear. So, I kept searching for it. After more than an hour of swimming, I spotted it. The ray had settled in much deeper water and was just resting on the seafloor looking up at me. Once again, I circled around trying to work up my courage to dive down and pull the spear out of the manta ray's back. After treading water and taking several deep breaths, I dove down to the bottom, yanked the spear out of the ray and swam back to the surface. Sheesh! I did it. With Dick's spear back in my hand, I circled around the ray one last time wondering if I should finish off the beast. I thought about driving the spear into the ray's head and bringing it back to shore. But, I didn't have the heart to put an end to the creature's life.

Chapter 44

Our next destination was Belize City. While we were driving south on the highway, Dick saw the car in front of us run over the head of a beautiful lime green iguana. He immediately pulled his car over to the side of the road, got out, grabbed the iguana and stuck it in his trunk. I asked him what he was going to do with the road kill and he told me he was going to gut it at a nearby cenote and then cook it up for dinner tonight. I immediately began to question the wisdom of this, but Dick assured me that they were delicious.

Soon, we pulled into a picnic area on the shore of a large cenote. Cenotes occurred in only a couple of places in the world and the Yucatan peninsula was one of them. They were created when ground water eroded a cavity in the underlying limestone rock causing the surface of the earth to sink into it. They are amazing little ecosystems with freshwater fish and plant life. Some of them are extremely deep providing wonderful places for skin diving. The only reason we needed this particular cenote was to wash out our iguana after Dick had gutted it. We continued driving until sundown when Dick pulled off the road and into a decent sized clearing where we made camp. Dick cut up the Iguana, stuck it into a large cast iron skillet and set it over our campfire. The iguana smelled delicious and it didn't take much effort on my part to try it. Mm, it tasted like, you guessed it bro, fried chicken!

The next day, we crossed into Belize. The road we were on deteriorated the farther we drove into the country. Soon there were huge potholes everywhere, and they were impossible to avoid. By the time we got to Belize City, the front end suspension on Dick's Chevy II needed to be repaired. We found a mechanic who agreed to let us camp out in his mechanic's yard until the parts came in and were installed. He said we could sleep in the back of a van that was parked on his property. Dude, we were stuck in that yard for five days.

Every morning, I woke up staring at a bunch of Hare Krishna posters that were taped on the inside of the van we were sleeping in. I saw and smelled more of Belize City than I had ever wanted to. Walking along the city's open sewers made me want to vomit. It was like living in a gigantic toilet. We walked to the central market every day and ate tamales and conch fritters. The food was delicious and I was happy to augment my meals with large Cadbury chocolate bars which were sold everywhere. The only mishap I had was a minor run in with a police officer who started yelling at me in creole. I had no idea what he was saying and I apologized to him for not understanding what he was trying to tell me. He suddenly began speaking English and I told him that I could understand him now. Dude, I think he was just messing with me.

When Dick's car was finally repaired, we decided to drive to Tikal. As soon as we crossed the border into Guatemala, we were back on well-maintained roads. Tikal was another Mayan ruin and it was an incredible sight. I climbed up the main pyramid, the Tikal Temple, and it provided a stunning 360 degree view of the entire area. Dick said that when things were not going well for the ancient Mayans they would sacrifice a virgin to their god. He said that they would cut out the heart of a young virgin and hand it to a runner who would race up to the top of the temple. If the heart was still beating once he reached the top, it was proof that their god was satisfied with the sacrifice. If not, they would continue making sacrifices until one of the hearts reached the top while it was still beating. Dude, this could have been the cause of the decline in the population of the ancient Mayan civilization. When it was time to camp, we just pulled Dick's car off the road onto a large open grassy area near the Tikal Temple.

Our next destination was Guatemala City. The first thing we did was hit the central Mercado. I was stunned by the incredible assortment of prepared foods that were available for sale. It was the most organized, clean and well-lit Mercado that

I had ever been to. The food was absolutely delicious and my one regret was having only one shot at sampling all the wonderful dishes that were available. Dick and I were excited to check out Mount Pacaya, which was just outside Guatemala City, and was erupting at the time. We drove as close to it as possible and found a farmer who was willing to rent us his donkey so Dick could travel closer to the base of the volcano. We hiked to the base of Mount Pacaya and Dick was satisfied waiting there until I scaled up the side of the mountain.

The mountain was covered in golf ball sized chunks of pumice stones. Climbing up that sucker was a real pain in the ass. I took three steps up and slid two steps back. I'm not shitting you dude! It was a frickin ordeal. Anyway, I got real close to the top when the wind suddenly stopped and the entire peak of the mountain was covered in a cloud of smoke mixed with sulfur dioxide, which smelled like rotten eggs. I sat down just below the cloud and waited for the wind to pick up and blow away the gas and smoke. It took quite a long time but finally a breeze came by that kept the smoke and sulfur dioxide away. I quickly scurried the rest of the way up to the top and was surprised to find a couple dudes running experiments on the edge of the caldera.

I asked them what they were doing up there and they told me that they were from the University of Chicago running experiments in conjunction with NASA measuring changes in specific gravity as the volcano erupted. I walked over to the caldera and saw glowing red magma bubbling below. Dude, it was totally cool! I was hoping that the volcano would eject some lava while I was up there. It took some patience but the volcano finally spit out some lava that solidified instantly and came raining down around us as glowing red stones. The two dudes were excitedly running around collecting specimens with tongs and placing them into specimen containers. They wanted to analyze the gasses that were being emitted from the glowing red stones. I bid them farewell and headed back down the mountain. Every step going down was like taking three steps because of all the sliding that occurred. It was a totally cool day bro.

Chapter 45

Dick wanted to spend some time in San Jose, Costa Rica and it was time for me to decide if I was going to continue my travels into South America or return home. I still had quite a bit of money left because traveling with Dick was very inexpensive. It had been three months since I first crossed over the border into Mexico and I was getting a bit homesick. But, I kept thinking about what I would do if I went back. The economy certainly wasn't going to be any better so I decided to split up with Dick and fly to Cartagena, Colombia with a stopover in San Andres which was a small island in the Caribbean.

San Jose, Costa Rica rests at an elevation of approximately 3.600 feet so when I stepped onto my plane to fly to San Andres, Colombia the weather was cool and dry. Stepping off the plane after arriving in San Andres was like stepping into a steaming hot bath. The air was thick and humid and harder to walk through. It didn't take me too long to adjust. After picking up my backpack, I asked a hippie dude who was on the same flight where he was planning on staying. He told me to follow him and he would show me a place in someone's home where the owners rented out rooms to tourists.

I followed him to a modest home that was run by a Colombian couple who not only rented us rooms but also cooked meals for us at very reasonable prices. All the tourists staying there were Americans and one of the guys suggested that we play poker after dinner. At the time, one American dollar would buy you a big stack of Colombian pesos in paper bills so some of the high betting hands looked like a high stakes table in Las Vegas. Sometimes the table would be piled so high with paper currency that the eyes of the workers, who served us meals and cleaned up after us, were filled with awe at the huge piles of cash sitting on our table. In American dollars, the biggest pots would total about five dollars. But dude, it was so much fun raking it all in when you won a hand!

We all got up late the next morning and I didn't get to the beach until noon. It was a crowded spot with tons of people sunbathing and playing in the water. After walking around a bit, I stepped into a casino to grab a fruit drink with a little paper umbrella in it and a long straw. I sat at a table and watched people gamble and drink and drink and gamble. Afterwards, I cruised around some more and then headed back to my room to clean up and get some dinner. After dinner, my new friend invited me into his room and pulled out a baggie of cocaine, a mirror, and a razor blade. He chopped up the crystals on the mirror with the razor blade and laid out a couple of lines for me to snort. I rolled up a bill and inhaled a line in each nostril. It was early evening and I decided to go out for a walk and check out the nightlife. The drug affected me differently than most people. It reminded me of the time that my friend Tim gave me an amphetamine tablet and all that happened was that I felt calmer and more lucid. As far as I was concerned, they were both pointless drugs.

Most of the Americans that I talked to in San Andres told me Colombia was a dangerous place to travel. Their advice was to head to Pasto, which was near the southern border of Colombia, and then head south to Ecuador which was a much safer country. They suggested that I stay in Quito and use it as a base to travel to other areas in Ecuador. The next morning, I flew into Cartagena, Colombia and I was astonished at the hustle and bustle outside the airport. There were several brightly colored busses loading and unloading passengers. Several young Colombians were climbing up and down ladders built onto the back of the busses as they were either loading or unloading baggage from large luggage racks built onto the rooves of the busses. I found a bus that was heading to my first stop which was Medellin.

When I got off the bus at Medellin, I immediately bought a ticket for the next bus leaving for Cali. I had a couple of hours to kill, so I walked around the city and it gave off an ominous vibe. It was a dark and dreary town and the people who worked in the stores all said the same thing to me as I entered, "A la ordin." I found it creepy. I grabbed a bite to eat and then headed back to the bus station for my next leg of the trip to Cali. By the time I got off the bus in Cali, it was dark. I was able to make a quick connection onto a bus heading to Pasto without leaving the station. The bus heading to Pasto had wooden benches as seats. Holy shit dude! They were terribly uncomfortable and I struggled for a long time trying to fall asleep.

The next morning when I woke up, I wasn't sure if I was still dreaming or not. I was incredibly groggy. As I stared out the bus window, I saw one of the most beautiful mountain settings that I had ever seen in my entire life! It was as though I woke up In some fairy tale land that consisted of dramatic mountains carpeted with lush, green grass. We must have been above the tree line because there were no trees to be seen. Dark green grass with no variation in color carpeted the steep and jagged mountaintops. There were no visible signs of erosion, or rocks, or creeks or trails. Slowly, I began to realize that I truly was awake and that everything I was seeing was real.

There were quite a few indigenous people sitting around me with sacks of produce at their feet and several of them were holding live chickens on their laps. Most of them wore navy blue ponchos, white cotton pants and cool looking fedoras. From time to time, people from one side of the bus rushed over to the other side while cackling and pointing out the windows. I had no idea what they were so excited about until a bunch of them rushed over to my side of the bus pushing my face into the cold glass of my window. As I stared a thousand feet down an incredibly steep cliff, my eyes began focusing on something rectangular and brightly colored. Holy shit dude! It was a frickin bus!

That totally woke me up and got my attention dude! Apparently several buses along the route suffered the same fate. The road we were traveling on was carved out of the side of a mountain. As I looked to my right, there was a steep mountain reaching up to the sky and to the left there was a shear drop off. The road was paved with cobblestones and barely wide enough to allow two busses to pass. Fortunately, we didn't encounter too many busses coming from the opposite direction but the few times we did, everyone on board took a deep breath and held it until we passed.

There was a section of the highway that had a good sized pull out and Colombian soldiers were motioning the bus driver to pull over. One of the soldiers entered the bus and ordered us to step outside where they checked our ID's. They pulled a couple people aside and let the rest of us back on the bus. FARC rebels were apparently active in the area and the soldiers found something suspicious about two of our fellow passengers. This country was indeed a dangerous place to travel for several reasons.

The bus took us to a border crossing where I walked over to a guard shack with my backpack and had my passport stamped. Afterwards, I grabbed the next bus heading to Quito. One of the Americans in San Andres recommended that I stay at the Hotel Grand Casino so that was my first destination. The Hotel was located in the old quarter of town just up the hill from an old town square. The streets were narrow and the front of the buildings were adjacent to the sidewalks creating a narrow little canyon to walk through. I became very fatigued carrying my backpack up the hill to the Hotel. I checked in, went to my room - which was on the second floor, took my backpack off, collapsed on a twin bed and passed out.

The next morning, I felt much better and began exploring the hotel. There was nothing in my room except a light and a bed. The bed was actually decent but there was no bathroom. Stepping outside my door I stood next to a railing overlooking an open plaza. Down below, I saw a few tables and chairs on the main floor where guests were sitting and eating. To the right, there was a communal bathroom with a toilet, sink and a shower allowing me the opportunity to wash my hands and face before heading downstairs to the hotel's café. A lean, friendly young man about my age took my order under the watchful glare of a rather humorless, overweight middle aged woman who was wiping her hands on her apron. Soon, I was handed a plate with a thin, well done steak sitting next to a pile of white rice. It was all rather tasteless but it filled me up.

The next morning I woke up feeling good and went downstairs to order some breakfast and drink some café con leche. I bought a newspaper and spent some time deciphering the Spanish language articles in it and came away with a basic understanding of what the news stories were about. After breakfast, I headed back down the hill where I found a newsstand across from an open town square and bought an English language "Time Magazine". I walked into a panaderia next to the newsstand and bought some bakery items which I devoured on the way back to my hotel. As I arrived at the arched entryway of the "Gran Casino", I was greeted by a pair of beautiful wrought iron gates which were opened and pressed against the side of the building's exterior. As I stepped into the hotel, I walked past a pair of solid wood doors which were both opened inwards in a welcoming gesture. The manager of the hotel was always at the front desk and ever watchful with his coal black eyes, his slicked back shiny hair and a black mustache. He reminded me of Gomez on the "Addams Family" except for the fact that he never smiled and wore a leather jacket instead of a coat and tie.

My short trip down the hill and back exhausted me and I was beginning to wonder if I had contracted hepatitis. There were some Americans sitting at a table at the hotel's café so I sat next to them and ordered another café con leche. They introduced themselves to me and we began chatting about our experiences traveling in Latin America. I mentioned that I felt totally exhausted just walking down the street and back. One of the guys asked me how long I had been in Quito and I told him that I arrived a couple of days ago. He said that the same thing happened to him until he got acclimated to the elevation. I had no idea what the elevation of Quito was and he told me that it was around 9,000 feet. Holy shit! It was a total shock to me. I thought that Denver, Colorado - at one mile high - was insane. Quito was nearly twice as high. Rocky Mountain high was kid's stuff, Andes Mountain high was the real deal bro!

Chapter 46

I met a dude named Casey who was staying at the hotel. He told me that he was a crane operator from Minnesota. It was January 1975 and Casey said that there wasn't much construction going on during the winter so he decided to spend some time in South America where he could live more cheaply. I also met Bernadette who was from Switzerland and was traveling through South America with a female friend of hers who lived in Paris. That night at dinner, the four of us sat at the same table and got to know one another better. Bernadette and her friend were telling us that they were heading to Banos, which was a small tourist town about a hundred miles south of Quito, and they asked us if we wanted to join them.

There were two big draws to Banos. One was a large public pool fed by a natural thermal hot spring that was located at the base of Mount Tungurahua. The other attraction was an unbelievable view of Mount Chimborazo which is the highest mountain in Ecuador - it's elevation is 20,548 feet! The elevation of Banos is 5,955 feet. When the four of us got off the bus, we all checked into the Hotel Americano which was more like a rooming house than a hotel. The woman who ran it was sweet and welcoming and she also provided us with meals. After dinner we went over to a little bar that specialized in serving up the local hard liquor. They served it to you in a shot glass that they lit on fire at your table. You were supposed to let it burn awhile to warm up the liquor and then down it while it was still on fire. One shot was enough for me bro. I'm glad I didn't set my face on fire!

Some tourists at the bar told us that it was a good night to sneak into the thermal pool because it had been drained that morning and was still filling up. They told us that sick people came to the pool to get healthy and their germs continued to multiply as the week progressed. It was safer to go into the fresh water before they opened the baths up to the public the following morning. We went back to our rooms, got into our swimsuits and proceeded to climb over the chain link fence that surrounded the pool. While we were testing the water, a security guard came by and told us that it was okay to go in as long as there were no Ecuadorians in our party. We told him that there weren't and then we all jumped in for a soak. Afterwards we headed back to the hotel for the night.

The next morning, Bernadette and her friend told us that they had to head back to Quito to catch their flight back to Europe. They took off right after breakfast while Casey and I lingered over our bowls of oatmeal. Some Canadian dudes came down to the dining area while we were sipping coffee and they started chatting with us. Maurice, Randy and Gordon were all construction workers from British Columbia and were spending the winter in South America. They said they were planning on renting some horses from a local guy and riding out of town after breakfast that morning. Maurice asked us if we wanted to join them and we said it sounded like fun.

A local farmer saddled us up. I was sitting astride a beautiful golden palomino and we were all riding high in our saddles. We rode down cobblestone streets as young children were chasing after us yelling "Macho Gringos!" It gave me an insight into how Spanish Conquistadors felt as they rode into town centuries ago. We rode along Via a Banos heading east until we found a nice spot next to a creek. We let our horses rest, drink and graze while we ate lunch. On the trip back, all the horses began galloping home to their farm. Dude, we all had a blast!

That night at dinner, Maurice told us that he and his buddies were going to head into the Amazon basin in the morning and he asked if Casey and I wanted to join them. They were planning on taking a bus to Tena and then catching a ride on a boat going down the Rio Napo to Coca. We all got along so well we decided that we would join them. Maurice told us,

"You know, for Americans, you guys are all right." 'Nuff said bro.

The next morning we bought tickets to Tena and boarded a colorful bus with a roof rack packed with sacks and suitcases. A couple of young guys grabbed our backpacks and secured them up on top of the bus. We rode for a couple hours and then the bus stopped. People started getting up and leaving. WTF? We were up in the middle of the Andes with nothing around us but road. I asked the bus driver what was going on and he said a huge landslide was blocking the road. He explained that we had to walk over the landslide and that there would be another bus waiting for us on the other side. Dude, this totally sucked!

There were four other Americans on the bus and they joined our group. We all grabbed our packs and began trudging in a single file line behind the locals who were clutching onto their belongings. Soon we were knee deep in soft soil stepping into two foot deep holes previous travelers had left behind. It was painstakingly slow. After a while, we began walking up and over the landslide which consisted of uncompacted dry soil. There was a huge bluff to the left of us and to the right there was a steep drop off. We all traveled on a footpath that was three feet wide and firm. I was in the lead.

As we walked, I began hearing a faint rumbling sound. Slowly, the rumbling grew louder and I began looking around to see where it was coming from. Soon, I could hear a diesel engine and clanking metal. I looked up to the top of the bluff while keeping my eyes peeled and focusing all my attention on the spot where the noise was coming from. A bulldozer began pushing a huge pile of tree stumps, rocks and dirt over the edge of the cliff directly above us. "Run!" I yelled as I started sprinting forward. I never looked back and was concentrating on putting as much distance between me and the tumbling landslide above me.

When I was safe, I turned around and saw two others directly behind me. Further behind them, four people were running in the opposite direction. Two people were unaccounted for. I set my pack down on the trail and started heading back to see what had happened to them. One of the guys was lying face down in the dirt with his hand stuck under a huge stump. A couple of the guys at the end of the line were digging at the base of the stump trying to free his hand. The dirt was super soft and they were soon pulling him away from the massive stump. A hundred feet down the side of the mountain, someone else was yelling for help. Randy and one of the other Americans began scooting down the steep slope. When they reached the last missing person, they found him buried up to his neck in dirt. The rescuers swiftly dug him out with their bare hands and came bounding up the mountainside.

The man whose hand was stuck under the massive stump was the only one who was injured. Fortunately, one of the Americans traveling with us was a nurse and she was tending to the man's hand as best as she could. I peered over her shoulder as she was pouring water out of her canteen onto the man's wounded finger. As the water began washing away the dirt, I could see about an inch of bone where the man's flesh was ripped away from his finger. I quickly turned my head away.

After the man's finger was bandaged, we all gathered our things and began heading along our path once again. We were all quiet and feeling a bit sullen. After more than an hour of walking, we came to a solid roadbed. This lifted our spirits and walking became much easier. Soon, we came upon a huge yellow dump truck parked on the side of the road. It had massive knobby tires that gave its underside a great deal of clearance. Just beyond the truck, the road switched back to the right and we were soon viewing the other side of the truck as we walked.

As we approached the next turn to the left, a construction worker wearing a white hard hat passed us walking in the opposite direction. He said nothing to us as we passed him. This seemed quite odd to me so I turned around and asked him in Spanish what was going on. He gave me a one word reply – "Dynamite".

Holy shit! We all immediately did an about face and followed the construction worker who stopped and leaned against the mountain at the side of the dirt road. Everyone lined up next to him staring at the yellow dump truck which was parked across the hairpin turn. As I stared at the massive yellow truck, I decided that I would feel safer standing on the opposite side of it. I walked back down the road, around the tight turn to the left and back up to where the truck was parked. I had a great view of the side of the mountain my friends were leaning against and as I looked father to the right of them there was an open vista allowing me to view all the way down to the base of the mountain. Suddenly, there was an enormous explosion and tons of earth shot out from the mountainside. Unfortunately, some of the debris was heading my way. I dove under the truck as a barrage of rocks began pinging off the side of it.

When the dust settled and the pinging stopped, I crawled out from under my fortress and headed back to my friends. The first thing they did was thank me. "if you hadn't talked to that construction worker we would have all been killed," said Maurice. I told him that I couldn't believe that the worker just walked by us without warning us. We were all shaken up but glad to be alive. After pulling ourselves together, we marched onward to the point where a truck with a canvas canopy was waiting for us. The driver asked us if we were the last passengers on the bus and we told him that we were. He started his truck and headed for Mera.

When we got to Mera, I told the driver that our friend hurt himself badly and needed to see a doctor to clean and

223

dress a wound on his finger. The driver said that there was a clinic in town that he would drive us to. We thanked him as we all bailed out of the back of the truck and into the clinic. The doctor wasn't busy at the time so he took a look at the wound, cleaned it out well, bandaged it, gave our friend a tetanus shot and handed him a bottle of antibiotics to guard against infection.

The next morning, we said goodbye to our American friends and the five of us caught a bus to Tena. We hired a guy with a dugout canoe, powered by a small outboard motor, to take us down the Rio Napo to Coca. As the man skillfully navigated his canoe down the river, we were enjoying our journey into the Amazon jungle. The first thing I saw when we stepped out of the canoe in Coca was a couple of young boys pulling a huge catfish out of the river. It was about five feet long and the boys were both struggling to carry the heavy fish to their home.

Coca was a small village mostly populated by indigenous people. There was, however a Chinese restaurant in town so not all the residents were locals. We stopped at a small restaurant located in a thatched hut and ordered some dinner. On the inside of the restaurant hanging on a wall was a ten foot blow pipe that the natives used for hunting game. We were all beat after traveling for the last couple of days and we asked our server where would be a good place to stay. She pointed out a wood frame structure across the road where we spent a couple of nights. Our stay in Coca was uneventful, and so was the return trip to Quito.

Chapter 47

The next morning at breakfast, back at the Hotel Grand Casino, Maurice was already talking about our next adventure. He wanted to go up to Ibarra, which was not too far north of Quito, and find some San Pedro Cactus to ingest. Apparently, this cactus is the Andes equivalent of peyote. He told us that it was growing in a city park fronting on a Street named "Simon Bolivar". He had already scoped out the bus schedule and we agreed to head up that way the next morning.

Upon arriving in Ibarra, we found an inexpensive Pension where we dropped off our packs and headed out to find the park on Simon Bolivar. We found it close to the center of town and it was one square block. Sure enough, there was quite a collection of San Pedro cactus growing there. Walking over to the specimens, we could see that chunks of cactus had been hacked off so we proceeded to do the same. After returning to the Pension, Gordon and I decided to catch a movie in town while the others were happy to prepare a cactus cocktail that we would all partake of the next morning.

When we returned, the guys had peeled off the dark green skin of the cactus and were cooking it up in a good sized pot. They had discarded the light green innards in a large stainless steel bowel that they had shoved under one of the beds. I slid the bowel out and began examining the pile of cucumber like pieces. After carefully searching for a piece that looked clean, I plucked a slice out of the bowel and scrutinized the specimen more closely. The cactus had been described as highly alkaline and bitter to the taste. The psychoactive ingredients were most potent in the skins.

While bringing the slice of cactus close to my nose, I noticed that it didn't have much of a smell to it. I carefully took a small bite of it and chewed it up. "Um... This is really good" I said and eagerly took another bite. "I thought this was supposed to be bitter." Of course it was, but I was pretending that it was delicious and kept chewing off chunks of cactus and exclaiming about the good taste. A couple of the guys grabbed some slices and shoved them into their mouths. They quickly made faces as the bitterness of the cactus made their faces pucker up. "Just kidding dudes!" We all had a good laugh and shortly after our cactus sampling party we went off to bed.

That night, I had the most vivid and colorful dream that I ever had in my entire life! In the dream, I was walking down a street toward an outdoor Mercado when I saw John, an American that I knew, who was also staying at the Hotel Grand Casino. He was wearing a black leather jacket and had a stick slung over his shoulder that held a large cloth bundle tied to the end of it. He was walking my direction. "Hey John, what are you up to?"

"I'm heading back to Quito."

"Oh, I'll be heading back there later today as well."

"Okay. See you back there."

"Okay, I'll see you later."

The next morning we were all a bit apprehensive about downing a cup of cactus juice. After getting dressed, we all pulled out our cups and filled them about half way and began drinking the bitter grog. After our ceremonial sipping of psychotropic cactus juice, we all headed outside and began walking to the central Mercado. Soon, we were all having stomach issues. Nausea mainly. Maurice suggested buying some lemons to counter the highly alkaline juice that was swirling in our stomachs. We bought some lemons and sucked on them for a while and that did the trick. We all felt better and we all began exclaiming about how vivid the colors were becoming. I felt more energetic and my spirits were lifted.

As I turned away from the Mercado, I caught a glimpse of John walking toward me. He was wearing a black leather

226

jacket and had a stick slung over his shoulder that held a large cloth bundle tied to the end of it. He was walking my direction. "Hey John, what are you up to?"

"I'm heading back to Quito."

"Oh, I'll be heading back there later today as well."

"Okay. See you back there."

"Okay, I'll see you later."

Dude, I was reliving my dream! Now, I understood why Native Americans used peyote for their religious ceremonies. I was totally blown away. We spent the rest of the morning taking in the sights and sounds of the city and we were all chatty and happy. By noon, the effect of the cactus began winding down and we all headed back to the bus station for our ride back to Quito.

Chapter 48

Shortly after my trip to Ibarra, I needed to make an important decision. I was running out of money. I had enough to get me to Brazil or turn around and head back to the U.S. I had been traveling for nearly six months and I was growing a bit weary. I didn't have the energy or desire to retrace my steps back up through Central America and Mexico so I decided that it would be quicker to fly from Cartagena, Colombia to Miami Beach, Florida and hitchhike across the U.S.

As it turned out, Maurice and the gang were at a turning point as well. Once again, we all decided to stick together and make our way north through Colombia. Our first destination was Popayan. Popayan was a beautiful Spanish style town with white stucco walls, red tile roofs and plenty of black, wrought iron railings and gates. You had the sense that you were in Europe rather than South America. The population of the town appeared more European than indigenous and they were happier and more affluent.

Gordon and I found a coffee shop where we ordered a couple cups of Columbian espresso that cost us a few pennies each. As we sipped our black coffees, we listened to all the chatter around us. There was a fairly young crowd hanging out there and I was trying as hard as I could to catch some of the conversations. The Columbians spoke Spanish clearly and at a moderate tempo. In Mexico, it was much harder to understand the language because of the staccato pace and the regional dialects.

After several cups of espresso, Maurice popped his head in the door and told us that Randy had been arrested for pot possession. Randy had told us he was going to meet a Columbian in a bar to buy some pot. I thought he was nuts for doing it and this proved me right. We went over to the local jail and asked to speak with our friend and they allowed us to do so. Randy told us that he was sitting at the bar with his

Columbian supplier having a drink when two cops came in and searched both of them. Randy hadn't taken possession of the pot yet but they found an ounce of it on the Columbian dude. The cops arrested both of them. We asked him to describe the cops that actually arrested him and then we left to confront them.

Gordon and I spotted them patrolling on foot along a boardwalk downtown. I approached the arresting officer and asked him how he was doing and we had a friendly little chat. I explained to him that we had just spoken to our friend who he had arrested earlier in the day and our friend told us that he didn't have any pot on him. I asked the cop if that was true and he acknowledged that it was. I could tell that he felt bad about it and I simply said that he should have only arrested the Columbian for possession and not our friend as well. Our friend was only being friendly and having a drink with one of the patrons in the bar. Now the cop felt really bad. I told him that we were going back to the jail and talk to the Captain around 4:30 that afternoon. Apparently, the cops had a change of shift at 5:00 pm.

When I was in Quito, I had met the wife of an American who was arrested for possession of drugs. She told me that prisoners typically slept on concrete slab floors and the only meals they got were from friends and relatives who delivered them daily. Sanitary conditions were horrible and there were many men who were in various stages of illness and some near death. Needless to say, these were not pleasant places and not somewhere you would want to be imprisoned for an extended period of time.

We all headed back to the jail at the appropriate time and there were quite a few officers standing around the Captain's desk answering the Captain's questions. I was the appointed liaison as my Spanish was much better than anyone else's and I had already developed a relationship with the arresting officer. I patiently waited outside the circle of cops until the Captain stopped speaking and looked me in the eye. I excused myself, and relayed my story to the Captain. He immediately called the arresting officer forward and asked him point blank if what I said was correct. The arresting officer looked at me and I stared directly into his eyes and he reluctantly nodded his head yes. The captain called out to the jailer and told him to release the Canadian.

When Randy walked out of that holding cell, he was the happiest dude I had ever seen in my entire life! He was thanking us and hugging us and telling us he was going to treat us all to a steak dinner at the most exclusive restaurant in Popayan. After cleaning up, we headed to the best restaurant in town and feasted on the most succulent filet mignon accompanied by some wonderful bottles of fine red wine. We were a rather rowdy and disheveled mob of foreigners and the locals looked at us with disdain. It was a warm evening and we were dining outside in a beautifully landscaped garden. The service was exceptional as we continued celebrating Randy's release from jail and brazenly disregarding the hard looks we were getting from those seated around us.

Chapter 49

The next morning, we took a bus to Cali where we spent a couple of days sightseeing and a couple of nights clubbing and grooving to the beat of hot salsa music while sipping on rum and cokes. We enjoyed dancing with some of the best looking women in Colombia as the nights slipped into day. One night we ate at a restaurant that served "La lengua de baca" or cow's tongue. I decided to be brave and I gave it a try. It was the softest piece of beef that I had ever eaten in my entire life bro!

As we headed up north, we blew through Medellin and bussed our way up to Cartagena which was a busy port town. We stayed at a place right along the beach that was close to the airport where I intended to catch a flight back to the U.S. After checking into an older hotel, the clerk walked me over to my room which was across a large, outdoor tiled patio. There was a good sized monkey tethered to a cable running along the edge of the patio. The monkey hopped off a short, pink stucco wall bordering the entire patio, ran over to me, jumped on my shoulder and started pulling my hair. Maybe it never saw a dude with long blonde hair before and just wanted to keep some of it as a souvenir. But I'll tell you what bro, it hurt like hell! The clerk provided no assistance, so I grabbed the monkey's arms, swung him over my head while battling with him to release my hair. The little prick wouldn't let go so I screamed at him. It scared him enough to loosen his grip and I was finally able to get him off me. He simply ran back to his perch and looked at me with a quizzical grin on his silly little face. WTF?

The next morning, we walked over to the Mercado where I found a "liquado" vendor that made me a tasty smoothie. After we all had breakfast, we checked out some of the sights around town. That evening, we found a club that had a live salsa band, a dancefloor, more rum and cokes and lots of young ladies to dance with. The next day, we headed out to the airport to arrange our flights. Maurice and his crew booked a flight to San Jose, Costa Rica, Casey booked a flight back to Minneapolis and I booked a flight to Miami. My flight was the last to leave the country.

On my last full day in South America, I was strolling down the road to the Mercado when a canvas covered troop carrier came to a screeching halt right beside me. Eight soldiers in camouflage uniforms surrounded me with their rifles pointed at me! Their leader started yelling at me, "Get in the back of the truck!" Dude, I kid you not, God sent me another one of his instant messages – Whatever you do, don't get in the back of that truck.

Remarkably, a sense of calm washed over me and I slowly lifted up my hand with my palm facing the soldiers and began speaking to them in Spanish, "Calm down, calm down, I have my papers here in my front pocket." I slowly lowered my hand to my right front cargo pocket on my Levis, unsnapped the metal button and slowly pulled out my passport. Holding it out in front of me, I just waited there until the leader lowered his rifle and took it. As he began examining it, I began telling him that today was my last day in Cartagena and that I had my airplane ticket in my other pocket which I slowly produced and handed to him.

I kept on talking slowly and calmly in Spanish telling him that I have had a wonderful visit to his beautiful country and that I found the people of Colombia to be "Muy buena gente." – Really good people. I went on to say that I loved their language and enjoyed speaking such beautiful words. I am leaving tomorrow to go back to the U.S.A. with wonderful memories of your country and your lovely people. As I spoke, the soldiers started relaxing, their guns came down and were resting on the ground pointing straight up instead of at me. They were beginning to smile, big, wide smiles. I saw lots of teeth and complete calmness overcoming them as their leader kept

232

examining my passport and my plane ticket. I could tell he was trying to figure out what to do next as he saw his men standing at ease and smiling. He finally handed my passport back to me with my plane ticket and sent me on my way. Sheesh! I never felt so totally relieved in my entire life bro! I continued walking to the Mercado, and happily ordered my last "liquado".

Chapter 50

My flight left early the next morning. So, after a long and solid sleep, I woke up feeling refreshed. I quickly packed my gear, checked out of my hotel and walked over to the airport where I grabbed a quick bite to eat. The plane took off smoothly and the flight was calm. I had a window seat providing me with great views. After a while, I recognized the island of Cuba as we approached it. The next thing I knew, there were two Cuban fighter jets next to us – one on each side. They held their positions until we flew past Cuba. Afterwards, they peeled off and headed back home.

I was told that the flights from Cartagena to Miami had a high percentage of passengers trying to smuggle cocaine into the U.S. As a result, U.S. customs in Miami looked like a grocery store with checkout lines and conveyor belts. Passengers were unpacking their luggage onto moving belts rolling past customs officers who were looking for anything suspicious. My customs officer was particularly interested in my tube of toothpaste. It was April 1975. A guy in the next checkout isle looked like a caveman. His long hair was unkempt and he sported a bushy black beard. He spoke in a slow and deep voice to the customs officer who was picking through the caveman's belongings, "I hear that Nixon isn't President anymore."

I couldn't help but laugh because Nixon resigned from office nine months previously. So I yelled out across to him, "Where you been dude, out in the jungle?"

He turned toward me with a big grin on his face and said, "Yeah!"

I noticed he had several paperbacks that were moving along his conveyor belt and I said, "Well, it looks like you had quite a bit of reading material with you anyway."

"Yeah, this one here was a great book," he said as he flung it over to me.

I had some paper backs as well so I grabbed one that I had read and threw it over to him, "Here, I'll trade you." We continued throwing books and bantering back and forth across the aisle. The customs officer checking out my stuff just started busting up. He quickly realized that I had nothing to hide and shoved the rest of my stuff off the conveyor belt and I began repacking my gear. When I was done, I grabbed my pack and walked over to Caveman and introduced myself. I asked him where he was heading and he said D.C. I asked him how he was planning on getting up there and he told me that he met a couple of long haired freaks on the plane who were making arrangements to get a "drive away" car and he was going to ride with them. I asked if I could join them and he said he would have to ask the dudes if it was alright.

He pointed to a couple of guys with super long hair down to their waists and super long beards to match. One guy was tall with red hair and the other was about six feet tall with black hair. The pair gave off the vibe that they had spent a really long time somewhere really remote. We walked over to their aisle as they were finishing repacking their stuff and I introduced myself. I told them that I only had $10 on me and I was trying to make it back to L.A. I asked them if I could join up with them on their trip north. The tall dude said it would be fine. I mentioned to them that I was thinking about heading west on highway 10 through the Southern States. They told me that it would be a mistake to do that because of my long hair. They told me I would be better off driving all the way up to New York City with them and taking highway 80 west.

These dudes were totally cool. The freakishly tall redhead was quite chatty and he told me that they had spent a year in the Amazon jungle in Peru searching for a lost city where an ancient civilization once lived. They ran out of supplies and were planning on going back. He said they needed to do some long term planning and more research before returning to search even deeper into the jungle. He also mentioned they needed to buy some high tech gear to take along as well. These guys shared their food with me and put me up for a couple of nights in their girlfriend's apartment in New York, before I hit the road again.

On my last night, they insisted that I take a huge bag of cashews, dates and apples to eat on the road. I still had my $10 bill in my pocket and a long way to go to the West Coast. So, I was unspeakably grateful for what they had done for me. I wanted to give them something. The only things that I had were a couple of embroidered wall hangings that I had bought as souvenirs in Ecuador. I got up super early the next morning, dug out my two embroidered wall hangings, left them on their couch and took off.

But dude, before I close this chapter I needed to share this item published in the "Daily Mail Reporter" dated December 3, 2008:

A lost city discovered deep in the Amazon rainforest could unlock the secrets of a legendary tribe.

Little is known about the Cloud People of Peru, an ancient, white-skinned civilisation wiped out by disease and war in the 16th century.

But now archaeologists have uncovered a fortified citadel in a remote mountainous area of Peru known for its isolated natural beauty.

It is thought this settlement may finally help historians unlock the secrets of the 'white warriors of the clouds'.

The tribe had white skin and blonde hair - features which intrigue historians, as there is no known European ancestry in the region, where most inhabitants are darker skinned.

The citadel is tucked away in one of the most far-flung areas of the Amazon. It sits at the edge of a chasm which the tribe may have used as a lookout to spy on enemies.

The main encampment is made up of circular stone houses overgrown by jungle over 12 acres, according to archaeologist Benedict Goicochea Perez.

Rock paintings cover some of the fortifications and next to the dwellings are platforms believed to have been used to grind seeds and plants for food and medicine.

The Cloud People once commanded a vast kingdom stretching across the Andes to the fringes of Peru's northern Amazon jungle, before it was conquered by the Incas.

Named because they lived in rainforests filled with cloud-like mist, the tribe later sided with the Spanish-colonialists to defeat the Incas.

But they were killed by epidemics of European diseases, such as measles and smallpox.

Much of their way of life, dating back to the ninth century, was also destroyed by pillaging, leaving little for archaeologists to examine.

Remains have been found before but scientists have high hopes of the latest find, made by an expedition to the Jamalca district in Peru's Utcubamba province, about 500 miles north-east of the capital, Lima. Until recently, much of what was known about the lost civilisation was from Inca legends. Even the name they called themselves is unknown. The term Chachapoyas, or 'Cloud People', was given to them by the Incas.

Their culture is best known for the Kuellap fortress on the top of a mountain in Utcubamba, which can only be compared in scale to the Incas' Machu Picchu retreat, built hundreds of years later.

Two years ago, archaeologists found an underground burial vault inside a cave with five mummies, two intact with skin and hair.

Chachapoyas chronicler Pedro Cieza de Leon wrote of the tribe: 'They are the whitest and most handsome of all the people that I have seen, and their wives were so beautiful that because of their gentleness, many of them deserved to be the Incas' wives and to also be taken to the Sun Temple.

'The women and their husbands always dressed in woollen clothes and in their heads they wear their llautos [a woollen turban], which are a sign they wear to be known everywhere.'

The Chachapoyas' territory was located in the northern regions of the Andes in present-day Peru.

It encompassed the triangular region formed by the confluence of the Maranon and Utcubamba rivers, in the zone of Bagua, up to the basin of the Abiseo river.

The Maranon's size and the mountainous terrain meant the region was relatively isolated.

Chapter 51

By seven o'clock in the morning, I was standing across the street from the entrance to the George Washington Bridge. It took a long time to get my first ride and that only took me down the road about 30 miles. I had vowed that I would only sleep while I was in a car moving across the U.S. It was discouraging to wait a long time for short little rides. By the time I got to the toll booths on the Pennsylvania and Ohio border it was 2:00 o'clock in the morning. So, it took me 19 hours to travel about 400 miles! WTF? That was like 20 miles per hour!

When I stepped out of my last ride, I realized that it got rather chilly in Ohio in April at 2:00 in the morning! I dug through my pack and put on several layers of clothes. Other dudes were trying to get rides as well. They finally gave up and walked down an embankment next to the highway where they rolled out their sleeping bags and crashed. I kept my vow and patiently stood on the highway with my thumb sticking out.

The frigid air was starting to turn my hands blue so I started praying that someone would pick me up and give me a long ride so I could warm up and get some sleep. A few minutes later, I saw a huge bus pulling over to my side of the highway. I thought they were having mechanical trouble or a flat tire. I stuck my hands in my pockets while the bus was slowing down. It came to a complete stop with the front door staring me in the face. WTF? The door opened up and a blast of heat from inside the bus engulfed me. It felt so good bro! I looked up at the driver who was a young dude with shoulder length hair wearing a frickin cowboy hat! My first though was these dudes must be a country music band on tour or something. Then the guy says, "Get in… Get in!" I wasn't going to argue with him so I jumped right in. He closed the door behind me and headed over to the toll booths. I turned to my left to check out the passengers and realized that there were no seats on the bus! Someone stripped all the seats out and built one huge platform bed running the entire length of the bus. As I was standing there, I was trying to figure out what was going on, so, I ask the driver, "How far are you going?"

He turned to look at me and said, "San Francisco."

Dude, I was so excited I yelled out at the top of my lungs, "No Shit?!" I saw people's arms and legs and bodies spasmodically reacting to the sudden noise as they were jarred awake.

"Shh, keep it down."

"Sorry. I couldn't help myself. I've been hitchhiking for about 20 hours and only made it from New York to here."

"Well, we'll be in San Francisco in a little over 48 hours. There are two of us driving and we only stop for food, gas and bathroom breaks. We're called the "Grey Rabbit" and we run back and forth from New York to San Francisco. We're a little light on passengers this trip, so we've been picking up hitchhikers and asking for donations to help pay for the cost of the trip."

"Wow. I'm so sorry dude. But... all I got is ten bucks."

"That's cool."

I pulled out my one and only $10 bill and handed it to him. He took it graciously and stuck it in his shirt pocket. "You're a life saver dude."

"Don't mention it. Just crawl on back and find a space to crash. We'll wake you up when we stop for breakfast."

"Thanks, bro."

Two days later, early in the morning, the "Grey Rabbit" popped off of highway 80 at University Avenue in Berkeley, dropped me off and got right back on highway 80 heading to San Francisco. My friend, Peter, lived on Blake Street which was about a two mile walk from where I was dropped off. I headed over to his apartment and knocked on his door. Nothing happened. I knocked louder and longer until I heard Peter yell something unintelligible. I waited politely until he staggered to the door and stuck his head out. "Richard! What are you doing here?"

"I just got back from South America. It's a long story."

"Yeah, well come on in and you can tell me all about it"

I hung out with Peter and visited with him and some of his friends who were sharing a big old house right next to Peter's apartment. They cooked me breakfast and made me coffee while I shared some of my adventures with them. Later that day, I headed over to the University to scan a ride board and jotted down some phone numbers. I made some calls when I got back to Peter's place and one guy wanted to meet me right away. He said that he had to drive his girlfriend's car down to Long Beach and wanted to meet me. I got his address and walked over to his place and chatted with him for a while. He said that he wanted to leave early the next morning and I told him that I was fine with that.

I spent the night at Peter's place, said my goodbyes the next morning and took off on foot to meet my ride. The guy let me in and told me that he really didn't want to drive to Long Beach. WTF? This dude just couldn't make up his mind. Then he said that he really didn't have the time to drive all the way down there and he really didn't want to have to pay for airfare to fly back up to Berkeley. He told me that he filled the tank with gas which should get me nearly to Long Beach. He handed me the keys to the car along with his girlfriend's contact information. I told him that it wasn't a problem and I would be happy to return the car for him.

I threw my backpack in the trunk and headed over to highway 80 via University Avenue. There were a ton of people hitchhiking just before the onramp to the freeway, so I pulled over and started asking where people were heading. Three guys said they needed a ride to San Luis Obispo and I told them that I would take them there if they each chipped in $15 for gas – which they did. I got out of the car and opened the trunk for them to stow away their backpacks. A gal standing close to them said that she needed a ride to Santa Barbara but didn't have $15 in cash. She went on to say that she did have $15 in food stamps that she could give me and I said that would be fine. The three guys piled into the backseat and the gal took the front passenger seat.

I dropped the guys off in SLO and continued south on highway 101. After arriving in Santa Barbara, I pulled off the road and let the gal out. At this point, the car was nearly out of gas. I stopped at an AM-PM, got $15 worth of gas, and bought some food using my food stamps. By the time I got back to the San Fernando Valley, I was exhausted. I drove home, parked the car in the street, phoned the owner and told her that she could pick up her car at my place. She said she would be there first thing in the morning. After six months of globetrotting, I was finally back home safe and sound. I breathed a huge sigh of relief and felt a profound sense of contentment. Mission accomplished bro!

Chapter 52

About three weeks later, I got a call from Maurice, my Canadian traveling buddy, and he told me that he was at the Ralph's Market in Panorama City. I told him to stay put and I would meet him there in 15 minutes. I took off out the door and walked over to Ralphs and we walked back to my place. The first words out of his mouth were, "Dude, this is the ugliest place that I have ever seen in my entire life!" We visited for a few hours and then he told me that he was going to catch a "Greyhound" bus in North Hollywood that would take him back up to British Columbia. He called a taxi and was gone about a half hour later.

I had discovered, upon my return, that my mom had planned a trip to Croatia. It was the first time that she would be visiting her country since escaping from the communists when she was in her late 20's. I was so excited for her! Then I found out that my friend Willy and his cousin were planning a trip to Europe as well. They were leaving on May 25th! So, I figured that I should go with them and then meet my mom in Split and visit with my relatives there for a few weeks. I quickly made travel arrangements and pulled out the remainder of my savings in travelers checks prior to leaving Los Angeles.

Randy drove us to LAX and he hung out with us for a while and then took off. I wasn't able to get a ticket on the same flight that Willy and his cousin, Jim, were taking. But, I was able to book a flight leaving four hours after theirs. They boarded there jet around midnight and I stepped on board mine at 4:00 am. I had a short layover in Chicago and then flew to Frankfurt. It was so cool flying over Germany and seeing cities that were separated by large swaths of forests. Los Angeles was simply a large swath of asphalt separated by invisible boundary lines dividing one city from another. As it turned out, I landed in Germany about 4:00 am the following day.

I was so parched when I got off the plane that I headed to a concession stand where a disheveled Frankfurter was leaning against the counter. He smelled of beer. Speaking in German, I asked the women behind the counter for an apple juice. The Frankfurter turned to me and said in slurred English, "We don't drink apple juice in Germany... we drink beer!" I just looked at him and smiled. After paying for my beverage, I quickly left to catch my train to Paris and rendezvous with Willy and Jim. They were staying with Willy's girlfriend, Tina, who had just finished her Sophomore year studying abroad.

I got on board the train and it dropped me off at the Metro line in Paris around 9:00 pm that evening. I had instructions to hop on the green line and take it to the last exit which I did. I walked up a bunch of stairs that took me up to street level and had no idea where to look for the address that I had written down. I saw a young couple standing next to a car chatting in French and asked them if they could tell me how to get to the address that I handed them. They told me that I got on the correct metro line, but I got off on the wrong end of the line! Then they told me not to worry they were headed that way and they would drop me off at the address. I can't tell you how thankful I was for their kindness!

It was about 10:00 pm when I knocked on Tina's door and I was utterly exhausted. I had been up for more than 48 hours and all I wanted to do was roll my sleeping bag out and crash. We spent a few days in Paris with Tina as our tour guide. The old section of Paris was wonderfully laid out and totally beautiful bro! The Eifel Tower, the Arch de Triumph, Napoleon's Tomb and the Louvre Museum were my favorite sites. I had no idea that they were all relatively close to one another. Paris is the most beautiful city that I have ever seen in my entire life!

I was told that the French were quite proud of their language and sometimes were irked when Americans asked them questions in English. So, whenever I needed some directions, I would stop a Parisian speaking to them in Spanish and ask if they spoke Spanish. The typical answer was, "Oh, no, no, no." Then I would ask them in German if they spoke German. This time it was a much louder and heartfelt, "Oh, no, no, no." usually accompanied with a vigorous shaking of their head. Then I would ask in English if they spoke English. At this point, they wanted to show me that they could indeed speak more than one language!

One of the most adorable cultural moments that I observed occurred immediately after work when most Parisians stopped at a local bakery to pick up a freshly baked baguette for their dinner. I never saw so many well-dressed people awkwardly juggling these long loaves of bread as they hurried home while carrying their briefcases and purses and other belongings. I could just imagine what it was like transporting all those loaves on the Metro!

Chapter 53

Soon, we were on our way to London where Willy, Jim and I bought a 1950's Austin Cambridge. We paid $150 for it and split the cost three ways which was equal to the price of a Eurailpass. It had a four speed manual transmission on the column. So, not only did the driver have to drive on the right side of the vehicle, he also had to shift left handed! Nobody wanted to drive the car through London traffic so I volunteered. It was trial by fire bro! But, I managed to navigate through London and drive out to the country.

Driving through the countryside was beautiful and relaxing as we headed toward our next destination. Around sunset, we pulled off the road and found a suitable place to camp. A police officer, on a motorcycle, pulled off the road and told us that we were not allowed to sleep there. We pleaded with him to let us stay, and we told him we would hit the road at sunrise. He acquiesced, but he made us promise to tell any other officer that came by that we pulled off the road after 11:00 o'clock. The nights were short that time of year, so, going to bed at sunset and waking up at sunrise gave us about five hours of sleep.

Stonehenge was our next destination. It was out in the middle of farmland, but it was a pretty cool sight! The thirteen foot columns all set in a circle with huge stones setting horizontally on top of them was rather bizarre to see just sitting in a huge, flat field. We ended up spending the night in a small village close to Stonehenge and headed back to London the next morning. Two cops pulled us over in the middle of London and asked to see our insurance. We told them that we didn't have any. They told us that it was mandatory and they made us follow them back to the police station.

The police said that we could buy insurance at any bank. They held Willy and Tina as hostages while Jim and I hunted around for a bank to buy insurance. We were leaving the country the next day, so we didn't want to spend too much money on a policy that we would use for only a day or two. There was a bank close to the police station so we went inside to see what the shortest term for an insurance policy would be. A bank clerk told us that the minimum term was eight days. It didn't cost much. So, we paid up and returned to the police station and presented the officers with a valid copy of our insurance policy. They released their hostages and we all beat it out of there.

The next morning, we drove Agnes, the name we gave our Austin Cambridge, onto a ferry that took us from Dover to Dunkirk. When we hit the mainland, Willy pointed Agnes toward Amsterdam where we intended to spend the night at a Christian youth hostel. There was quite a long line of cars at the Belgium border and when we came to a stop, I got out of the car and started asking other drivers what the Border Patrol was looking for. The main things they were looking for were evidence of an auto insurance policy, valid for a period of 60 days or longer, and a passport.

I hopped back into the passenger seat and fished out our eight day policy from the glove compartment and studied it for a while. As I read through the policy, I noticed there was a blank for the number 8 and there was a blank for the number spelled out - E I G H T - which designated the term of the policy. Aha! I thought to myself. I took a pen out of the glove compartment that matched the black ink on the insurance policy. I carefully added a 0 next to the 8 on our policy and carefully added a Y next to the word EIGHT thereby lengthening the term of our policy to 80 days! We handed the policy to an officer who took it to his supervisor. After glancing at it quickly, he motioned us to proceed.

When we arrived in Amsterdam, we discovered that the Christian youth hostel was smack-dab in the middle of the red light district! I guess whoever chose the sight completely ignored the phrase in the "Lord's Prayer" about leading us not into temptation but delivering us from evil! We spent a few days in Amsterdam and we were all astonished to find out that it was apparently legal to smoke pot in restaurants! WTF? This was like 1976! Another cool thing we noticed was that most of the cops had long hair and drove around in Porsches. Unbelievable! The canals and bridges were pretty trippy but the best part of our stay was visiting the Van Gogh Museum. There was just so much of his work to admire and I never realized that he had produced so many wonderful drawings. Amsterdam was a charming place but we had to head back to Paris so Tina could catch a flight back to Los Angeles.

Chapter 54

After dropping Tina off, the three amigos headed south through Southern France where we drove through a vast area of farmland and small towns on our way to Cannes where we spent a couple of days touring around town and walking along the beach. I found it amusing that people would walk onto the beach dressed in formal attire – suit and tie – and then disrobe once they picked a spot to sunbathe. At first I was wondering WTF? Then I realized that they were wearing their bathing suits under their formalwear!

On our way to Turin, we picked up a hitchhiker in Nice who spoke decent English and was a bit older than we were. We got a late start and ended up stopping at a restaurant in one of the coastal towns of Italy. After looking at the menu we all ordered lunch but I was a bit dumbfounded by their pricing scheme. I ordered lasagna for $5.00 but they had a T-bone steak on the menu for $3.00. Dude, this made no sense to me whatsoever! Anyway, Willy and Jim ordered some pasta and our hitchhiker ordered the steak.

When the waiter delivered our meals, we were all astonished at the size of the steak that they set in front of our new traveling companion. His eyes lit up and we all commented that $3 was a huge bargain for the size of steak he got. He ate his steak with gusto and we enjoyed our meals as well. The waiter brought us our individual checks and our newest companion suddenly looked quite confused. He said that he didn't understand why his check was for $18. He signaled for the waiter to come over and they started speaking in French to one another.

I didn't have a clue what they were saying but I could see that they were both growing louder and more animated – especially the waiter. The Italian was making big hand gestures as he was getting angrier and suddenly ended up hitting our new friend accidentally in the shoulder. I thought, oh shit, this is going to end in a fist fight! They both had surprised looks on their faces and they stopped talking momentarily. The waiter, quite humbly, said "Scusi," and our hitchhiker accepted his apology and they began arguing heatedly once again! Disaster averted bro! As our new buddy explained to us in English, after they settled their argument, there was a small asterisk on the $3* with some very fine print at the bottom of the menu explaining that the price of the steak was $3 per every two ounces of steak. His steak was 12 ounces and therefore the bill was $18. Our French companion paid the bill but complained about it the rest of the way to Turin where we said our goodbyes to him.

We parked Agnes just outside an older quarter of town where the streets were paved with stones and only wide enough for one lane of traffic. Jim pulled out a handy little Italian phrase book from his pack and figured out how to ask in Italian, "Where is a cheap place to stay nearby." After getting directions from a passersby, we selected a place to spend the night, got cleaned up and headed back to the old part of town to do some sightseeing. Afterwards, we found a pleasant Café with some outdoor tables and ordered some dinner. As we waited for our food, we heard motorcycles coming. In no time, a herd of café racers came screaming around a curve in the road with their bodies hugging their brightly painted gas tanks and their hands firmly gripping the low and narrow handlebars in front of them. Sheesh, what a racket!

The next morning we stopped at a bakery before heading up to Zermatt, Switzerland to check out the Matterhorn. I smelled fresh baked bread and bought a two pound loaf of whole wheat French bread. I sat in the back seat while Willy was driving and I started nibbling on my loaf of bread. Dude, it was totally gone before we got to the Matterhorn! The rest of the day I felt like I had swallowed a bowling ball! We found a place to spend the night and the next morning we stopped at a market to buy some food to take on our hike up to the Matterhorn. After the loaf of bread I ate the day before, all I wanted was fruit!

One of the first things I noticed as we hiked up the mountain, was the sound of cowbells. They weren't the clanking unmelodious type that you hear on cattle in the U.S. They were actually tuned to a musical scale. It was absolutely marvelous listening to random notes echoing in the canyon that we were sharing with our bovine buddies. Everything was lush green and the cows were quite busy munching on grass as they slowly moved along the alpine meadows. And indeed bro, the hills were alive with the sound of music!

The next day, we headed to Salzburg, Austria. We drove through some of the most amazing scenery on winding two lane highways that snaked through the Alps. Our trip was filled with views of stunning snowcapped peaks, glaciers, ravines and majestic panoramas. After arriving in Salzburg, we came up with plans for our stay in Austria. Our most memorable moment was attending a chamber orchestra performance at the Mozarteum. The performance took place in a relatively small room that felt like a huge living room. It was intimate and charming and the music was beautifully performed. Salzburg, after Paris, was the second most beautiful place that I had ever seen in my entire life!

Agnes began overheating in the Alps, so we stopped in Munich to have a mechanic take a look at the radiator and make some repairs. After he did what he could, we drove over to the 1972 Munich Olympic Village to check it out. It was the site of a terrible terrorist attack by a group called Black September – a faction of the Palestine Liberation Organization – who murdered 11 Israeli athletes. Afterwards, we were back on the road again heading north.

Chapter 55

Our next stop was Wurzburg, Germany where Willy and Jim wanted to visit a cousin stationed on a U.S. Army base. We stayed in his apartment for a few days and got a taste of what life was like on a U.S. military base. Picture someone picking up a few square blocks of a U.S. city and transplanting it onto German soil. Everyone on base spoke English, not German, and the Army PX had all the usual products that you would find back in the USA. They also used U.S. dollars as currency. It was a tight knit community and it seemed like kids were constantly running from apartment to apartment.

His cousin showed us around town and invited us to a barbeque hosted by a German couple who were good friends of his. We also spent time in some of the German pubs drinking beer from huge steins which could hold a liter of beer. Jim wanted to spend more time visiting his cousin in Wurzburg before catching a return flight back to the good old U.S.A. His flight back took off from Brussels which was about a five hour drive from Wurzburg. So, it was time for Willy and me to say our goodbyes to Jim before heading to Lyon, France. Our tight little trio was now a duet.

We drove through several small towns in Southern Germany displaying huge banners boasting about brewing beer since 1482 or 1395 or 1421. It didn't appear as though much had changed in the intervening years. Perhaps a conclusion could be drawn that beer drinking hinders progress? When we got to Lyon, Willy informed me that he wanted to visit a female friend by himself. Well, shit! If I had known, I would have purchased a magazine or book to read while waiting for him to have his "visit". Instead, I spent the most boring time in my entire life waiting for him to return. He came back smiling, but I was totally pissed off and I let him know it.

From there, we headed to Geneva where I had hoped to visit a cousin of mine from Croatia. Unfortunately, he was on a business trip. So, I crossed that item off my agenda. We hung around Geneva for a day and then headed just outside of town to visit Bernadette who I spent some time with in Banos, Ecuador. We met Bernadette at her home in the morning and she was excited to show us around. After climbing into our car, she gave us directions to a beautiful clearing overlooking a wonderful alpine valley. She reached into a bag that she had brought along and pulled out a bottle of red wine. We walked over to a bench, uncorked the bottle and began sipping wine. It was a gorgeous, sunny day and Bernadette and I had a chance to reminisce and chat about our South American adventures. Afterwards, we returned to her parent's stone home.

Upon entering her home, it was apparent that Bernadette came from an affluent family. The living room and dining room were huge and well-appointed with all the furniture resting on polished oak floors. Her family was seated in the dining room around a huge oak table waiting for us to arrive. They were dressed in formal attire and staring at us with eye piercing indignity. The three of us joined them after formal introductions were made.

We ate a huge meal that her mother so graciously prepared for us. Everything was delicious except for some wild boar that I had tasted. I'm not one for wild game and the meat had a very pungent taste that I was not accustomed to. Apparently, my displeasure was plainly registering on my face because Bernadette asked me if the wild boar was okay. I told her it tasted like "mierda", which was the Spanish word for "shit". Everyone at the table paused and looked at me with contempt. I put my head down and continued eating without making eye contact with anyone until we were all through with the meal. Later, when none of her family was around, Bernadette informed me that the French word for shit was "merde". Dude, I was so embarrassed! I felt like crawling under a rock.

In spite of my rudeness, Bernadette invited us to spend the night at her family's home. She apologized about having to go to work the next day and I said it wasn't a problem and that Willy and I were planning on heading to Croatia in the morning. That evening, we sat in the living room chatting with Bernadette and her family and the topic of jazz came up and I told them that I really enjoyed playing Dave Brubeck's composition "Blue Rondo a la Turk" on the piano. Bernadette's brother-in-law said he was not familiar with that piece and asked me to play it for them on their beautiful, natural wood baby grand piano. He had a smug look on his face communicating that he didn't believe that I could play the piano at all. It happened to be my favorite piano piece and I had fully mastered it in the summer prior to my travels. I also had the chance to refresh my skills prior to leaving for Europe.

I stood up, walked over to their piano and played the piece flawlessly. Upon finishing my performance, I received exuberant compliments and warm applause from Bernadette's entire family. Somehow, I felt that this had redeemed me for my rude comment about the wild boar over lunch. A family member asked Willy about the colorful red, white and blue stripped socks with white stars that he was wearing that evening. He told them he was preparing for America's Bicentennial celebration in 1976. Bernadette looked at him and said, "What's 200 years? Our home is more than 200 years old!" She had a point bro.

Afterwards, Bernadette showed us to our rooms. She told us that she would be getting up early in the morning and that she would be immediately leaving for work. She told me not to worry about getting up early to say good-bye to her and then gave me a warm hug and smile. I said that I was grateful for her hospitality and that I would always remember her warmth and kindness. She gave me a kiss on the cheek and said goodnight.

Chapter 56

The next morning, Willy and I climbed into Agnes and headed to our next destination which was Venice, Italy. I wanted to see Saint Mark's Square so we found a place to stay close by and headed over there on foot. It was a bit breezy under clear blue skies and the plaza and the Basilica were remarkable. The scale was perfect and the plaza was filled with people from all over the world. We bought some tea and sat outside just watching the crowds milling about on the plaza with Saint Mark's Basilica staring at us in the background. After the drive, we were both happy just sitting stationary for a while and relaxing.

After our tea, we walked into the Basilica and marveled at all the varying patterns in the tiled floors and the beautiful frescos looking down upon us. It was an amazing place to spend time studying all the incredible craftsmanship that went into creating such a masterpiece. After all, I was used to staring at rolled vinyl flooring that was cheap, unexciting and created without much imagination or any sense of craftsmanship whatsoever! I was fascinated with the precision of the cut marble that showed no discernable gaps between the varying colors and shapes. Tiles in the U.S. had huge grout lines and so did mosaics. Without power tools for cutting and grinding and shaping each individual tiny piece of marble that were fitted together so perfectly, it must have taken a tremendous number of man-hours to complete this three dimensional work of art!

Willy and I were getting quite hungry and we found a cafeteria style restaurant that served plenty of Italian pasta dishes at a reasonable price. We both bought the lasagna because it looked really good and picked a table that was next to a couple of young ladies from the U.S. After eating more than our fill we started chatting with the young ladies and trading stories of our travels. We were pretty exhausted and they looked like they were worn out from traveling as well. The conversation flowed into dinnertime so we all got up and bought food for dinner. Dude, it was the only time in my entire life that I had stayed in the same restaurant for both lunch and dinner!

The next day, Willy and I walked along the sidewalks and crossed canals over beautiful foot bridges. Our tour of Venice, of course, would not have been complete without a ride in a gondola which was memorable. We walked around town nearly the entire day never growing tired of taking in our surroundings and the people and the shops and the cafes. I was a bit apprehensive about entering Croatia the next day. It was a communist country, at the time, and was ruled by a dictator named Josip Broz Tito. I had grown up speaking Croatian and that gave me some confidence but I had no idea what to expect. Willy and I would be separating once we got to Split and I would be staying with my mom and our relatives there while Willy would keep heading south to Greece. In any event, Croatia was our next destination.

The next morning we headed to Trieste, Italy where we got out of the car for a while, had lunch and roamed around town. By late afternoon, we were ready to climb into Agnes for a short trip to the border of Yugoslavia. Upon our arrival, we parked the car and entered a small building that housed the customs office. A young lady with long black hair and olive complexion greeted us unenthusiastically. I said good day in Croatian as Willy and I presented our passports. She looked up at us with an expressionless face and began speaking to me in Croatian. She asked questions and I provided her with answers. I told her we were heading to Split and she said that she recognized my accent as coming from there – who knew? She stamped our passports and I had my first experience with a communist bureaucrat!

We drove a short way through Slovenia and then into Croatia stopping at the northern most tip of the Adriatic Sea. I got out of the car and began walking over jagged rocks carefully making my way down to the water. I found a decent spot to sit allowing me to slip my feet into the sea. As soon as I did, a dolphin shot out of the water and dove back down again bestowing a wonderful welcome to me as I gazed at the beauty of my ancestral home! I decided to jump into the water and swim to a large rock outcropping about a hundred feet from shore. As I climbed out of the water my friendly dolphin provided me with more entertaining surfacing and diving while swimming around the rock that I was perched on. Dude, it was a wonderful homecoming!

Willy and I got back into the car and drove south to Rijeka where we made a quick stop to grab some dinner. The sun was setting as we continued our journey south. Willy noticed a farmer walking up a dirt road on the left side of the highway. He turned left pulling onto the road and attracting the attention of the farmer who turned around and started walking toward Agnes. Willy suggested that we ask the farmer if we could camp in his field and I agreed that it was a good idea to do so. We climbed out of the car and headed up the hill toward the farmer. I said good evening to him in Croatian and we had a pleasant little conversation that culminated with the farmer granting us permission to leave our car on the road and camp in his field.

As the farmer turned to head home, we turned and headed back toward Agnes. Willy asked me what the guy was so angry about and I was a bit taken aback. I told him the guy wasn't angry at all. As a matter of fact, he's letting us leave our car on the road and camp in his field. Willy just shook his head and told me that it sure sounded like he was angry about something. We got our gear out of the car, pitched our tents, rolled out our sleeping bags and hit the sack. When I awoke the next morning, I noticed that I had a little companion nestled next to me in my sleeping bag. It was a furry little black and white mottled field mouse! I touched his soft little body with my index finger and he quickly scooted out of my tent. Yet another warm welcome home from a furry friend!

Chapter 57

After packing up our gear, we headed south to Split along the coastal road. I was surprised to see how rocky and rugged the coastline was. It was almost entirely limestone! Looking across the white rocks, to the dark blue of the Adriatic Sea, we were provided with a stunning and dramatic view as we continued south. It took us less than four hours to get to Split. When we arrived, we pulled into a parking space alongside the highway and stretched our legs a bit while taking in the scenery. The air was fresh and clean and so was the beach and sea below us.

After a while, I got out my backpack and searched for the address of where my mother was staying. Once I retrieved my address book and a map of Split, Willy and I figured out where we were and where we needed to be. We found the home with no trouble and parked in front of it on the street. The house had solid limestone walls forming a near perfect square. It was two stories and had a red tile roof that contrasted nicely with the light colored limestone and the mature evergreen pine trees surrounding it.

Soon, Willy and I were seated at a kitchen table sipping black tea with milk and eating lunch while chatting with my mom, Helen, and her aunt who was my grandmother's sister. She was a lovely, self-assured and solidly built older woman with grey hair who seemed to have a permanently cheerful disposition, a wonderful sense of humor and a slight touch of mischievousness. She was a delightful and generous host to my mother and me. We spoke in Croatian and Willy was good-natured about not being able to understand a word of what we were saying. Dude, I was totally blown away by how graciously we were received by relatives that I had never met before!

Willy hung around for a couple of days and then took off to continue his solo run to Greece leaving me to hang out with my mother's and my father's relatives. After Willy took off, my mom and I were invited to my dad's brother's home for dinner. His name was Jerko which, as it turned out, was a rather appropriate description of how I was treated by him. Needless to say, I didn't want to have anything to do with the man after witnessing his total lack of character. I loved my mom's side of the family as they were totally fun loving, kind, gracious and upright.

I had the pleasure of meeting my mom's cousin, Miljenko Smoje, who was a columnist for a local newspaper in Split. He invited us to have lunch at a small café located in the oldest part of Split. Outside the restaurant, there was a large plaza with a number of wrought iron tables and chairs resting on travertine tile imported from Italy. We were sitting in the middle of Diocletian's palace walls! He was a Roman emperor who ruled from his palace in Split. Apparently, he had bad allergies and settled on the Dalmatian coast because he could breathe more easily there. We had a fine meal served to us under warm, sunny skies while Miljenko asked us questions about life in the United States and our travels. The next day, we were featured in his column outlining how practical Americans were. I have included a brief excerpt from Wikipedia outlining my cousins life and accomplishments below:

Miljenko Smoje (February 14, 1923 – October 25, 1995) was a Croatian writer and journalist.

Smoje was born in Split, at the time in the Kingdom of Yugoslavia, in a family of poor laborers. The neighborhood where he grew up was known for its support for anarchism, socialism and other left-wing ideologies. This would later influence Smoje's work and help him develop a strong dislike of authorities and the establishment.

Smoje finished high school in Split in 1941, but his further education was interrupted by the Axis invasion of Yugoslavia and Split being occupied by Italy. Smoje joined the Communist Party of Yugoslavia and took part in the local resistance movement. However, due to his rebellious nature, he was expelled from the Party, but he survived that, as well as brief incarceration by Italian authorities. After the end of the war he finished college and worked as a teacher. In 1950 he took a job as a reporter for the Split daily newspaper Slobodna Dalmacija, where he would write until his formal retirement in 1979.

As a reporter, Smoje developed a specific style that included use of Čakavština dialect in his articles. His specialty was articles about ordinary people and through the decades he travelled over Dalmatia chronicling many aspects of its life. Later he used many of those experiences as the basis for his short stories, plays and novels. He liked to inject all of his work with a strong dose of humor, laced with elements of every-day tragedy. All this helped Smoje become one of the most respected and more popular writers of former Yugoslavia, as well as arguably the greatest humorist of Croatian literature.

It was the medium of television which helped Smoje become famous. In 1970 he wrote the script for Naše malo misto (also known as Malo misto), a mini-series chronicling three decades of life in a small Dalmatian coastal town. The series featured many memorable characters that would later become part of local culture. Smoje also showed the ability to use broad comedy as a way to criticize aspects of Communism. The series nevertheless became an instant hit and grew in popularity through the decades.

In 1980 Smoje tried to repeat the success with Velo misto, a more ambitious project chronicling life in Split between 1910 and 1947. Velo misto became very popular and developed a cult status of its own.

After his retirement Smoje continued to write for Slobodna Dalmacija and Nedjeljna Dalmacija weekly. In the late 1980s and early 1990s he opposed Croatian nationalism and for that reason he was snubbed by the media controlled by Franjo

Tuđman and his ruling Croatian Democratic Union. When Tuđman's supporter Miroslav Kutle took over Slobodna Dalmacija in 1993, Smoje began to write for the satirical weekly Feral Tribune.

The semi-official snub of Miljenko Smoje ended in the late 1990s when his shows were allowed to be aired on Croatian Radiotelevision.

Smoje was married twice. He is buried in Žrnovnica near Split.

Chapter 58

My mom and I went to Vodice, a small coastal village, where my dad's family lived. While we were there, my mom made arrangements for my accommodations including paying a small café owner to provide meals for me during my stay. The beach house I was staying in was old, but clean with plenty of natural light pouring through the windows. The furnishings were minimal but sturdy and rested on natural wood floors.

It was a short walk to the beach. I had brought ample reading material so I spent most of my time sunbathing and reading. There were many German tourists at the beach and it allowed me to brush up on my German. Unbeknownst to the locals, I could understand every word that they were saying and they were constantly making nasty comments about me behind my back. After a few days of observations, I found Croatians to be extremely arrogant without any apparent reason to be so. Farmers, for example, were still using farm animals to haul produce to market in old broken down wooden carts! Seeing that they were so far behind much of the world when it came to agricultural practices, the question in my mind was: Why were they so arrogant? The only explanation was that they completely lacked any understanding of their circumstances. Thus, they were both ignorant and arrogant... A bad combination bro!

Growing up as an immigrant in America, I was living my life with one foot in American culture and one foot in Croatian culture. At school, I spoke English but at home I spoke Croatian. The first time that I was invited to eat dinner at a friend's house, I was served "SpaghettiOs", cottage cheese with canned peaches and a Jell-o salad! At home, we never ate SpaghettiOs, Jell-o or canned peaches. My mom always prepared meals from scratch and they included a cooked vegetable and a tossed green salad! Another time a friend asked me if I wanted a pop? All I could think of was that I already had a pop, and a mom too!

Growing up in two cultures and speaking two languages always made me wonder if I were more American or more Croatian. Spending a few days in Vodice helped me answer that question – I was totally, 100% American bro!

After my stay in Vodice, I headed back to Split and ended up taking a trip to Dubrovnik with my mom. Dubrovnik was the crown jewel of the Croatian coastline. The old part of the town had a huge wall that surrounded it and you could walk along the top of it. Once again, limestone was the main building material along with red tile roofs. The dark blue Adriatic in the background contrasting with the light colored limestone produced a stunning sight.

I spent more time visiting with relatives in Split. One of my cousins, Sretchko, was close to my age and I ended up hanging out with him for a day. He was studying chemistry in college and he took me out sailing on the Adriatic. Afterwards, Sretchko wanted to introduce me to a friend of his who lived in a multi-story, government subsidized housing complex. As we approached his friend's home, Sretchko wanted me to pretend that I was a Vietnam Veteran. His friend greeted us at the door and ushered us into his room where Sretchko began making up stories about my time in Vietnam. His friend was buying the stories and Sretchko was getting into the graphic details surrounding the killings that I was responsible for. He finally ran out of material and his friend looked at me with a mixture of fear and reverence. I finally told him that I wasn't a veteran and that Sretchko made the whole thing up. Sretchko exploded with laughter and his friend took it all rather well.

My mom was terrified of flying. So, on our return trip to the U.S., she booked a cabin for us on a cargo ship. Our port of entry was New York, the same port my grandparents docked at when they arrived in America. The ship was designed to take on about 100 passengers as well as cargo. The only problem was, its scheduled departure time was two weeks down the road! I couldn't see hanging around Split for two weeks so I hopped on a ferry that took me across the Adriatic to Ancona, Italy. From there, I traveled to Rome.

Upon my arrival, I felt like I had been dropped into a sea of anarchy. There were protesters carrying signs and chanting slogans that I couldn't understand and drivers were buzzing around me beeping their horns in noisy little Fiats. I took a minute and did a complete 360 degree turn to get a big picture of my surroundings. I saw walls built during the second century, beautiful churches built in the 1500's and a modern train station that was completed in 1940. People were shoving flyers into my hands and everyone seemed to be yelling and screaming.

There was so much chaos and tension surrounding me that all I wanted to do was remove myself from all of it. So, I started walking away from the train station and didn't stop until I found a quieter and more peaceful place. I got my travel guide out, found an inexpensive place to stay and checked into a room there. Sheesh! I had never experienced anything like that in my entire life! I gathered from the flyers and posters that there must have been an election of some sort coming up and all the different parties and factions were out on the streets campaigning for their various causes. I spent the rest of the afternoon quietly scoping out my new neighborhood.

First thing the next morning, I took a hike to the Sistine Chapel. As I slowly walked through it, I was overwhelmed at all the beautiful frescoes on the walls and ceilings painted by Botticelli and Michelangelo. There were some windows that opened up to Vatican City and I could see some of the most beautifully landscaped areas that I had ever seen! It was absolutely gorgeous. I also explored one of the Roman catacombs where many Christians were buried, the Colosseum, Trevi Fountain and the Spanish Steps.

From Rome, I headed north to Pisa to visit the leaning tower of Pisa and then headed east to Florence. The Florence

Cathedral was totally stunning and so where the covered bridges over the Arno River which was close by. The people in Florence were great and more friendly and relaxed than those in Rome. They always seemed to be happy and laughing and having a good time and the food was fantastic.

Everything in Italy was tastefully planned and executed. Their freeways, for example, were built with great respect for the environment. Instead of following the U.S. method of cutting hills and filling in valleys to form a pathway for cars, the Italians built bridges over their valleys connecting one hill to another. It must have cost a fortune, but the results were amazing! The beauty of their countryside was left intact and there were no ugly scars caused by cutting into mountainsides and hillsides. There were also no ugly rock filled roadbeds to stare at either. Of all the people that I had met and all the countries that I had visited, Italy was by far my favorite. There was so much diversity of geography and culture. The food and dress and architecture and history and art were all fused together forming an incredibly vibrant, fun loving and rich environment.

Chapter 59

Our voyage back to the United States began in Rijeka, Croatia where we boarded a huge cargo vessel with a load of copper in its hold. It was riding low in the water. We were greeted by an officer and his crew who were in charge of the ship's passengers. The officer was a friendly, middle aged fellow with a stout build and a full head of black hair which stood in stark contrast to his white uniform and cap. He was an amiable and chatty fellow who enjoyed laughing and he made us feel comfortable and at ease. We were shown to our cabin by one of the crewmen who carried my mom's luggage, in a down to business manner, through the ship's narrow hallways.

My mom tipped him and he smiled and turned around leaving us alone in a compact but comfortable cabin. It had two single beds, a blonde table, which was round, and came with two matching stuffed chairs upholstered in pale green fabric. It also had a tiny bathroom and a good sized window looking out to sea with cream colored curtains hanging over it. The carpeting was dark green with a short nap that went nicely with the lighter green chairs. It was a fine place to hang out for three weeks while sailing down the Adriatic, through the Mediterranean and across the Atlantic.

It was a warm and sunny day as we set sail and I decided to explore the ship and see what it had to offer. There was a nice sized sundeck with plenty of lounge chairs, tables and umbrellas situated around a large pool. I went back to our cabin and put on my swimming trunks, a tee shirt and my Panama hat. I grabbed a book as I left and returned to the pool. I spotted a young lady in a lounge chair and asked her if I could join her and she said sure. She was from Santa Fe, New Mexico and probably a few years older than I was with sandy blonde hair that was curly and hung down a little past her shoulders. She was rather average looking and she wore no makeup. We chatted for a while and I found her to be quite dull. Something told me that it was going to be a long three weeks bro!

Our first meal was lunch and consisted of soup, chicken with mashed potatoes and vegetables and lots of French bread with plenty of butter. The sea was calm and the ship was cutting through it slow and steady. Lunch was served on white linen table cloths and matching white linen napkins. The food was good but not outstanding. As I looked around the dining room, I realized that I was the youngest passenger on board which concerned me. Over time, I found out that the older passengers were quite friendly, interesting to chat with and great company.

My favorite passenger was a woman in her sixties with grey curly hair formed in a soft afro who walked with a pronounced limp. She was quite lively and friendly and she loved to play cards. I spent hours and hours and hours playing cards with her and whoever else was around at the time. An older gentleman who appeared to be in his mid-seventies and his Filipino wife, who was half his age, frequently joined us to play bridge. I had never played bridge before and my traveling companion was kind and patient enough to teach me the game. We were usually partners when we played. It was a great game and a wonderful way to pass the time and listen to stories that other passengers shared about their lives.

I spent some time walking around the ship to get a bit of exercise and occasionally I spotted the young lady from Santa Fe sneaking out of one of the crew member's cabins. After spending several days chugging across the Atlantic, I had an epiphany bro: The Atlantic Ocean is one frickin huge body of water! We had about a week remaining before reaching New York and all I could do was pray that this ship wouldn't sink.

A few days later, I noticed that the ship had done a 180 degree turn overnight and was heading back out to sea! WTF? I asked the officer at breakfast what was going on and he said that the Captain was trying to avoid a hurricane that was working its way up the coast of the U.S. Apparently, it was traveling much farther north than had been anticipated. Shit! That wasn't good news! But, I figured that the ship was heavily laden with copper and it would be difficult to tip it far enough over to take on water.

At lunchtime we were hitting some heavy waves. After I ate, I walked up to the bow of the ship and hung onto the guard rail as the ship was being lifted and lowered by the huge swells. I estimated that it was bouncing about 100 feet from the bow's low point to its highpoint. It was like riding a fast elevator up and down a ten story building. It was quite fun! I hung out for an hour as the ship was bobbing up and down like a float on a fishing line. Except, there was no fishing line and no one to reel us in.

The storm we were in was increasing in intensity as the afternoon progressed. By dinner time, you couldn't be out on the deck because the splash from the ship cutting through the waves was rising about 100 feet above the deck and blowing across it and even splashing the windows of the dining room! The ship's Officer had swung up wooden side rails that were fastened to the underside of the dining room tables providing a two inch lip that kept the dinner dishes from sliding into your lap! I figured hitting this kind of storm was to be expected when you sailed across the seas.

After dinner, I was invited to play bridge so I followed my partner back to her cabin. As we walked down the narrow hallway you could feel the ship listing gently from side to side. Four of us sat around her small round table which was exactly like the one in our cabin. Two people sat on the bed and two sat in the heavy, upholstered chairs. We switched partners so I was sitting on one of the chairs next to my usual partner. As time went on, the ship began listing more and more. No one seemed concerned. After a while, the listing became even more pronounced. At one point, I was watching my usual bridge partner as the ship listed so severely that it pushed us back into our chairs. I leaned forward so that I wouldn't tip over backward. I watched my partner's chair tipping back so far that she fell over backwards while never letting go of her hand! She just started laughing, stood up, set her chair back up at the table and proceeded with the game.

About ten o'clock in the evening, we broke up the game and I headed back to my cabin. It was impossible to walk completely upright down the hallway of the ship at this point. When the ship listed to the right, I had to face the wall and put both hands against it or I would have fallen over. Once the ship returned to level, I could take three or four steps and then turn to the left wall placing both hands against it until it finished listing to the left. I repeated this several times before entering our cabin. My mom was laying in her bed reading a book when I came in so I decided to do the same. The listing was not problematic when you were laying down.

After a short while, there was a knock at our door. I got up and opened it and a couple of the crewmen said that they needed to secure the furniture in our room so I let them in. When I looked at their faces and saw the fear that was in their eyes, I started to get concerned. I guess this wasn't business as usual bro! I had often wondered, when reading news accounts of ships lost at sea, why they had "broken up". I mean, there was nothing out here to run into that would cause ships to break apart. Well, shortly after pondering this conundrum, I was enlightened.

Once the men had fastened down the furniture and left, I went back to my bed and resumed my reading for a while. Suddenly, I heard the oddest thing. It was a whining noise that picked up in speed and pitch and intensity. The noise was ear piercing and then it stopped instantly. The entire ship shook violently and was accompanied by a thunderous rumbling! Shit dude, this was not good! WTF was that? Then it happened again and again and again! I finally figured out what was going on. The waves had grown so enormous that they were lifting the propeller out of the water. When the propeller hit the air, there was less resistance against it and began spinning much faster. So, the RPM's skyrocketed just like it does when you're racing your car and the tachometer gets way into the red zone! Once the propeller hit the water, all that extra power forced the ship to lurch forward like it was trying to pull a wheelie. Sometimes that force was so strong that it literally broke ships in half! And that dude, was how ships broke apart at sea!

After that unpleasant realization, I prayed that all would be well and I went to sleep. In the morning, it was calm. I was grateful to be alive. I was also grateful that it was pitch black outside as we hit the worst of the hurricane. I am sure my anxiety level would have spiked if I had seen how huge those waves were!

Chapter 60

It was a huge relief seeing the Statue of Liberty off in the distance as we approached New York City! After three weeks at sea, I was so grateful to have reached our destination safely. After disembarking, we took a taxi to Jersey City, NJ to my aunt Gabriella's home. It was a stout, red brick house in a middle class neighborhood and it was quite well maintained. My aunt was in her seventies and she lived alone. My uncle, Ivo, who had been the Minister of Finance of Yugoslavia prior to the communists taking over the country during WWII had died a few years earlier. She had prepared a nice meal for us and showed us our room afterwards. It was the first time that I had seen her.

She let me use her phone to call a friend that I had made while traveling in Ecuador. His name was Neal and he had made a point of giving me his phone number and telling me to look him up if I ever made it to New York. As it turned out, he had just returned from South America and had plenty of free time to show me around. We met the next day and he showed me the two main places that I wanted to see while in New York – The United Nations and the New York Stock Exchange.

Neal had never seen either place and was enjoying being a tourist in his own backyard. I asked him how the rest of his trip went and he told me about hiring some of the indigenous men in the Amazon basin to build him a raft to float down the Amazon River! I asked him where he slept and he said he slept on the raft as it drifted along. I told him that he was nuts. He wanted to show me around Queens where some of his friends lived so we hopped on a ferry and we spent a day hanging out with them. I also wanted to visit Harlem but he refused to take me there. I asked him, "What? You float down the Amazon on a handmade raft but you're afraid to go into Harlem?"

"Yep." Was all he had to say. That night, he invited me to stay at his parents' house so we went back to Manhattan, caught a subway train and rode it to the outskirts of town. When we left the station, we walked along a four lane highway with cars whizzing past us at 65 MPH. It was loud and I didn't see any houses around. All I saw were high rise towers standing several blocks away. When I asked him where his folks lived he pointed over to one of the towers. I thought he was kidding me! But, no, he wasn't. We went up to the 65th floor of a towering condominium building and that's where we spent the night. Dude, that was so different from the suburban lifestyle of the San Fernando Valley!

I asked Neal if he knew of an inexpensive bus line that would take me down to Los Angeles and he recommended the "Blue Rabbit". After making some phone calls, I found out their schedule and it was quite reasonable. My mom wanted to see me off so we went to the bus line at the appointed time and found a medium size converted school bus that was painted blue. I paid for a ticket and the bus driver stowed my backpack in the luggage area and I hopped on the bus. My mom wanted to visit with my aunt for a while longer so I waved goodbye to her as the bus pulled out of the station.

When I stepped on board the bus, I was surprised to see the same young lady from Santa Fe who I met on the ship. I was polite and said hello again and that was about the extent of our conversation for the duration of our trip. Some of the seats from the bus were rearranged and a table was installed for playing games and eating. I politely chatted with some of the other travelers but I was pretty wiped out after walking all around Manhattan and other parts of New York City. I slept well on the bus seats and the trip only took two and a half days.

After pulling into Los Angeles, the driver asked me where I wanted to be dropped off. I told him that it would be great if he could take the 170 into the San Fernando Valley and drop me off at the Roscoe exit. He told me that worked out great for him because he needed to drop the rest of the passengers off in the Bay Area. I told him that there was an on-ramp directly across the street from the off-ramp and that made him smile. After pulling off the 170, it took him less than a minute to grab my backpack out of the cargo area and step back into the bus. There wasn't much traffic at that end of Roscoe and the newly completed Hollywood Freeway wasn't carrying many cars either. It felt great to be walking, after sitting for so many hours, and my home was only two miles away. I walked down Roscoe toward Van Nuys Boulevard and turned left on Hazeltine then right on Stansbury and then left on Wakefield. My mom had given me her key to the house, so I let myself in. Dude, I traveled across the entire U.S. by bus two times within five months! Sheesh, I was totally exhausted!

Chapter 61

The next morning, I woke up in my own bed. It felt wonderful to be somewhere I was familiar with. It was nice and refreshing to have some space to myself for a while. I didn't have any motorized transportation. So, I had to walk to Ralph's to buy some groceries and it was reassuring to walk along familiar streets. I could still hear the General Motors plant making noise 24/7 but it didn't bother me. I fell asleep that night listening to the familiar drone of the 405. Yep, home sweet home. ☺

I started taking long morning walks before the air pollution got out of hand. On one of those walks, I ran into my friend Jacey and he told me that he had graduated from CSUN. He was still playing electric bass with his own band and filling in for some pretty well known rock bands performing at the Santa Monica Civic Auditorium. We started taking long walks together and chatting while we got some exercise. He had grown his hair out and it was about as long as mine at the time. We both talked about what our next step in life was going to be. I still had a few hundred dollars left, but I needed the money to buy a motorcycle and some money for living expenses until I could find a job.

My mom came home a few days later. She took a Greyhound Bus back to North Hollywood and then took a bus back home. My brother Joe stopped in to visit us and said that he was planning on taking a trip to Colorado and asked me if I wanted to come along. I told him that I would like to think about it and asked if I could bring a friend along with us and he said sure. The next time I went on a walk with Jacey, I asked him if he would be interested in taking a road trip to Denver and he said sure. I told Joe we would go along with him and I could help with the driving. He was happy about that. He told me that he would be ready to leave on the first of November which was a couple of weeks away.

During the meantime, I was just hanging around home, playing the piano and going on long walks with Jacey. When the appointed time came, We hopped into my brother's Ford van and we headed east on Roscoe. We spent the first night in Flagstaff, Arizona. The second day, we drove through Albuquerque, Santa Fe and on up to Taos New Mexico. It was nighttime when we pulled off the road just outside Taos We rolled out our sleeping bags and crashed by the side of the road.

The next morning, it was 16 degrees and I didn't want to get out of my sleeping bag and neither did Jacey. We both decided not to proceed farther north because of the cold. I told my brother that we were parting ways and heading back south. He was fine with that. So, Jacey and I hitched a ride to El Paso where we hung out at the University of Texas. After it got dark, we hunted around campus until stumbling upon a large fir tree. It's long, low hanging branches provided us with great cover so we rolled out our sleeping bags and fell asleep under the tree's protective wings.

The next morning, at first light, we packed our bags and headed to a border crossing. After walking over the Rio Grande and stepping into Ciudad Juarez, we caught a bus heading to Chihuahua. Once we reached our destination we headed to a train station and bought two first class tickets to Topolobampo. The train took us through beautiful scenery as it wound its way through the Sierra Madre Mountains. It was super rugged territory with lots of red rock canyons and gorgeous mountain views. Jacey and I spent most of our day hanging on to a steel railing at the very end of the train and soaking up the incredible vistas.

We arrived in Topolobampo, a small town located on the Gulf of California, where everything was closed for the night. A full moon lit our path as we made our way across a dry lakebed. After rolling out our sleeping bags, we realized that we were both thirsty. I dug through my backpack and the only thing I could find was a cucumber. I cut it in two and we each ate our half. It tasted fantastic and there was just enough moisture in it to satisfy our thirst.

The next morning, we walked back into town and bought a ticket for the ferry to La Paz which was located on the Baja California peninsula. A worker, standing on the dock, had just untied the ferry and it was slowly slipping away. He motioned for us to jump as the gap widened. We looked at each other then ran and successfully leaped onto the ship. It was lucky for us because the ferry just made one crossing **per** day. We were both thankful that we didn't have to spend another day in Topolobampo.

La Paz lay warm and sunny under beautiful blue skies. After renting a cheap hotel room for the night, we ended up spending the afternoon looking around town for an interesting place to eat dinner. We met a young man and a young woman inside and had fun sharing stories about our travels. The woman was a nurse from Vancouver, British Columbia and the guy was from California. After dinner, we walked back toward our hotels and the guy from California peeled off to his room first. A little further on, the young woman from Canada asked if I would like to see some of the souvenirs that she had purchased on her trip. I said sure and told Jacey that I would catch up with him later on. As it turned out dude, later on was the next morning around ten o'clock.

Jacey and I bought bus tickets to Tijuana. It took over 20 hours to drive and we ended up singing nearly every Beatles' song ever written. The people on the bus applauded us and kept asking us to sing more. By the time we were done singing, we passed out and slept until morning. Upon arriving in Tijuana, we grabbed our backpacks and walked across the border. We began hitchhiking north and a young woman picked us up and drove us to San Diego.

From there, we caught a ride from a guy driving a Dodge van. I sat in the front seat and Jacey hopped in back. I asked the driver where he was headed and he said San Francisco. We were planning on ending our trip that day, but I turned and asked Jacey if he wanted to go to San Francisco. He started laughing and said sure. We drove to my friend Peter's apartment in Berkeley which was on Blake Street. It was dark by the time we arrived. Our driver asked if it would be okay to leave his van parked in front of Peter's place for the night. I told him it would be fine and gave him Peter's name and apartment number if he needed anything. We said good-bye and the next morning his van was gone by the time we headed out for breakfast.

Chapter 62

Back in Panorama City, I sat on my bed and started plotting out my next moves. First, I needed to acquire a motorcycle and second, I needed a job immediately. I called Willy up and told him that my traveling days were over. I was broke and I needed to buy a motorcycle and get a job. He laughed and told me that he could get me a job at "Hang Ten" a company that produced tee shirts, polo shirts and socks. He said that it paid minimum wage. I told him that I would take it. Willy drove me around as we went searching for a motorcycle to buy. I settled for a slightly modified Honda 350 that had some extra chrome, and custom handle bars. It also had a beautiful custom gas tank painted metallic blue with powder blue pin striping.

At "Hang Ten", I worked in the warehouse packing orders, unloading and loading trucks and stocking shelves. The time went by quickly because we were always busy. Soon, I had saved up enough money to buy a Pontiac Le Mans which could seat four across the front bench seat. I bought it from Willy. It hadn't been parked in a garage so the paint was totally oxidized and it looked bad but Willy said that it was in good mechanical shape.

One day, my brother, Tony, stopped in to see my mom. He was on his way home from Schlitz brewery where he worked. He asked me how I was doing and I told him that I was working at a warehouse for minimum wage. He told me to sign up at the Teamsters union downtown and get on their waiting list. He said that the Teamsters were threatening to go on strike at the Budweiser brewery in Van Nuys because their demand for higher wages was not being met. He said that if they did go on strike, Schlitz would be hiring a bunch of people. At the time, it was the second best selling beer in America. I figured it couldn't hurt to try so I took time off from work and ran downtown to sign up. The guys at the Teamster's office knew

Tony and my dad. They put me on their list and said they would try to push me toward the top if they could.

I worked at "Hang Ten" for a couple more months. In my spare time I designed a line of pen and ink greeting cards. I had them professionally printed and started selling them to family, friends and even coworkers at Hang Ten. After saving up more money, I quit my job and devoted full time to selling my greeting cards. They were well received at stationery stores and gift stores but I only had a line of ten different cards that I sold in packs of twelve. After factoring in my time and expenses, I realized that it was costing me money to sell my cards! It was a losing proposition. There were two solutions to my problem. I could either produce more greeting cards or take on other products to sell along with my cards. After pondering my predicament, I realized that neither option appealed to me.

The next morning, as I was lying in bed wondering what to do, the phone rang. It was Schlitz brewery. They asked me if I could come to their office for an interview that morning. Of course I said yes! Once again, God came to my rescue. After my interview, they told me that they would let me know in a day or two if I had the job. However, before the day was over, they called me back and asked if I could start working the next morning. "Sure," I said. I was earning $2.00 per hour at "Hang Ten" and now I would be starting at $7.00 per hour! That was over three and a half times what I had been making! Plus, there were shift differentials, time and a half for overtime, double time for working on weekends and triple time for holidays!

My first day of work at Schlitz was quite traumatic dude. The brewery was incredibly loud, steamy and dangerous. One of the foreman took me aside and gave me earplugs and a plastic face shield. He showed me where to pick up a large hopper that I could roll around. Next we went to an area where I was given a big aluminum scoop shovel and a push broom. I was told that I was in charge of keeping a certain area of the plant clear of any beer cans and bottles that accidentally fell off the production line. I had to duck under conveyor belts that had both cans and bottles whizzing by at top speeds.

I was also tasked with unblocking cans and bottles that were jamming the production lines. If a can or bottle was not removed quickly enough, a pileup would occur and cans would come tumbling down onto the plant floor. If I saw a line blocked, I was to clear it as quickly as possible and then sweep and shovel up the cans or glass into their respective hoppers. Sometimes the shovel would poke a hole in a can turning it into a pinwheel spraying pressurized beer out and propelling it across the brewery floor. It was actually quite amusing and provided me with some entertainment as I labored away. When a hopper of cans was full, I would wheel it over to a huge machine that cut and compacted the aluminum cans turning them into large disks of compressed aluminum. A guy driving a forklift would lift the hopper and dump it into the mouth of the machine. Afterwards, I would wheel it back to my workstation and fill it up again.

Sometimes, the brewery was shorthanded and a foreman would come over and move me to a production line. One day, someone didn't show up for their shift on a bottle line and a foreman asked me to cover for the guy. I was working swing shift at the time and the guy working days gave me a quick rundown on what to do. He told me that sometimes a bottle would fall over and block the line and that my first priority was to remove that bottle as fast as possible. I worked at the pasteurizer making sure that the bottles were being fed onto a conveyor belt. He told me to be careful because the bottles coming out of the pasteurizer were under quite a bit of pressure and prone to explode!

I was totally stressed out. Bottles would frequently fall over requiring me to remove the blockage while making sure that bottles were being fed onto the line. About half way through my shift, I grabbed a bottle that had fallen over without noticing that the bottom of it had been completely blown out. As I was grabbing the broken bottle, it cut right through my glove and sliced my hand. Blood instantly started streaming down my arm. I knew enough to raise it above my head so that gravity wouldn't increase the blood loss. I was bleeding so badly that my entire arm was covered in blood as I worked my way to the nurse's station. She helped stop the bleeding, bandaged me up and told one of the foremen to take me to the emergency room. One of the emergency room doctors sewed my hand up and told me not to get it wet until they pulled the stiches out in ten days.

The next day, I was working on a can loader that was located on the front end of a can line. There were no liquids to deal with just pallets and pallets of empty cans with no lids. The pallets were about ten feet high and they filled up a semitruck trailer from floor to ceiling and wall to wall. They were unloaded onto a conveyor belt and transferred onto a remote controlled trolley car that fed the pallets into an elevator. The elevator would raise the pallet up to a point where the bottom of the cans were flush with a huge conveyor table. A flat metal arm would push an entire layer of cans onto the conveyor.

There were hydraulic suction cups on the back side of the arm that would pop down and remove a sheet of poster board that separated the various layers of cans stacked on top of one another. When the arm finished retracting, it would release the poster board onto a pallet that rested on top of a steel shelf located behind the mechanical arm. The elevator would then rise so that the next layer of cans could be pushed onto the conveyor table. The table was designed like a funnel guiding the cans into a single file line and whisking them away to be filled with beer.

Next, the cans were moved to a machine that hammered on the lids. This machine was so loud and fast that it sounded like a machine gun. The workers manning that machine, even if they wore earplugs, must have sustained some hearing loss. The cans were then fed to another machine that arranged them into six packs and snapped a plastic top on them. At the far end of the line, workers were grabbing the six packs and placing four of them onto a cardboard case and then stacking the cases onto pallets. It was all in a day's work at the brewery bro.

Chapter 63

My brother, Tony, had a great deal of seniority at Schlitz. As a result, he worked the dayshift and was positioned at the can machine. It hammered lids onto cans and sounded like a machinegun. The canning machine was the loudest piece of equipment in the entire plant and could be heard throughout the facility. Tony had worked in the brewery for over fifteen years and wasn't that far from collecting a pension at the twenty year mark but, he hated his job. He thought it was dangerous and demeaning.

During the time I spent shuffling around the brewery, I noticed that one of the workers was always watching me. It was weird dude! It was like, what the hell did I do to make this guy want to stare at me? He never smiled, he just watched what I was doing. Finally, after about a month or so of this, I was sitting in a breakroom eating lunch with my back to a wall where a swinging door was installed that muffled much of the noise from the factory floor. The mystery man that was watching me was sitting across the breakroom from me. His back was turned to an exterior wall and he was facing my direction. One of the foremen stuck his head in the room and yelled at no one in particular, "Has anyone seen Sain?"

They mystery man replied, "Which one, the one that works or the one that doesn't?" So, that was it! He was checking me out to see if I was a hard worker or not. I knew that I was a hard worker and I had been reprimanded by the shop steward a few times for working too hard. He told me to slow it down. Finally, after about the third time he told me to slow down, I told him that I just had one speed and told him to get over it.

After working on the front end of the can line for a couple of months, a foreman came by and said he was going to pull me off the line. He thought that it should only take one man to run the line. I told him that he was out of his mind and explained to him why he was wrong. He turned and stomped away. A couple days later, there was a guy who was standing on a catwalk next to the can line watching me and my coworker. He was there for about a week and I finally asked him what he was doing. He said that he was trying to figure out why the shift that I was working was operating at 96% capacity and the day shift was operating at only 70%. I told him that the answer was simple – we worked harder than the day shift. I never saw him again bro!

Shortly after starting at the brewery, I had made a point to give each of the foremen my name and phone number. I told them that I only lived ten minutes away from the plant and if someone missed their shift I would be happy to fill in for them. Over the remainder of the time that I worked there, I was called in frequently. In the middle of summer, at peak production time, I worked twelve hour shifts every day of the week for seven weeks! On the fourth of July, I earned triple time working a twelve hour shift. That was nearly a week's worth of pay for one day of work!

I loved working swing shift. We got six ten minute "beer" breaks during our shift. The breakroom was stocked with cans and bottles of beer that were rejected because they were under filled. They called them "shorts" and we were allowed to drink them while we were in the breakroom. We were not allowed to drink while we were on the factory floor. During my entire time on the job, I only saw one guy chug a beer while he was working on a labeling machine. If he had been caught, he would have been fired on the spot!

Anyway, I never drank beer until my last break when I popped the top off a bottle and sipped it during the last ten minutes of my shift. It was my reward for putting in a good day's work. My shift ended at ten. On Friday and Saturday nights, I would grab a couple extra bottles of beer and stick them in my lunch sack and take them home. I sipped the beers at home while showering and getting ready to go clubbing. I loved to dance and I usually got to a club about a quarter to 11:00. After three beers, I was on par with everyone else at that hour. Usually, there was a one dollar cover charge that went to the band. It was a cheap night out and I had a great time dancing until 2:00 am when the clubs shut down. There was never a shortage of willing partners because most guys didn't like to dance. I loved it bro, and I ended up dating several of the young ladies I danced with.

In November of 1976, Leslie invited me to her birthday party where I met Mary Jo. She was Leslie's best friend and she was beautiful, smart and fun loving. After saying goodnight to Leslie, Mary Jo followed me outside and invited me to a Christmas party at her mom's house. I told her that I would love to go. The party was in Thousand Oaks. Mary Jo picked me up in her cool little MG sports car and drove me to the party. She told me that her mom worked at Amgen which was headquartered in Thousand Oaks. It was a fun party and it was the first time that I had ever seen an entire wheel of Jarlsberg cheese being served to guests. Mary Jo said that it was delicious cheese and encouraged me to try it, so I did. She was absolutely right dude! It instantly became my all-time favorite cheese!

Schlitz laid me off just before Christmas but I was thankful that I had the opportunity to work so many hours over the six months that I had worked there. I was able to pay off my school loans and started to invest some money in the stock market. John, my brother, found out that I had been laid off. He offered to hire me as a foreman to run one of his construction crews. He was willing to pay me well so I agreed to start work after the first of the year.

During the holidays, I was spending more time hanging out with my friend Paul who introduced me to Fred. I knew who he was because we had some classes together in high school. Fred had just graduated from Stanford with a degree in English, but his true love was movies. The three of us started going out to Westwood to watch newly released films. We had a great time together and we decided to become housemates. As it turned out, Mary Jo and her roommates had just given a 30 day notice to their landlord and the three of us ended up moving into their vacated rental home. It was located on Chastain Avenue, in Reseda, just south of Roscoe Boulevard.

Chapter 64

Shortly after Christmas, in 1977, my mom was diagnosed with Lymphoma. She agreed to be treated with chemo therapy. I was greatly concerned. I told her that even though I was moving out with my friends, I would stop by regularly to see how she was doing and help her with her shopping. She always insisted on fixing me dinner whenever I came by. She never learned how to drive and was too poor to afford the cost of owning and operating a car. Typically, she walked to Ralph's market to buy her food and shopped at the Panorama Mall for shoes and clothing.

I started working for my brother, John, after New Year's day. While he was out bidding on jobs, two other guys and I did the framing on various remodel jobs in Beverly Hills and Bell Air. I learned quite a bit about real estate prices, quality improvements and how some people made a great deal of money buying, refurbishing and reselling real estate. We worked mostly on single family homes but occasionally we worked on upgrading apartment units as well. John had joined AA and was doing much better than he ever had. One of my coworkers was also a former alcoholic. He was a nice guy that was quite amusing and helped make our day go by quickly. Once, he told me that he got so drunk that he couldn't remember where or what he did for an entire week! Dude, I didn't know that was even possible! We worked well together and John was happy with our production.

Meanwhile, Paul, Fred and I moved into our three bedroom two bath rental home. My bedroom was on the north side of the house and the neighbor to the north of us had a fiesta going on 24/7. They were always out grilling meat, drinking alcohol, playing Mexican music, talking loudly and laughing even more loudly. Sometimes I would get up at 2:00 or 3:00 o'clock in the morning to go to the bathroom and the lights in their backyard were still on and they were still having a great time. I actually enjoyed the energy and the joyfulness of my new neighbors even though I never met them in person.

None of us were using the two car garage at our rental, so I asked John if he would be interested in renting it for $50 per month for storing tools and construction supplies. He was happy to do so and we were all grateful to be paying a little less for rent. I enjoyed the physical nature of construction work and I found that working with my hands was rewarding. Every day, before leaving our job site, I would check out the progress that we made and that brought me a great deal of pleasure. It was hard work but that had its benefits as well. I felt relaxed after a full day's work. I was also getting stronger and I slept like a rock!

My girlfriend, Leslie, ended up moving up to Northern California to go to school at U.C. Berkeley. As a result, I ended up seeing more of her best friend. Mary Jo had moved out to a cool older home in the MacArthur Park neighborhood but she still kept her job in the Valley. We got together on the weekends and she would come over to our place after work. I found out quickly that she was neither a truthful person nor a faithful girlfriend and I broke up with her.

Paul was working at a plant that separated the components of blood in a lab in Westwood and Fred was pressured by his father to sign up as a premed student at CSUN. Fred hated the classes and dropped out of the program entirely within a few weeks. He ended up getting a job for a new pay TV station called "On TV". It was a sales job that involved answering calls from people who were responding to TV commercials sponsored by "On TV" and signing them up for the service. It was a broadcast station that required a special piece of equipment that needed to be installed on subscriber's TV sets.

I had signed up for a couple of evening classes at CSUN that were required to obtain a California Real Estate Broker's license. I was taking a real estate law class and a principles and practices of real estate class. Each class met once a week and I found them interesting and informative. My real estate law professor was a practicing attorney and he presented many real world examples of real estate and contract law. Occasionally, he would bring in guest lecturers who were involved in the real estate industry to provide case studies of projects that they were working on. One of the guests spoke about the importance of "OPM" or "Other People's Money". It was a presentation that pointed out the importance of financial leverage in real estate ownership. After taking that class, I was motivated to become a real estate broker and real estate investor!

By summer, I had saved up enough money to buy a better car. I called up my friend Willy for some advice. I told him that I had $3,000 and wanted to buy the best car that I could find in that price range. He told me that he had just seen an ad for a new 1977 Chevy Vega for sale at a new car dealership in the Valley for $2,888. GM stopped manufacturing the Vega and the dealer was just trying to unload the last two Vegas on his lot. The Vega had an aluminum block engine that didn't have the greatest reputation but they were offering a six year 60,000 mile warrantee on the car so I went over to the dealer to check it out.

The only two models left were both painted a bright orange! Luckily, orange was my favorite color. One of the cars was a hatchback and the other was a two door coupe. I test drove the hatchback because I liked the idea of having extra hauling space when the backseat was folded down. It also looked way cooler. I was surprised at how well the car handled and I loved the four speed stick. I told the salesman that I would buy it. He said that he had to check with his manager. WTF? Check for what I wondered? Anyway, he came back and said that since the hatchback had custom aluminum wheels on it they would have to charge me an extra $50. I told him to just swap the wheels with the standard coupe because I didn't want to pay the extra money. He went back to check with his manager and came back and told me that they would just sell me the car for the advertised price of $2,888.

Chapter 65

It was a hot summer. The Valley was getting into the 100's, and I was getting fed up with driving my brother's truck around in Los Angeles traffic without air conditioning. I didn't want to get sunburned so I wore a straw hat and a long-sleeved shirt which made it even hotter. John was also beginning to get abusive and I told him that I was quitting. He took it well. I told Fred that I quit and he said that they were hiring at "On TV" if I wanted to work there. I applied for the job and was hired. It was fun to be working together with Fred that summer and the sales job was easy, indoors and air conditioned! Meanwhile, Paul had been accepted into a PhD program in inorganic chemistry and he had taken off for Corvallis, Oregon to study at OSU. His main interest was studying crystals used for lasers. His sponsoring professor was a leader in that field. Fred and I found a new roommate named Bill and we all got along well.

During that summer, I ended up spending weekends at Oviatt Library at California State University at Northridge. I was working on improving my writing skills and ended up meeting Pam there. She was a wonderful and attractive young Christian woman who had recently moved to Sun Valley where she was living with her aunt. Pam grew up in Minnesota and her parents were Polish. She invited me to go to a Polish picnic and I accepted. We had a great time. We both liked the outdoors and we both enjoyed doing yoga together at her aunt's home. There were also hiking trails close by in Sun Valley and we enjoyed spending time walking and talking together.

Fall came rolling around and Fred signed up for a film making class at CSUN. After a few weeks of instruction, the professor told the class to divide up into groups and go out and produce a short movie. Fred talked his group into making a parody of the movie "Night of the Living Dead" and called it

"Night of the Loving Dead". The movie was mostly shot at our place and I was nominated to be the head zombie. I also, ended up getting credits for the film score and my contribution to the screenplay. We shot the film over several nights and my new girlfriend, Pam, also played a part in our student film. We recruited a few other high school friends to help us as well. We had a blast making the film and Fred told me that his professor thought that I was a professional actor!

Pam and I were getting pretty serious about each other and one afternoon when we were out jogging around CSUN she told me that she had something important to tell me. She acknowledged that we were becoming quite close and she said that before it went any further she needed to tell me that she couldn't have children. I felt like I was hit by a ton of bricks! It took me a while to gather myself together. I couldn't speak because I had a huge lump in my throat. Somehow, I choked out that I was sorry to hear that. I didn't ask any questions and neither one of us said anything for a long time. It was devastating information and I knew at once that our relationship was over because I wanted to have children. As deeply as I felt for Pam, I knew that I couldn't overcome my desire to be a father. Sometimes life just sucks bro.

I met Patricia while working at "On TV". She was a young African American woman who sat directly in front of me in the "phone room". She was absolutely gorgeous! We started flirting around at work and that quickly turned into dating each other. She was smart, witty and a lot of fun to be with. We ended up growing close very quickly and she wanted to introduce me to her folks. I didn't have a problem with that but apparently her father did. He wouldn't even come out to greet me. After assessing the situation, I decided that getting more serious with Patty was not going to work out in the long run. Marrying into a family with a hostile father-in-law did not sound like a good idea.

My mom had not been doing well and the doctors said that she wasn't responding to the chemo therapy. She quickly fell into a deep depression and told me that she couldn't go on any longer. She showed me a dress and a pair of shoes that she wanted to be buried in and we both held each other and cried. Shortly after that, she passed away at UCLA Medical Center. It was September of 1977. She was 63 years old.

After my mom's funeral, my brothers asked me if I would be the administrator for my mom's estate. They said that I could live in our mom's home for free as long as I kept it neat and tidy and maintained the yards. I realized that my older brothers were well into their lives and that it would be easier for me to take on the responsibility of dealing with my mom's estate. I apologized to Fred and told him what the situation was and he was gracious about it. We gave our landlord 30 days' notice and we went our separate ways.

Moving back into my mom's home was emotionally difficult. I was having dreams of her walking around the house. When I woke up, I was totally freaked out dude! I would just lay in bed afraid to do anything until I fell asleep again. After a while, I felt like I had to do something to stop these fearful dreams. One night, I told myself that I needed to confront my fear. Sure enough, I had another dream of my mom brushing her hair in the bathroom and I woke up. This time, I forced myself to get out of bed and walk into the bathroom and turn the light on. As soon as I did, the fear vanished. I felt silly, but it stopped the dreams from reoccurring!

Chapter 66

As the administrator of my mom's estate, I needed to find an attorney to handle the probate filing. My brother, Joe, wanted me to use his friend to handle our case. I acquiesced. I contacted the attorney and he said that he would get the process started. I didn't hear back from him for about a week, so I called him again. He said that he was busy and didn't have time to start the case. I told him that I would like to meet with him and get this process started. We made an appointment to meet at the courthouse in downtown Los Angeles the following week. I was not happy to drive all the way downtown in traffic, find a parking place and hike over to the courthouse. When we met, he apologized again and said that he had not done the paperwork yet. I was pissed off bro!

I talked to my brother, John, and told him that I was thinking of replacing our attorney. He said fine so I called my real estate law professor and asked him if he would be interested in handling our probate case. He said that he had a legal assistant that did nothing but process probate cases. I asked him how long it would take and asked if he could file the case at the courthouse in Van Nuys. He said that I could come into his office the next day to sign the paperwork and he could file it at the Van Nuys Courthouse the following morning. I agreed to do so.

I was thrilled. I called Joe's friend back and left a message telling him that his services were no longer needed. When Joe found out that I had fired his friend he went ballistic! I told Joe that I was the one handling our mom's estate and I wanted to get it done as soon as possible so that I could get on with my life. His friend ultimately apologized to Joe for not moving more quickly so my brother felt better about what I had done.

Taking control of the situation felt good. I decided that I needed to get more control over other areas of my life as well. I decided to get more involved with jogging so I read a book about it and I began running regularly. The shoes that I was running in weren't that great so I bought my first pair of running shoes. I was astonished at the huge difference the shoes made. They had way more cushion and jogging became fun!

It took a while to switch my running style from sprinting on the balls of my feet to running heel to toe. I needed to slow my pace down in order to run longer distances. It was a difficult transition for me. Little by little, I slowed it down until I could run for three miles without stopping or gasping for air. Once I was able to do that, I began interval training. I would spend about five minutes warming up and then start alternating between sprinting and jogging. This helped me increase my jogging speed to eight minute miles. Running made me feel great. I was hooked bro. It also helped me trim down my weight and build up my leg muscles. Running became my daily routine helping me to keep my spirits up and my mind focused.

Next, I decided to do a one day fast while isolating myself from all outside distractions. I had been sleeping on a twin bed that doubled as a couch in our family room. My old bedroom was completely vacant. It had been cleared out by my brothers as we divided up the furniture and the few personal possessions that my mom had. I hauled my sleeping bag, pillow, foam mat, a gallon of water and a bucket into my old bedroom. I poured some water into the bucket so that I could use it as a portable toilet.

The following morning, I began my 24 hour confinement. I closed my bedroom door and windows so I wouldn't be distracted by outside noise. Sitting down on my rolled up sleeping bag and leaning against a wall I began my day of solitude. All kinds of thoughts began to wander through my mind. Some were more important than others and some were not important at all. My brain began cycling through my thoughts and sifting out the ones that were not important. This process took some time resulting in three main life goals that I needed to address: 1. I wanted to get married. 2. I needed to find a better job. 3. I had to decide where I was going to live after my mom's house sold.

Well dude, I never thought that 24 hours of isolation would be so hard to handle! It felt like I had been locked away for weeks! The next morning, I went outside, got into my old Pontiac, drove it down Van Nuys Boulevard and pulled into Magic Muffler to get an estimate on a new muffler. When I walked into the office, I was overwhelmed with joy to see another human being! Shaking hands and interacting with my fellow man was exhilarating. I felt so thankful not to be alone! The words: "Man does not live by bread alone," echoed in my brain.

Chapter 67

I decided to start working on finding a job that would lead to a career path. So, the first thing I did was quit my job at "On TV" allowing me to focus full time on my job search! I began by heading over to the CSUN Career Center to check out job postings. When I returned home, I decided to turn our kitchen table into my work station. So, I spread out my notes and began the long arduous task of crafting a resume and a cover letter. Day after day, I mailed out letters and after a while I began to get responses and began scheduling interviews. I was determined to find my career path!

I interviewed with Motorola, Panasonic and National Cash register and decided to give being a salesman for Panasonic a shot. The first few days consisted of learning about company procedures and learning about the products that I would be selling. I began questioning my choice after examining the products that I was expected to peddle. Soon after that, I was sent off to tag along with one of the salesmen. One or two days of that told me that this was not the correct career path for me. So, I kept on looking.

Meanwhile, we found a buyer for my mom's home which sold for $56,000. By the time we paid for attorney's fees, closing costs and paying off the loan on the home, my brothers and I each netted approximately $10,000 from our mom's estate. I was also paid an administrator's fee of $1600. It wasn't much, but it was enough for a down payment on a home. Soon afterwards, I accepted an offer to work for the Carnation Company as a credit manager. I asked my attorney if he could recommend a real estate broker that could help me find a home to buy. He suggested Jennie Stabile who found a three bedroom one bath home for me located at 20451 Hartland Street in Canoga Park near Pierce College.

I asked my friend, Fred, if he would be interested in renting a room in my new home and he said yes. So, we moved into the property once it closed escrow in the spring of 1978. I bought the home from a graduate student who had neglected the property during the time he was attending college. As a result, there was quite a bit of deferred maintenance and the exterior of the home needed painting and the yards were just weeds. The home had an attached garage, an RV access on the side of it and a children's playhouse in the backyard. The playhouse was about eight feet by eight feet with a locking entry door, an operable window, carpeting and it was wired with an overhead ceiling fixture. The house was your basic fixer upper – it was the ugliest house in the neighborhood and the asking price reflected it. Home prices in the late seventies were increasing by double digits each year so buying a home was a good investment.

The Carnation Company was located on the north side of Wilshire Boulevard a block west of Highland Avenue. It was about 20 miles from my new home. It was a 30 minute drive with no traffic but my commute took an hour! I tried several alternate routes each morning and finally settled on taking the 101 east to Coldwater Canyon where I turned right and headed for the Hollywood Hills. When I reached Mulholland Drive, I turned left and drove along the crest of the mountains which provided me with fantastic views of both the San Fernando Valley and the Los Angeles basin. My Vega, with its low center of gravity, handled the curves remarkably well allowing me to drive much faster than the posted speed limit! I took a right onto Outpost Drive and then worked my way over to Highland Avenue. It still took me an hour to get to work, but there was no traffic on Mulholland and the views were stunning!

Bill was the name of my boss and he was the head of the credit department at Carnation. He was a great guy but was completely engrossed in planning his wedding. He had graciously invited me to the ceremony and I accepted. I sat at an old metal desk that was surrounded by a sea of other metal desks piloted by other workers! Music was pumped through our office and it was provided free of advertisements by a company called Muzak. Pop songs were arranged for strings and soft piano. We called it elevator music. One day they were playing a Muzak version of Creedence Clearwater's song "Proud Mary". I found it utterly repulsive dude! Marilyn was a coworker who sat behind me in a desk that was placed so close to my chair that I could barely squeeze into my seat. She was a chain smoker and blew her second hand smoke over my shoulder all day long making my head spin! Ralph, another coworker, sat next to her and he couldn't stand the smoke either.

By 1978, most large corporations had computers handling their accounting records but not Carnation! They still had accounts receivable clerks that recorded each transaction by hand on card files! Apparently, the CEO at the time was so old that he didn't want to deal with learning about computers and he was close to retirement age. He had been running the company ever since the founder passed the baton on to him. Bill told me that the heirs to the Carnation Company had no interest in running the company themselves and said that they intended to sell the company whenever their CEO chose to retire or die. One of the heirs was the President of the company who usually came in around 10:00 in the morning, took a two hour lunch at noon and then left at 3:00.

I was in charge of managing $60 million dollars in accounts receivable from customers that were spread out over a third of the United States. When I agreed to take the job, I had assumed that I would be working with numbers and analyzing financial statements and updating files. This was the part of the job that I liked. What I was totally incapable of doing, was remembering all the names of the hundreds of companies I was responsible for managing! Dude, I sucked at remembering names! It was totally embarrassing.

Richard was Bill's boss. He was the Executive Vice President of Finance whose office was located one floor above us and he was a smart guy! The finance department was swamped and Richard asked me to handle a project for him. The Carnation Company was interested in acquiring a company that manufactured and distributed cookies and they had narrowed their choice down to two companies. One of those companies was Mother's Cookies. This was the company that Richard wanted to buy, but his boss was more interested in acquiring another company.

I was called upstairs to meet with Richard. He wanted me to analyze the financial statements of both companies and create a graphic display emphasizing the merits of Mother's Cookies when compared to the rival cookie company. He told me that Bill would drive me over to the closest stationery store to buy whatever supplies I needed. After my analysis, I made graphs that made Mother's Cookies look like the obvious choice as the best acquisition for the Carnation Company. Richard won the argument and Mother's Cookies became a part of the Carnation Company. He was quite pleased with my work. It was a fun project for me and it made me realize that I was in the wrong department!

The credit department, consisting of Bill, Marilyn, Ralph and me, ate lunch together at the company's cafeteria. One day, Bill told me that the Personnel Director would be joining us. After grabbing a grilled cheese sandwich and a salad, being a vegetarian at the time, I joined my associates at our table. Bill introduced me to the Personnel Director who stuck out her hand for me to shake and I jumped back in horror! No one had bothered to tell me that the Personnel Director's hand was deformed. The woman's hand was the size of a baby's and it was missing some fingers! It came at me like a snake ready to strike! The jaws of the snake hand were wide open and threatening. It totally freaked me out dude. The snake hand was quickly retracted and I felt like crawling under a rock and dying.

The Carnation Company also had a dining room for executives. It was far superior to the employee cafeteria but my boss only wanted to eat there on Fridays. It was all quite formal with white linen table cloths, matching napkins, real silverware, and fine china. Lunch was served buffet style while women in maid's outfits walked around taking our drink orders and bussing our dishes. I liked eating there because the quality and variety of the food was much better and so was the service. I asked Bill why we didn't eat in the executive's dining room every day and he said that it cost two dollars more than the cafeteria. I felt like saying, "So what?" But, I didn't.

Chapter 68

My job at the Carnation Company was more stressful than I had anticipated. When I came home from work I was so stressed out that I had chest pains! I ended up falling into a routine of going for a jog as soon as I got home. Each afternoon, I tried a different route around my new neighborhood. One day, I discovered the cross country course at Pierce College and I fell in love with it. It snaked through a natural setting that provided a quiet and peaceful place to run in the midst of the concrete and asphalt surrounding it.

After running, I showered and fixed myself a large salad accompanied by cheese and nuts that I purchased from Trader Joes on Riverside Drive between Woodman and Van Nuys Boulevard in Sherman Oaks. Salads required a great deal of chewing so I read the L.A. Times while eating my dinner. Fred usually got home quite a bit after I did and we spent a good part of the evening chatting or going out for ice cream or catching a movie.

On weekends, I worked on fixing up my new place. After painting and installing flooring in the kitchen, I removed an accordion door that separated the living room from a third bedroom. I ordered a custom set of louver doors that I stained to match the existing trim and then installed them. Once I finished replacing the accordion doors, I found a new roommate named David who was interested in renting the third bedroom.

As it turned out, David was a young alcoholic who stopped paying rent after a couple of months and I was forced to evict him and I changed the locks on the front door. Fred and I hauled all of his stuff out of the house and set it on a covered patio in the back yard. He eventually showed up when we were at work and picked up his belongings. Afterwards, I found another roommate. His name was Ben and he managed a yogurt shop in the Valley for his dad. He worked out fine and we all got along well. I also ended up renting out our two car garage for $50 per month. The rent I collected from the garage and my two roommates covered my monthly mortgage payment!

December of 1978 was an incredibly wet month. It rained every day for three weeks and the commute from work was taking two hours. It was driving me nuts dude! So, on a Friday afternoon I decided to take Mulholland Drive all the way across the Valley to Hayvenhurst Avenue where it turned into a dirt road. I was thrilled to be moving and I made such good time that I decided to test the dirt roadbed on the other side of Hayvenhurst. It was quite solid. Now, I had a choice to make. I could either drive back down the hill and into the horrific traffic in the Valley, or continue on Mulholland to Topanga Canyon. I chose to continue on Mulholland.

It was about ten miles from Hayvenhurst to Topanga Canyon with no cross streets intersecting Mulholland at that time. It was a big gamble but I decided it was worth the risk. I drove about five miles and everything was going great and I knew that I had made the right choice. But the solid dirt road suddenly turned into soft mud with no warning! My front tires started throwing so much mud onto my windshield that it overwhelmed my wipers. I quickly rolled down my window, stuck out my arm and began wiping the mud off a porthole sized section of the windshield. My left hand was moving up and down as fast as it could to give me a view of the road ahead.

I drove like this for about a mile. Up ahead, I saw a car stranded in the middle of the road. There was just enough room to squeak by the stranded vehicle and the edge of the road. If I didn't make it, my car would plunge down a steep cliff. The rear end of my car was drifting side to side in the mud. I took a deep breath, held the car as steady as possible and barely squeezed by the stalled vehicle! I was in first gear and heading up a long steep section of road. My foot was steady on the gas pedal. As I approached the top of the hill, my car started to lug and I had to press down on the accelerator. As soon as I did, the rear wheels started spinning. My car went into a spin and slid sideways ending up stuck in some deep muck.

Having just gotten off work, I was wearing my best three piece wool suit. I rolled up my pant legs before getting out of my car. Upon taking my first tentative step outside, my foot sunk into the soft mud all the way up to my knee! The bottom of my car was resting completely in the mud and it was still raining! I began tearing off chunks of bushes that were pressing against the side of my car and trying to shove them under my rear wheels. It was useless! I couldn't get anywhere near the bottom of my tires. So, I began jacking up the rear of the car. I quickly realized that all I was doing was sending the base of the jack farther and farther into the mud. The car didn't budge.

It was starting to get dark, I was soaking wet and I was about five miles away from Topanga Canyon. I looked up and prayed to myself, "What I need is a four wheel drive with a winch to come down the road and pull me out of here." And, just as I said that prayer, I heard the sound of an engine off in the distance. Soon, a set of headlights peaked around the corner of a hill. As the engine noise grew louder and the headlights got bigger, I saw a four wheel drive Jeep with a winch secured to the front bumper! The Jeep stopped on level ground just above me and an African American dude stepped out of his vehicle.

I asked him if he could pull me out and he said sure. He grabbed the hook on his winch, pulled the cable down to where I was standing and secured it to the front end of my car. Soon, he began reeling my car in like a fish until it stood nose to nose with his Jeep. I asked him how the road was the rest of the way to Topanga. He said it was a little dicey for a couple of miles but good and solid after that. I asked him if he could follow me until the road got better and he said he would if I could chip in for some gas money. I gave him twenty bucks and he escorted me back then flashed his high beams and turned around. Dude, I can't tell you how happy I was! After driving the rest of the way home, I parked my car in the driveway and headed straight for the shower!

The next morning, Willy was ringing our front doorbell. It was Saturday and we had planned to go cross country skiing that day. When I opened the door, Willy was laughing his head off while pointing at my car. The first words out of his mouth were: "There's got to be a story about that!" I stepped outside to see my orange Vega completely covered in mud. It was nearly unrecognizable as a car. It looked more like something out of a cartoon show. I started cracking up at the sight of it as well.

Willy had been working at the Farmers Insurance Office on Sepulveda Boulevard for about a year and was sharing a house with his friend Skip out in Simi Valley. Skip was in the process of selling his home and purchasing a new one that wasn't completed yet. As a result, Willy needed a place to live for a couple of months. He asked me if he could stay with us. I didn't hesitate. Sure, I told him. You could rent the playhouse in the back yard including full house privileges for $150 per month. He accepted the offer.

Chapter 69

By the time the first of February 1979 rolled around, the winter rains had ended and we returned to our typical warm days and cloudless skies. I had my clock radio tuned in to a news station and every workday morning the first thing I heard was this: "Unhealthy air quality predicted for the Los Angeles basin today." So, what else was new dude? I got ready for work, climbed into my car and listened to more news on the radio. The guys hosting the show were taking bets on who killed J.R. and I was thinking WTF? Are these guys for real? And, who the hell was J.R.? Since I didn't watch TV, I had no idea that they were talking about a fictional character in the popular TV show "Dallas".

So, I continued driving to work and when I got up onto Mullholland Drive, on a section of road overlooking the Valley, I took a good look at the view. I couldn't believe what I was seeing! It was mesmerizing. I couldn't take my eyes off it! Hovering above the Valley was a flying saucer! Just kidding bro. What was covering the entire San Fernando Valley was a green cloud layer! I kid you not. Really? Green air? I had lived in the Valley for nearly 27 years and had never seen green air. It truly looked like something you would expect to see on the planet Venus. I just shook my head in disbelief thinking... that can't be good to breathe.

I had been working at the Carnation Company for about eight months and I had my doubts that I could hang in there for an entire year. I already knew that I hated the job and I knew that this was no way to live. It was getting to the point that the closer I got to work the higher my anxiety level grew. Upon arriving at the Carnation building, I frequently would circle the parking lot questioning whether I could do this another day. But, I told myself, I drove all the way over here so I might as well park and go in. Fred and I referred to the Carnation Company as "Carnico". It sounded more ominous and less flowery like some carnivorous beast that stripped its employees of their humanity and supped on their soul! Dude, the job was killing me!

The outside of my house was looking drab and dreary. It needed to be freshened up with a new coat of paint. I wanted something bright and cheery so I chose a paint color that was halfway between bright yellow and the color of Dijon mustard. I painted a test patch and thought that it was just perfect! After spending a couple of weekends prepping the exterior of the house, I began painting it near the end of February. I had forgotten how much I loved working with my hands and being outdoors. After spending a weekend painting, I decided that I enjoyed it so much that I called in sick. I told them that I had a toothache.

On Tuesday the toothache got worse and I needed to see a dentist. On Wednesday, I had an appointment and was told that I needed to get my wisdom tooth pulled on Thursday and wouldn't be back to work until Monday. I spent long hours every day working on my house and by the end of the week, the entire home was painted and it looked marvelous. I was exhausted and actually looking forward to sitting at my desk at work on Monday. By the end of the week, I decided that I was going to put my house up for sale.

I called up Jenny Stabile and asked her to come over and list my house. I priced the home so that I would net $10,000 after all my expenses including commissions and closing costs. Jenny seemed to think that it would sell at that price so we put it on the market in March. I was surprised the home sold so quickly and that the deal would close escrow in mid-May.

I immediately quit my job at "Carnico" and had to decide where I wanted to live. Moving to a smaller city with less traffic and less pollution sounded appealing to me. I made more money fixing up my home and selling it than I made from working at the Carnation company for nine months. I also enjoyed doing it! My mind was set. I would start my own real estate company with the $20,000 that I would be getting when my escrow closed. I did some research and found that Sacramento was growing at twice the rate of California at the time. The average price of a home there was nearly half of what it was in the Los Angeles area and that also sounded appealing to me.

My friend Peter was doing a one year internship up in Sacramento working on a California water atlas for the California Department of Water Resources. Peter had been living up in Sacramento for about six months so I gave him a call. I told him that I was thinking about moving up there and starting a real estate company. He told me that he really liked living in Sacramento. He said that it was a mellow place and was much prettier than the San Fernando Valley. He also said that the weather was fairly similar except hotter in the summers. Peter graciously offered to let me stay with him until I could find a place of my own and I quickly accepted his offer.

I began selling my furniture which basically consisted of a piano, a couch, a bedroom set, a desk, a coffee table and a few other items. I called my niece, Katherine, to see if there was anything that she would like to have and she came over and picked out a few odds and ends. She was living in an apartment in the Valley and working as a receptionist at the same Farmers insurance building that Willy worked at. Her dad, my brother Tony, had taken his inheritance and bought a home up in Placerville, CA which was just a bit east of Sacramento. By the time May rolled around, I sold most of the big pieces of furniture and left the rest behind including a large inventory of unsold greeting cards!

Horace Greeley, an American author and newspaper editor, once wrote: "Go West young man." In 1885. Nearly 100 years later, I would be doing just that! Except, in order to go farther west I also had to travel north as well. So, after picking up my cashier's check from the title company on May 15, 1979, I stuffed whatever belongings would fit in my Vega hatchback and headed North on the 405 to start a new chapter in my life and possibly a new book! ☺

Made in the USA
Las Vegas, NV
18 August 2022

53513597R00174